New World Modernisms

New World Modernisms

T. S. Eliot, Derek Walcott, and Kamau Brathwaite

Charles W. Pollard

New World Studies
A. James Arnold, editor

University of Virginia Press
Charlottesville and London

University of Virginia Press

Printed in the United States of America on acid-free paper
First published 2004

9 8 7 6 5 4 3 2 1

Library of Congress Cataloging-in-Publication Data

Pollard, Charles W., 1963–
New world modernisms : T.S. Eliot, Derek Walcott, and Kamau Brathwaite / Charles W. Pollard.
p. cm. — (New World studies)
Includes bibliographical references and index.
ISBN 0-8139-2277-1 (alk. paper) — ISBN 0-8139-2278-X (pbk. : alk. paper)
1. Walcott, Derek—Criticism and interpretation. 2. Brathwaite, Kamau, 1930—Criticism and interpretation. 3. Eliot, T. S. (Thomas Stearns), 1888–1965—Influence. 4. Caribbean literature (English)—American influences. 5. Caribbean Area—Intellectual life—20th century. 6. Modernism (Literature)—Caribbean Area. 7. Postcolonialism—Caribbean Area. 8. Caribbean Area—In literature. 9. Postcolonialism in literature. I. Title. II. Series.
PR9272.9.W3Z82 2004
811'.54099729—dc22

2003026773

For Carey, whose love sustains and sweetens it all

Contents

Acknowledgments

I AM DEEPLY grateful to Calvin College, which generously provided research support through its McGregor Program and a Calvin Research Fellowship.

I would also like to acknowledge the editors and publishers who have kindly granted permission to reprint previously printed material. Revised sections of the introduction and chapter 1 originally appeared in *Twentieth Century Literature* 47, no. 2 (2001) and have been reprinted with permission. Excerpts from Derek Walcott's *Collected Poems, 1948–1984,* © 1986 by Derek Walcott, and *The Arkansas Testament,* © 1987 by Derek Walcott, are reprinted by permission of Farrar, Strauss & Giroux, LLC, and Faber and Faber Ltd. Kamau Brathwaite's "Letter Sycorax," from *MiddlePassages,* © 1993 by Kamau Brathwaite, is reprinted by permission of the New Directions Publishing Corporation. Excerpts from Kamau Brathwaite's "Wings of a Dove," "The Dust," and "Ogun," from *The Arrivants: A New World Trilogy,* © 1969 by Kamau Brathwaite, are reprinted by permission of Oxford University Press.

My personal debts are many. From the earliest stages of this project Jahan Ramazani has given freely of his time, intelligence, enthusiasm, and wisdom to help me improve this book in countless ways, for which I will always be deeply grateful. Laurence Breiner also read the manuscript with a thoroughness and depth of insight that helped sharpen immeasurably the structure and argument of the work. Richard Mallon, Daniel Wenger, and Mark McWilliams generously offered their warm friendship and critical acumen in ways that encouraged and sustained the initial conception and drafting of the book. My colleagues in the English Department at Calvin College have also been generous with their time and goodwill. I have also benefited from the comments of J. C. Levenson, Tejumola Olaniyan, and A. James Arnold and from the research assistance of Krista Betts and Janae

Salecker. I appreciate Cathie Brettschneider, Mark Mones, and Joanne Allen for their scrupulous and cheerful editorial work, and Denice O'Heron who worked on multiple versions of the manuscript with professionalism, care, and good humor.

Finally, I thank my family: my parents, Bill and Judy, for your love, support, and encouragement; my children, Chad, Ben, Emma, and James, for your patience with Dad as he worked on the "big" book but also for your pleasant interruptions, which put the work into proper perspective; and my wife, Carey, for your perceptive comments, your inexhaustible faith in me, and your love, which sustains and sweetens it all.

New World Modernisms

Introduction

THE BOOK form of the *Southern Review*'s anniversary issue on T. S. Eliot features a picture of Eliot standing cautiously on the rail of a cruise ship as it comes into port in Hamilton, Bermuda, in January 1959 (Olney 8). It is a stereotypical photo of the retired tourist. Eliot looks old, somewhat frail, with a weary smile on his face. His sports jacket stretches noticeably to cover the results of a sedentary lifestyle; he does not wear a tie, and his shirt collar is open to the third button; he wears what appear to be deck shoes without laces and a straw hat to protect himself from the sun. He stands on several shuffleboard cues to position himself squarely against the rail, and the harbor is framed symmetrically in the background of the picture. A circular life buoy, to his right, innocently documents the paradoxes of neocolonialism: the name of the cruise ship is *Queen Bermuda,* but its homeport is London. It is a far different picture of Eliot than is usually included in biographies or on the covers of critical works, far different from the fastidious Eliot that Virginia Woolf mocks as the man in the "four-piece suit" (quoted in Gordon, *Eliot's Early Years* 84). It is Eliot on vacation in the islands.

Eliot and his second wife, Valerie, actually made three trips to the islands toward the end of his life: this trip to Bermuda in 1959, a leisurely cruise and two-month vacation in Jamaica during the winter of 1961, and a similar trip to Barbados in 1962 (Gordon, *Eliot's New Life* 261). These trips had become necessary because of Eliot's fragile health; he had a bronchial condition that was aggravated by the smog and dampness of the harsh British winters. To many people, this picture of an ailing Eliot in the islands would aptly represent any potential relationship he might have with postcolonial Caribbean poetry. The elderly, weakened voice of European modernism comes to the Caribbean only as a sick tourist, a person with seemingly little appreciation of, and little to offer to, the vibrant life and culture of the region. Indeed, Eliot's own comments about these trips reinforce such a view: he tells a friend that he found nothing attractive in the West Indies except the weather (Gordon, *Eliot's New Life* 261). In the early sixties, the demise of the influence of Eliot and his modernism seemed imminent for Anglo-American poetry and irrelevant to the emerging postcolonial poetry of the Caribbean.

It is striking, then, that two young, talented Caribbean poets as different as Kamau Brathwaite and Derek Walcott would both speak so favorably of Eliot.[1] Brathwaite claims that Eliot is the "only 'European influence' I can detect and will acknowledge" ("Edward Brathwaite" 129), and Walcott asserts that "there is no writer of poetry in English who does not owe him a debt" ("T. S. Eliot"). What could these Caribbean poets find so attractive in the ideas and techniques of this elderly, somewhat fragile, and dismissive poet-tourist from Europe? Even if the first part of the twentieth century could arguably be called the age of Eliot in Anglo-American poetry, was Eliot's modernism not already a tired, somewhat fragile and worn-out aesthetic by the time Walcott and Brathwaite began to formulate their own poetic ideas?[2] Does not the dominant critical narrative of Anglo-American poetry for the last forty years—what James Longenbach aptly calls the "breakthrough narrative" (7)—describe Eliot and his modernism as the burdensome heritage that contemporary poets must overthrow in order to develop their liberating theories of confessional, postmodern, or postcolonial poetry?

In fact, Brathwaite and Walcott have recast modernism in general and Eliot in particular because aspects of his modernist aesthetic enable them to understand and to represent better their postcolonial experience of modernity, what Edouard Glissant calls the New World's "irruption into modernity" (*Caribbean Discourse* 146). With Eliot, they articulate an aesthetic theory that represents the intellectual and emotional contradictions of contemporary experience; they desire to identify a "tradition" and a "mythical method" that control, order, and give shape to the anarchy of the Caribbean's colonial history; they seek to revitalize poetic language with the rhythm and diction of common Caribbean speech; and they aspire to assume the role of the public poet in order to imagine and speak for a unified cultural community. The heart of this book explores how Brathwaite and Walcott reshape these three principles to represent their corresponding but different understandings of the New World experience, but the fact that they reshape Eliot's modernist principles at all should significantly revise how we describe and categorize writers of the twentieth century. It is a fascinating example of cross-cultural intertextuality that clarifies the central contributions of Walcott and Brathwaite in imagining complementary New World Caribbean poetics, poetics that in turn fundamentally reconfigure our understanding of modernism.

Not enough attention has been devoted to trying to understand the larger regional and theoretical contexts of Caribbean writers in general and Caribbean poets in particular. Clearly, the complexity of the Caribbean's multiple colonial experiences, languages, and literary traditions has made it more difficult to make these larger connections. However, recent incisive works, such as J. Michael Dash's *The Other America,* Silvio Torres-Saillant's *Caribbean Poetics,* and many of the essays in the ambitious and timely *History of Literature in the Caribbean,* edited by A. James Arnold, have begun to establish a comparative framework for studying Caribbean writers in a more multilingual, regional context. This new approach, which has come to be called New World studies,[3] serves as a framing context for the more specific focus of this study. In particular, Dash's work is important because it identifies and broadly traces the "Caribbean's modernist legacy within its New World context" (20). The strengths and limitations of Dash's argument are discussed more fully in the next chapter's detailed discussion of Caribbean modernism, but it complements felicitously the work in this study and reveals the promise of one type of New World studies.

Indeed, the present volume helps to cultivate this vital new field by emphasizing poetry and by providing Eliot's modernism as a distinguishing point of reference. New World studies has tended to examine theory and fiction more than poetry, and the relatively few references to poetry have often been conceptual rather than linguistic evaluations.[4] This study of Caribbean poetry calls for a sharper linguistic focus because it seeks to make comparative and specific claims about the poets' aural and figurative use of language, and not just their ideas. Moreover, Walcott and Brathwaite have clearly developed their poetics in relation not only to each other but also to Eliot and other writers outside the region. New World studies has rightly stressed a larger regional approach to the study of Caribbean literature, but it should not ignore other cultural, even global, contexts in which Caribbean writers work and through which we can gain useful perspectives. In other words, there is much to learn about the New World modernisms of Brathwaite and Walcott by comparing them with the European modernism of Eliot, and vice versa.

Eliot serves Brathwaite and Walcott as a useful though by no means exclusive spokesperson for modernism for many of the same reasons that he dominated Anglo-American literature in the first part of the twentieth century. His reputation as a cosmopolitan poetic innovator and magisterial critic was advanced by the New Critics in Anglo-American universities and by their students teaching in colonial preparatory schools around the world.[5] Eliot's influence also spread because of the power of the British Empire's channels of cultural distribution. For instance, the British Council distributed recordings of Eliot reading his poetry throughout the commonwealth. In other words, Eliot's relationship to these writers was shaped by the two features that Arjun Appadurai identifies as the conditions of cultural globalization: mass migration and electronic mediation (4). Indeed, examining the relationships between Eliot, Walcott, and Brathwaite contributes an important chapter to "the story of the globalization of English-language poetry," which Jahan Ramazani contends "remains largely untold" because "postcolonial criticism is largely grounded in mimetic presuppositions about literature. But since poetry mediates experience through a language of exceptional figural and formal density, it is a less transparent medium by which to recuperate the history, politics, and sociology of postcolonial societies" (*Hybrid Muse* 1, 4). It is just this figural and formal density that makes poets such as Walcott and Brathwaite so valuable in representing the complexity of the Caribbean experience. While the oeuvres of Walcott and Brathwaite have often been compared in a summary fashion, this book offers the first sustained study of their complementary poetics in a larger theoretical context.[6] It pays close attention to the formal qualities of individual poems, a courtesy too rarely extended to these poets,[7] as it describes and assesses the larger regional and global significance of their ideas.

While Brathwaite and Walcott come of age as poets at the end of the age of Eliot, they are not overwhelmed or stifled by his reputation or his ideology, as so many of their Anglo-American contemporaries are.[8] Instead, they find the comprehensiveness and contingency of his modernism strategically helpful in stimulating their own thinking about poetry's social function. They freely and selectively reshape Eliot's modernism—they creolize it—to achieve their own purposes; in the process, they create vibrant and complementary New World modernist poetics. *Creolization* is, of course, a theoretical term that has emerged from, and been uniquely shaped by, the experience of colonization in the Caribbean.[9] However, it is also a term that links that Caribbean experience with the methods of modernism. As Neil ten Kortenaar rightly suggests, "Creolization is best understood . . . as the form that modernist ambivalence takes in the Caribbean" (19). The writings of Edouard Glissant and James Clifford help to make this broader connection between creolization and modernism.

Glissant, one of the leading Caribbean writers and theorists, describes creolization, not as a static "category" of identity "halfway between 'pure' extremes," but as "the unceasing process of transformation" through which people create a collective sense of identity from multiple cultural sources (*Caribbean Discourse* 142, 140). *Creolization* identifies a process by which something is created in the colonies that is neither indigenous to the region nor identical with its counterpart in the culture of origin, so it serves as a fitting description for Walcott's and Brathwaite's transforming of some of Eliot's modernist principles. They create New World poetics that are not truly indigenous because they draw upon several diaspora cultures including European modernism but that are also not identical with European modernism because they have naturalized those principles to reflect their New World, Caribbean experience. This creolization does not, as some popular versions would have it, easily homogenize cultures to eliminate ethnic, cultural, national, or ideological conflict, but it also does not ignore the cultural exchanges that occur despite these conflicts (Dash, "Psychology" 47). Creolization recognizes the possibility of contiguity and discrepancy, interdependence and resistance, in the relationship of these writers.

As Dash suggests, Glissant subsequently extends this idea of creolization to a "new global level" in developing his "poetics of relation" (*Edouard Glissant* 179). Glissant defines this term by offering a simple historical narrative of the trajectories of cultural exchange, first a trajectory from the center to the peripheries, then a movement from the peripheries to the center, and finally, in the "poetics of relation," the "trajectory is abolished" and the "poet's word" reproduces a "circular nomadism; that is, it makes every periphery into a center; . . . it abolishes the very notion of center and periphery" (*Poetics of Relation* 29). Glissant's poetics of relation aptly describes the ambition of examining the relationships between Walcott, Brathwaite, and Eliot, an examination in which the trajectory is neither from the center (Eliot) to the peripheries (Walcott and Brathwaite) nor from the peripheries to the center, but a collocating of the contributions of, and interactions between, these writers to describe a broader, more comprehensive modernist poetics.

Glissant's poetics of relation is a particularly useful concept in this context because it bears such a strong resemblance to the method of Eliot's modernism, what Michael Levenson calls the principle of "provisional" unity in Eliot's modernism, "the principle of order . . . [which] depends on . . . an ever-increasing series of points of view, which struggle towards an emergent unity and then continue to struggle past that unity" (*A Genealogy*

192–93). Eliot identifies this provisional unity with a variety of terms—"the theory of points of view," "the historical sense," and the "mythical method."[10] Readers of Eliot have, in turn, offered other useful synonyms, describing Eliot's "dialectical imagination," his "logic of complementarity," his "constructivist aesthetic," his "ambivalence," and even his "relative poetics."[11] In all of these descriptions the essential elements of Eliot's modernist method remain the same: it is a poetics that collocates an increasingly diverse set of cultural resources and perspectives to imagine an increasingly comprehensive but still contingent sense of cultural wholeness. Brathwaite and Walcott find this collocating method attractive because it recognizes not only the reality of cultural fragmentation but also the aspiration for cultural unity; in other words, it is a method that recognizes their New World experience as central and representative of the modern condition. As Glissant contends, the Caribbean experience is so important because the Caribbean is "one of the places in the world where Relation presents itself most visibly" (*Poetics of Relation* 33).

James Clifford, a leading American cultural anthropologist, has made a similar journey in his thought. For instance, Glissant asserts that creolization is a "cross-cultural process" from which "no people has been spared" (*Caribbean Discourse* 140), and Clifford claims that "we are all Caribbeans now in our urban archipelagos" (*The Predicament* 173). The force of Clifford's plural pronoun must be examined carefully. He is not glibly appropriating creolization and/or the Caribbean experience to homogenize all the different experiences of interculturation throughout the world. Like Glissant, Clifford recognizes that Caribbean creolization was uniquely shaped by the involuntary and violent experience of colonialism in the region. Even so, he believes that Caribbean creolization offers an important model for understanding the process of interculturation occurring elsewhere. He uses creolization to identify a process that he sees as increasingly transcultural, while still recognizing that this process takes different forms in different cultural contexts.

In his more recent work Clifford has been more explicit in recognizing the violence that has shaped the complementarity of creolization. In his influential essay "Traveling Cultures" he argues that the process of "displacement and transplantation" in "diaspora cultures"—the process, in other words, of creolization—"[is] inseparable from specific, often violent, histories of economic, political, and cultural interaction—histories that generate what might be called discrepant cosmopolitanisms" (*Routes* 36). He favors this new phrase because he thinks it avoids both an "excessive localism" and an "overly global vision of a capitalist or technocratic monoculture" (36). Stated more positively, Clifford coins the term *discrepant cosmopolitanisms* to identify common patterns of responses to interculturation that find different, even contradictory expression in different cultural contexts.[12] Indeed, the *discrepant* in Clifford's concept of discrepant cosmopolitanisms conveys more of the grit of resistance involved in intercultural exchange, a resistance to the potential homogenizing effect of that exchange.

Clifford has not been alone in trying to articulate a nonuniversalist, non-Western understanding of cosmopolitanism. His fellow anthropologist Paul Rabinow urges the need for more "critical, cosmopolitan intellectuals" who can sensitively balance "the specificity of historical experience and place" and the "macro-interdependency encompassing any local particularity," for a cosmopolitanism that is "always suspicious of its imperial tendencies" (238). David Hollinger describes his "postethnic perspective" as a form of *rooted cosmopolitanism,* which he contends recognizes, accepts, and eagerly explores diversity (5). Kwame Anthony Appiah's term is *cosmopolitan patriotism,* which he defines as an attachment to the "cultural particularities" of one's own home and a "pleasure in the presence of other, different places [and] other, different people" ("Cosmopolitan Patriots" 618). Homi Bhabha offers *vernacular cosmopolitanism* as the appropriate phrase to describe this experience of simultaneously participating in a transnational and an indigenous cultural community ("Unsatisfied" 194–97). Whether this cosmopolitanism is described as *discrepant, rooted, patriotic,* or *vernacular* is not that important; each of these terms rightly encourages an approach to the cultural migrations of the twentieth century that recognizes the more prevalent experience of being settled and traveling, local and international, discrepant and cosmopolitan. Clifford and these others writers set the rightly theoretical trajectory in renewing an interest in a localized cosmopolitanism, but it is a concept that is sorely lacking in descriptive thickness because of the dearth of examples. As Bruce Robbins challenges, others need to take up the "scholarly project of accumulating instances of cosmopolitanism from around the globe" to test Clifford's claims about discrepant cosmopolitanism (195). This study takes up that challenge and establishes the modernist roots of discrepant cosmopolitanism.

Of course, this renewed interest in cosmopolitanism has not been without its critics. Timothy Brennan has been one of the most articulate and wide-ranging. He sees this renewed cosmopolitanism as threatening the nationalism that has animated the resistance of existing and emerging third-world political movements. He faults Clifford for failing to "hold out a sophisticated theoretical space for a defensive nationalism" and reproaches

Rabinow for not seeing the "practical difficulties and inappropriateness of living by [a cosmopolitan] ethic as a participant in anticolonial war" (17, 18). Brennan rightly warns against cosmopolitanism's homogenizing tendency—the conflating of cosmopolitanism with Euro-American universalism is always a risk—but he does not sufficiently recognize the *discrepancy* in Clifford's discrepant cosmopolitanism.[13] Insurgency, contestation, and divergence are embedded in Clifford's concept. His discrepancy involves recognizing national, linguistic, and cultural differences, but he does not conceive of these differences as the *exclusive* way to understand cultural resistance and formation. His cosmopolitanism suggests that cultural change occurs through strategic collaboration, as well as direct opposition.

Brennan also rightly notes that this renewed interest in cosmopolitanism is inextricably shaped by the historical realities of colonialism and neocolonialism. The "traveling" of people and cultures has not always been voluntary; slavery, indentured servitude, imperial conflicts, and immigration policies are all forces of displacement that have influenced the possibilities of this new cosmopolitanism. In addition, while English may have emerged as the world language of this cosmopolitanism, it has done so in no small part because of the economic, technological, and military power of the British Empire and, more recently, of the United States. This cosmopolitanism also depends upon metropolitan channels of cultural distribution—the networks of publishers, reviewers, editors, and universities—that condition, in part, its expression. Clifford recognizes the historical taintedness of terms such as *cosmopolitanism* and *travel,* but as he rightly counters, there are "no neutral, uncontaminated terms," so any "comparative cultural studies needs to work, self-critically, with compromised, historically encumbered tools" (*Routes* 39). Whereas Anglo-American critics tend to view Eliot's modernism as too contaminated by his ideology to be of use, Walcott and Brathwaite approach it as a compromised but useful tool. As Bruce King, a prolific and early critic of Caribbean literature, recognizes, Caribbean writers find in Eliot's "*avant-garde* techniques and attitudes" a way "to express the cultural concerns" of the region: "the style of European alienation has become that of colonial liberation" (*New English Literatures* 137).

Indeed, Clifford's discrepant cosmopolitanism essentially restates and reorients the modernist ideal, an ideal that recognizes the fragmentation and diversity of any contemporary culture but also seeks to bring those fragments together to form new, provisional and transnational cultural wholes. Clifford probably would not object to this characterization—claiming, as he does, that his interest "in cultural collage and incongruity derives quite explicitly from *modernist* art and poetry" (*Routes* 180)—but he does not work out the implications of this connection either for modernism or for discrepant cosmopolitanism. He does not recognize that modernism may well continue to be a vital contemporary aesthetic in the Caribbean and elsewhere precisely because its methods offer writers a better way to perceive and represent their experience of discrepant cosmopolitanism. And as Caribbean writers have transformed the methods of modernism, modernism itself has become a more discrepant cosmopolitan literary movement.

Eliot, Brathwaite, and Walcott bring together different cultural fragments, so their visions of cultural wholeness are discrepant. Eliot shores together the fragments of Euro-American culture to reimagine a new, provisional "Western" cultural unity. Brathwaite develops his insurgent Afro-Caribbean folk tradition by piecing together the remnants of Afro-Caribbean cultural connections. Walcott envisions an ironic New World classicism that represents a provisional cultural wholeness emerging from the different diaspora cultures of Europe, Africa, and Asia. While these visions are discrepant, they are also cosmopolitan and modernist: cosmopolitan in that they imagine a cultural wholeness that is not limited by national borders and modernist in that they share common aesthetic methods and ideas to represent these discrepant visions. By juxtaposing Eliot, Brathwaite, and Walcott we can more clearly see both the cosmopolitan scope of modernism and the inevitable partiality of any individual expression of it. It illustrates how modernism has migrated as a cultural ideal and how it has been changed through this migration.

In the first chapter I show how this theory of discrepant cosmopolitan modernism challenges the dominant theoretical approach to the relationship between modernism and postcolonialism. This dominant approach too easily relies on a faulty historical parallel to conclude that modernism is to postmodernism as colonialism is to postcolonialism. Instead, we should ask why and how Eliot's modernism was revised to further the aesthetic projects of these two Caribbean writers. It is a reorienting of these critical concepts that calls into question the demise of Eliot's influence and clarifies the complementary poetics offered by Brathwaite and Walcott. Brathwaite and Walcott are not derivative of Eliot; instead they create modernisms that augment, rival, and complement his European modernism. The goal is to offer an account of the relationships between Eliot's ambivalent European modernism, Brathwaite's creolized Afro-Caribbean folk tradition, and Walcott's New World mimicry that respects the variety of poetic practices without necessarily demanding a choice between them; honors the opportunities for poetic exchange, while acknowledging the depth of ideological disagreement; and envisions both truly discrepant and truly cosmopolitan modernisms. It is an account that recognizes poetic exchange not exclusively in terms of anxiety and competition, but also in terms of creative ambiguity, open generosity and strategic synergies. It is an account that seeks to read these poets, in Edward Said's term, "contrapuntally" (*Culture and Imperialism* 66–67), to explore the imaginative possibilities and growing interdependence of literatures written in English.

Chapters 2–4 each focus on how Walcott and Brathwaite rework a specific principle in Eliot's modernism—poetry's relationship to tradition, poetry's relationship to speech, and poetry's social function—to thicken the description of this discrepant cosmopolitan modernism. Chapter 2, "Not Borrowers, But Bearers of a Tradition," examines how Brathwaite and Walcott appropriate and recast Eliot's concept of tradition and the mythical method to create their own cultural home. Eliot conceives of a tradition, not as a fixed set of texts as many critics have claimed, but as a contingent ideal order of the relations between writers that subsequent participants construct and reorient with their own work. It is an ideal that Eliot himself reorders by fusing together fragments from many cultural traditions—Augustine and Buddha speak with one voice in *The Waste Land.* Brathwaite and Walcott are drawn to this constructivist approach to tradition because they too aspire to build a coherent cultural tradition from their even more fragmented experience of modernity in the New World. They build, of course, with different fragments. Brathwaite develops his insurgent Afro-Caribbean folk tradition more by examining forms of popular culture in the region, whereas Walcott conceives of his ironic New World classicism more through mimicking conventional European literary figures. Eliot poetically embodies his concept of tradition in the figure of Tiresias, a conditional persona in whom the multiple perspectives of *The Waste Land* surface, momentarily cohere, and quickly dissipate. Brathwaite uses Harriet Beecher Stowe's Uncle Tom and Walcott employs Daniel Defoe's Robinson Crusoe to serve similar organizing functions for their poetry early in their careers, choices that underscore the different ethnic and class orientations of their complementary modernisms. Brathwaite and Walcott both recognize the genius of this modernist concept of tradition: it is flexible enough to incorporate a wide variety of cultural sources and coherent enough to set these cultural sources in relation to one another in a contingent tradition. This flexible coherence is one of the key features of modernism's cosmopolitan appeal.

Chapter 3, “Listening to Eliot: Poetic Revolution and Common Speech,” explores the ambivalence of Eliot’s response to the question of poetry’s relationship to speech. The younger Eliot argues that part of the poet’s task is to bring poetic diction up to date with the spoken language. Indeed, the different voices of *The Waste Land* are not only different points of view that cohere in Tiresias but also different levels of spoken diction. However, the older Eliot contends that the poet should “purify the dialect of the tribe” in order to give his or her audience a more refined language (*Little Gidding, Complete Poems* 141). Brathwaite and Walcott both testify to the influence of Eliot’s actual spoken voice, for they both recall hearing a recording of Eliot reading his poetry as one of the formative events of their poetic careers. They learn, however, different lessons from listening to Eliot. Brathwaite hears the “riddims of St. Louis” in Eliot’s voice, a sound that encourages him to write in Afro-Caribbean dialect, or *nation language* (“History of the Voice” 266). His nation-language poetry seeks both to resist the hegemony of Standard English and to renew poetry with the common speech of the region. His later experiments with what he terms *Sycorax video-style* extend this initial insight to alter the graphic conventions of writing in order to convey the sound of nation language more precisely and to resist the authority of Standard English more directly. Walcott, on the other hand, hears the Eliot of *Four Quartets* and adopts a concern for speech that impels him to “purify” the dialects of the tribes in the New World. However, whereas Eliot speaks of this purification as “developing” and “refining” common speech, Walcott asserts that his poetry “purifies” speech by amalgamating and fusing the different dialects of the region. In blending the linguistic differences of indigenous and imperial forms of speech, Walcott aspires to contribute the sound of his own accent to the common, transnational, and interethnic language of the New World. Eliot initiates both the modernist revolution to update poetic language with modern speech and the subsequent consolidation of that revolution through the poetic refining of modern speech. Brathwaite reorients Eliot’s revolutionary precepts to advocate an insurgent New World poetry of nation language, whereas Walcott recasts Eliot’s subsequent advice into a New World poetry that transforms culture by fusing forms of speech. This strategic listening to Eliot is instructive, not only in understanding the different ways in which Brathwaite and Walcott have appropriated modernism’s poetic revolution but also in rethinking the relationship between poetry, speech, and identity in a world in which more and more people speak English, but speak it differently from one another.

Chapter 4, "Public Poets," examines how each of these writers conceives of poetry's social function. Eliot turns to Dante as his model. In *Little Gidding* he transmutes Dante's dramatic encounter with his poetic master, Brunetto Latini, to suggest that the public poet fuses diverse traditions and renews common languages to bring people to the point of recognizing both their individual and their collective need for spiritual wholeness. In *Omeros,* Walcott mimics Eliot's homage to Dante by imagining a reunion with his own "familiar compound ghost"—the ghost of his dead father—a composite figure that represents a tradition that includes Homer, Virgil, Dante, Shakespeare, Eliot, Joyce, and others. Walcott sharpens Eliot's conclusions about poetry's social function to reflect the astringency of his New World experience of colonialism. He speaks for and about those who endured the injustices of colonialism, but he also recognizes the dangers and limits of poetry's public role. He believes that cultural wholeness can be achieved, not through evoking revenge or guilt, but through remembering and honoring the inner strength of those who survived. In *Barabajan Poems* Brathwaite takes a different approach in that he recasts and explicates his earlier poetry to make a case for its social function. Instead of appealing to Dante, he looks again to his great-uncle Robert, the carpenter/sculptor, who intuitively recognizes, recovers, and represents the African heritage of Caribbean culture in sculpting his "folk" art, as a model of the public poet. Similarly, Brathwaite believes that his poetry can best cultivate individual and cultural wholeness by recasting the oral and graphic conditions of poetic language to represent the African distinctiveness of the region.

The epilogue explores the ways all three poets rely on tropes of traveling to express how art can unite the fragments of experience to create the possibility of a transnational, interethnic, cross-cultural sense of individual and collective wholeness. It is an ideal that is best expressed through poetry because poetic metaphors can more readily convey the complexities of experience and poetic language can more adeptly register the linguistic strategies needed to achieve this provisional wholeness. It is the ideal that best unites these writers in a discrepant cosmopolitan modernist tradition and that best serves as a standard by which to judge the success of their work.

Placing these writers in a discrepant cosmopolitan modernist tradition involves risks: the risk of conflating too easily Eliot's expatriate experience in Europe with Brathwaite's and Walcott's colonial and neocolonial experiences in the New World; the risk of reinscribing the cultural hierarchy of colonialism so that Europe remains central and the New World derivative;

the risk of blurring these writers' ideological differences by highlighting the congruence of their methods. Critics should not, however, be more timid than the writers they study, and each of the writers in this study has risked misunderstanding to conceive of new possibilities for poetry. In particular, comparing the complementary modernisms of Eliot, Brathwaite, and Walcott should deepen our appreciation for the possibility of transcultural poetic exchange despite principled ideological disagreement. This appreciation can be cultivated only if the analysis is not wholly removed from, nor easily conflated with, cultural politics; instead, the critic must carefully parse ideological commitments and poetic strategies in evaluating these writers' achievements. It is a critical approach that will need to be more widely accepted if we are to begin to understand better not only the discrepant and cosmopolitan nature of modernism but, more importantly, the growing interdependence of, and differences between, literatures written in English.

James Clifford urges cultural critics to turn their attention to "traveling cultures." Even though Eliot once dismissed the idea of a "distinctive" Caribbean literature as "a question that lies in too remote a future to be discussed" ("Tradition and the Practice of Poetry" 15), his modernist tradition now depends in part on the work of poets who are recasting his ideas to create a vibrant Caribbean literature. Even though Brathwaite and Walcott reject the neocolonial tourism that brings Eliot to the islands, they adapt his strategies to imagine a provisional sense of cultural wholeness among those islands. Eliot only visits the Caribbean; his ideas emigrate and are naturalized by Brathwaite and Walcott. Brathwaite and Walcott visit, either literally or figuratively, the Old Worlds of Africa, Europe, and Asia, but they collect ideas from these places in order to represent the unique contribution of Caribbean culture and experience to the New World. Discrepant cosmopolitan modernism emerges as the poetic passport for the imaginative travels of these twentieth-century writers of literature in English.

1 Postcolonial Modernism/Modernist Postcolonialism

ANGLO-AMERICAN postcolonial theory has failed to see the implicit modernism in Caribbean literature because it has relied too readily on a faulty historical parallel (i.e., that modernism is to postmodernism as colonialism is to postcolonialism). This reliance has blinded too many postcolonial theorists to the possibility of a postcolonial modernism or a modernist postcolonialism, a possibility that a theory of discrepant cosmopolitan modernism not only encompasses but also encourages. This chapter considers first the shortcomings of the current theoretical definitions of *postcolonialism* and of the critical discussions about postcolonial writers in thinking about the relationships between Eliot, Walcott, and Brathwaite; it then identifies the potential of a growing body of criticism that recognizes a recasting of European modernism by Caribbean writers; and finally it articulates the advantages of seeing the specific features of Eliot's modernist ambivalence, Brathwaite's creolization, and Walcott's mimicry in the larger framework of discrepant cosmopolitan modernism.

The ubiquitous *post* of contemporary critical discourse underscores our troubled relationship to the past, an anxiety readily apparent in the contentious debates over defining *postcoloniality.* At its most basic, the *post* in *postcolonial* signifies simple historical chronology—the postcolonial as the time "after" colonial rule, after the political independence of the former colonies. However, this historical definition of *postcolonial* raises more problems than it solves. For example, Anne McClintock contends that it is "prematurely celebratory and obfuscatory" because it fails to recognize the continued influence of colonialism and neocolonialism around the world; it unduly homogenizes very different colonial experiences; and it still orients its analysis in a way that puts Europe at the center (298). She calls for a "*proliferation* of historically nuanced theories and strategies" to replace *postcolonial* as a critical term (303). It is a call, however, that avoids rather than solves the problem of definition. All theories, even historically nuanced ones, abstract from particular examples to generate their explanatory framework. Even though critical labels such as *modernism* and *postcolonialism* oversimplify the heterogeneity of writers, these terms still serve a useful function in identifying common contexts, questions, and strategies employed by different writers.

Others have sought to offer a more ideological definition of *postcolonial,* namely, "*against* colonialism." For example, the authors of *The Empire Writes Back* contend that "postcolonial" texts share a "foregrounding of the tension with the imperial power" (3). Their ideological definition is not prematurely celebratory, but it still asserts a single, simplified understanding of the postcolonial experience. In their review of *The Empire Writes Back,* Vijay Mishra and Bob Hodge rightly criticize this totalizing approach and offer as an alternative a distinction between "oppositional" and "complicit" postcolonialisms. They define the "oppositional" postcolonialism as the more defiant approach of writers who are more likely to have endured a racist colonial experience, more ready to employ a nonimperial language, and more concerned with direct political struggle (286). They describe "complicit" postcolonialism as a more symbiotic understanding of the relationship between, on the one hand, the postcolonial writer who creatively engages the imperial language and tradition to create hybrid, syncretized, and pluralist forms and, on the other hand, the dominant literary tradition (288–90). Mishra and Hodge's categories are useful because they provide a starting place to distinguish between Brathwaite's more "oppositional" and Walcott's more "complicit" postcolonial poetics, but they need qualification. The pejorative connotation of *complicit* is misleading when the term is applied to Walcott's poetics, for he does not feel guilty about mastering and revising the dominant literary tradition. Mishra and Hodge also define their categories only in relationship to colonialism (the obvious foil of oppositional postcolonialism) or postmodernism (the questionable ally of complicit postcolonialism); however, Brathwaite's more oppositional and Walcott's more complicit postcolonialism both have deep affinities with modernism. Recognizing these affinities undermines the questionable binary logic of these theorists' historical parallels.

In fact, the ubiquitous *post* has made this parallelism too easy to assert. For example, Stephen Slemon claims that the "armed version" of modernism is colonialism and that postmodernism and postcolonialism have emerged in reaction to this single cultural event (3). Postmodernism reacts by asserting the "constructedness" of all texts, whereas postcolonialism makes strategic truth claims to expose the "constructedness" of the colonial "social text" (9). Slemon favors the postcolonial approach on ideological grounds and castigates postmodernism for joining "hands with its modernist precursor" to assert a "universalizing, assimilative impulse" and to continue a "politics of colonialist control" (14). In other words, postmodernism is bad because it is too modernist, and modernism is a form of cultural imperialism. He concludes wistfully that postmodernism may still find a way to "join, not assimilate, post-colonial critical discourse in . . . decolonizing Western culture," by which he means "decolonizing it . . . from a residual modernism" (15). Unfortunately, Slemon is not alone in strapping modernism to the whipping post of contemporary theory.[1]

Kwame Anthony Appiah offers a more sophisticated and compelling response to the question whether "the post- in postmodernism [is] the post- in postcolonial," but he still represents modernism as the evil to be overcome. He concurs with Slemon and others that the *post* signifies a common methodological need to make a "space-clearing gesture," the need that "drives the underlying dynamic of cultural modernity" (*In My Father's House* 149, 145). He also agrees that both discourses challenge "earlier legitimating narratives," but he contends that postcolonialism has something to teach postmodernism because it challenges these narratives in the terms of an "ethical universal"—in terms of "*humanism*" (155). He quickly qualifies this humanism, describing it as "provisional, historically contingent, antiessentialist," and then suggests that it could become the common ground for postmodernism and postcolonial discourse (155). Unfortunately, he too succumbs to making modernism the scapegoat to achieve this synthesis, arguing that postcolonialism and postmodernism should affirm together this contingent humanism by expressing a common "concern for human suffering . . . while still rejecting the master narratives of modernism" (155). Appiah's contingent humanism is a compelling concept. It resonates with the work of Brathwaite and Walcott in various ways, but they do not see it as being in conflict with their revised understanding of modernism. By assuming that *post* implicitly means "against modernism," Slemon, Appiah, and others have oversimplified the nature of modernism and so have obscured the ways in which Brathwaite and Walcott have productively adapted modernist strategies and ideals to forge their own discrepant cosmopolitan modernisms.[2]

While these theoretical definitions of postcolonialism have tended to castigate modernism, critical studies of "minority" or postcolonial writers have been more willing to employ modernism as a useful conceptual category. Consider, for example, the work of Houston Baker Jr. and Simon

Gikandi. In *Modernism and the Harlem Renaissance* Baker contends that African American writers at the beginning of the twentieth century employed two complementary strategies to construct a liberating modernist poetics: the mastering of standard forms (the method of minstrelsy) and the deformation of mastery (the opposing of those same forms). He asserts that the "essence of black discursive modernism" is "poetic mastery discovered as a function of deformative *folk* sound" (xv), a definition of modernism that resonates with aspects of Brathwaite's and Walcott's methods. Even more apropos, Gikandi develops a theory of "Caribbean modernism" to explain the similarities between novelists in the region. He contends that Caribbean modernism develops from an anxiety about the history, language, and ideology of colonialism, an anxiety that it responds to by creolizing imperial and ancestral sources of culture to resist colonial domination (5). Similarly to Baker, he concludes that Caribbean writers employ "the language of modernism" to reclaim "colonial modernism" as a "narrative of liberation" (256). Gikandi's theory resonates closely with the complementary poetics offered by Brathwaite and Walcott, and he cites both poets liberally as supporting evidence for his theory.

While Baker and Gikandi are more willing to use modernism as a critical concept, they still adamantly define their concepts of modernism in opposition to "Western," "European," or "high" modernism. Baker rightly contends that African American modernism should not be judged as merely an emulation of Anglo-American modernism, but he overstates the case when he argues that "Africans and Afro-Americans . . . have little in common with Joycean or Eliotic projects" and that their theories are, in fact, "radically opposed" (xv–xvi). Similarly, Gikandi claims that Caribbean modernism must be conceived as "opposed to . . . European notions of modernism" in general and to the "high modernist aesthetic" of Pound, Eliot, and Joyce in particular (4–5). He concludes that "only by subverting colonial modernism could these [Caribbean] writers become modernists" (256). The example of Brathwaite, Walcott, and Eliot testifies to a more complex relationship between these forms of modernism than Baker and Gikandi are able to distinguish with their theories of opposition. Brathwaite feels no compulsion to set up a binary opposition between his own work and that of the "high" modernist. He willingly aligns his efforts with the "colonial breakthrough already achieved by Eliot, Pound and Joyce" ("Jazz" 73). Walcott is similarly uninhibited in recognizing his debt to modernism in interviews and poetic allusions. Neither of them sets out to oppose European modernism; instead, each creates a modernist poetics that diverges from European modernism because it responds to the Caribbean/New World cultural situation. An understanding of modernism as discrepant and cosmopolitan better recognizes the subtle duality of this synergy and divergence.

Gikandi seems particularly culpable for resorting to this simple, binary distinction between Caribbean and European modernisms because his familiarity with Brathwaite's and Walcott's work should convince him otherwise. For instance, he cites approvingly Baker's description of European modernism as "exclusively Western, preeminently bourgeois, and optically white" (5) even though he should know that Brathwaite speaks of Eliot's European modernism as being deeply influenced by Africa and by popular culture ("Jazz" 74). In addition, Gikandi recognizes that Walcott cites Joyce as the epigraph for his influential essay "The Muse of History," but he labors to distinguish Walcott's argument from Joyce's, claiming that Walcott "really" negates Joyce's "European model of history anchored in the notions of progress and temporal closure" (9). More accurately, Walcott recognizes what Gikandi refuses to accept: that the modernism of Pound, Joyce, or Eliot could be useful to a Caribbean writer precisely because it expresses deep doubts about the "European model of history," including the "notions of progress and temporal closure" (9). Gikandi is right to see Caribbean modernism as different from European modernism, but the differences emerge more through their representation of the Caribbean than through their opposition to European modernism. Unlike these postcolonial theorists and critics, Brathwaite and Walcott seem less anxious to sweep away the burden of modernism and more anxious to exploit its resources for new purposes. Instead of accepting the monolithic caricatures of modernism, they resonate with its multifaceted ambivalence as they respond to the complexities of the Caribbean experience.

In fact, it has been the critics of Caribbean literature who have initiated this examining of the overlapping concerns and complementary strategies of Caribbean and European modernism. For instance, A. James Arnold led the way by convincingly showing how Aimé Césaire's early poetics of negritude paralleled and extended the aesthetic primitivism of European modernism. He contends that "modernist culture" was the "principal source of [Césaire's] inspiration and even of his techniques" in his earlier work (*Modernism and Negritude* 70). Arnold subsequently qualifies this assertion with respect to Césaire's late work *i, laminaria . . .* , describing it as "postmodern" in its "deconstruction of the negritude myth" and its expression of a West Indian sense of the "dispersion of the self," but he still suggests that even in this work Césaire's "nostalgia for the sacred, . . . belongs to and expresses another world," a world still closely related to modernism (Introduction xxxiv, xxxv, xl).[3] Arnold's reading of Césaire is important, not only because it offers a concrete example of a Caribbean writer adapting modernist strategies but also because Brathwaite and Walcott struggle to define the salient points of Césaire's work in forming their own modernist poetics.

Dash's *The Other America* is probably the most important new work in this area. He makes a broad historical and comparative argument to examine what he describes as the "Caribbean's modernist legacy within its New World context" (20). Historically, he finds this "modernist impulse" in the invention of the Caribbean as a European ideal, in the poetics and politics of Haitian independence, in Caribbean writers' longing for a cultural origin and their creation of a New World Mediterranean myth, and in the contemporary aesthetic and ideological position of Martinique (17). Comparatively, he discusses Caribbean modernism in relation to writers working in each of the major languages of the region—French, English, and Spanish. However, the impressive historical and cultural breadth of Dash's work is also its primary limitation, for he touches only briefly on the details of any individual Caribbean writer's modernist aesthetic, particularly as it is represented through modernist literary techniques.

The ways in which Dash handles Brathwaite and Walcott reveal both the strength and the limitation of his work. For instance, he rightly sets Brathwaite's Afro-Caribbean modernist poetics in the intellectual context of Eliot's "Anglo-American modernist tradition" and an "adopted Césairean aesthetic" (71), but he does not explore how this combination of ideas shapes Brathwaite's poetic technique, such as his shifting personae, his representation of nation language, or his experiments with Sycorax video-style. Indeed, Dash only quotes a few lines from Brathwaite's *The Arrivants* to illustrate his larger conceptual point. His handling of Walcott is similar. Again, he rightly conceives of Walcott's general aesthetic as "translational and intertextual," describing him as a "critical criollist" who seeks to "inflect, rather than efface, European culture" (100). He then nicely points to Walcott's vision of the Caribbean as a "New World Mediterranean," particularly in *Omeros,* as a good example of this translational and intertextual aesthetic. However, he concludes by importing the theory of Mikhail Bakhtin and suggesting that "perhaps Walcott's verse should not be read as poems at all—at least in the strict definition of the genre—but as an indeterminate form that constantly drifts toward the novel" (104). Walcott's intertextuality and shifting personae bear a resemblance to what Bakhtin identifies as the "polyglossic" nature of the novel, but Dash's claim obscures the figurative and formal excellence of

Walcott's achievement as a poet, particular in his shorter lyric work. In fact, as the close textual analysis in this study shows, Walcott actually draws on modernist *poetic* strategies and techniques to represent this New World polyglossia. It is in such details that this study offers a deepening richness and an occasional corrective to the impressive intellectual history of Caribbean modernism traced by Dash.

Neil ten Kortenaar has also filled in some of those details in the most thoughtful article to date on the relationship between Eliot and Brathwaite.[4] He extends Paul Gilroy's concept of the Black Atlantic to investigate what he calls the "Greater Atlantic," his term to describe a common perception of modernity that includes a variety of racial and ethnic experiences but is not limited to any one of them. He identifies this common perception as "ambivalence," an awareness of the allure and the impossibility of modernity's humanist ideal. He contends that this ambivalence characterizes literary modernism in all its forms, a proposition that he illustrates by comparing the modernisms of Eliot and Brathwaite. His conclusion suggests both the advantages and the limitations of this method:

> If Eliot's modernism is a function of his creolization, may not the converse also be true—that creolization is best understood, not as the expression of an indigenous West Indian soul, but as the form that modernist ambivalence takes in the Caribbean? The advantage of seeing modernism not as the European contribution to Caribbean creolization but as something that the Caribbean and Europe share is that in describing Caribbean modernism we establish the limits of its European equivalent, which are not the limits of modernism itself. If we are going to understand the modernism of the Greater Atlantic, we will have to look at its appeal for Césaire as well as Breton, for Brathwaite as well as for Eliot. (19)

Ten Kortenaar rightly employs modernism's own collocating method to contend for Brathwaite and Eliot as equal contributors to the modernism of the Greater Atlantic, or what I have been calling cosmopolitan modernism; however, he still feels compelled to oppose these modernisms. Does Caribbean modernism have to "limit" European modernism in order to be discrepant? Why can the different expressions of modernism not qualify, extend, renew, or intensify other expressions of it? Should our understanding of the modernism of the "Greater Atlantic" not be greater than the sum of that modernism's parts?

With this reservation in mind, this study expands the scope and promise of the approach briefly sketched out by ten Kortenaar. It resists the temptation to ignore or oppose the relationships between Eliot, Brathwaite, and Walcott; instead, it seeks to collocate their different responses to modernity so as to identify the common and disparate features of literary modernism as a cosmopolitan intellectual movement. Models of literary influence that isolate writers by geography or race or that oppose writers in Oedipal struggles are simply not multifaceted enough to describe the transcultural relationships between writers in the twentieth century.[5] Brathwaite and Walcott are neither exclusively literary orphans unrelated to Eliot and European modernism nor exclusively rebel sons rejecting his and its authority; instead, they are more like second cousins whose distinctly individual responses to modernity bear a common family resemblance. Accordingly, at its broadest level this study challenges the proposition that postcolonial writing must oppose modernist strategies and ideals, and in the process it reorients our understanding of modernism's discrepant cosmopolitanism.

Recuperating Eliot?

While some may agree that postcolonialism should not be equated with antimodernism, they still might hesitate about the choice of Eliot as a representative figure of modernism. Why not James Joyce or W. B. Yeats, whose Irish historical, political, geographical, and linguistic heritage seems more plausibly aligned with the postcolonial condition of writers from the Caribbean?[6] What could Brathwaite and Walcott possibly find useful in the work of this self-proclaimed Anglo-Catholic, royalist, and classicist and critically disparaged anti-Semite?[7] Indeed, is Fredric Jameson's approach to modernism not more acceptable? He is willing to rewrite Joyce as a "feminist," "creole," "multiethnic," "Third World," and "anti-imperialist" writer but wonders whether "all the classics of yesteryear [are] rewritable in this fashion? . . . is T. S. Eliot recuperable?" (*Postmodernism* 302–3).

This animus against Eliot in contemporary Anglo-American criticism runs deep and wide, and chief among his antagonistic readers has been Harold Bloom. In defending romanticism Bloom has attacked Eliot consistently and vitriolically to the point of caricature. Consider, for example, a historical sampling of his comments about Eliot: in 1966, "We need to thrust aside utterly, once and for all, the critical absurdities of the Age of Eliot"; in 1970, "We still need to clear our minds of Eliotic cant"; in 1982, "The malign influence of T. S. Eliot still lingers on" ("Central Man" 37; "Internalization" 32; *Breaking* 17). In 1985 Bloom made explicit the motivation of his attack: "To speak out of even narrower personal experience, anyone adopting the profession of teaching literature in the early nineteen fifties entered a discipline virtually enslaved . . . by the entire span of [Eliot's] preferences and prejudices. . . . The ascendancy of Eliot, as a fact of cultural politics, is something many among us could not wish to see return" ("Introduction" 1–2). By Eliot's centenary, in 1988, Bloom considers his devaluation of Eliot to be a success. He concludes that Eliot "has ceased to be the spiritual enemy," so he can magnanimously extend a place in the canon to *The Waste Land* (but not to *Four Quartets*) because it expresses the vision of a "late Romantic poet" ("Reflections" 71, 87).

The exaggeration and repression in Bloom's attack on Eliot invites, as Bloom's own theory of influence suggests, speculation about his subconscious motives to slay the critical father.[8] In fact, his theory of influence essentially restates what Eliot has to say in "Tradition and the Individual Talent" in more exotic and affective terms. However, even putting aside such speculation, Bloom nicely exemplifies the anti-Eliot sentiment among an influential segment of Anglo-American critics during the last couple of decades, a sentiment that caricatures Eliot's modernism as rigidly monolithic, conflates it almost completely with New Criticism, and criticizes Eliot's poetics primarily on the basis of his ideology.[9]

Brathwaite and Walcott encounter Eliot in a different context, and they are more open to the ambivalence of his modernism and more willing to adapt selectively from his contrary positions to advance their own poetics. They are willing to see him as both a New World colonial and a European imperialist, both a classicist and a romantic, both an elite and a popular artist, both a member of the literary avant-garde and a cultural conservative. They feel no compulsion to resolve these polarities because they are quite ready to appropriate selectively from his poetic techniques and ideological positions. While Jameson, Bloom, and other contemporary Anglo-American critics see Eliot's modernism primarily as a cultural *politics* that must be resisted, Brathwaite and Walcott consider it primarily as a cultural *poetics* that can be revised and redeployed to advance their own cultural ends. Indeed, Walcott expresses impatience with Bloom in particular and anti-Eliot sentiment in general. He scoffs at an interviewer who asks him whether he suffers from an "anxiety of influence," describing it as an "ambitious, careerist phrase" that means "nothing" to a practicing poet (Walcott, "Thinking Poetry" 186). Instead of laboring through Bloom's revisionary ratios, Walcott contends that people should reread Eliot and Coleridge because they are "poet-critics" (186). When the intrepid but slow-witted interviewer asserts that contemporary critics were "devaluing" Eliot's work, Walcott responds irritably: "I know, but Eliot is solid. Why are you knocking Eliot?" (187).

Brathwaite and Walcott seem to develop this critical appreciation of Eliot because they mature as poets at an oblique angle to the institutions of Anglo-American culture. On the one hand, the colonial education system and channels of cultural distribution reinforce modernism as a liberating poetics and Eliot as a representative voice of modernism. Brathwaite decries "the English Romantic / Victorian cultural tradition" taught in Caribbean schools and aligns his alternative cultural tradition with the "colonial breakthrough" of modernism ("Jazz" 72–73). Walcott remembers fondly holding "actual volumes of Eliot" and experiencing the "physical pleasure of seeing living poetry in print" (Walcott, "An Interview" [Hirsch] 53). Both of them claim that listening to British Council recordings of Eliot reading his poetry was formative in their development as young poets (Brathwaite, "History of the Voice" 286n34; Walcott, "Leaving School" 31). On the other hand, they were also less exposed to, and so less likely to react against, the pervasive simplifying of Eliot by his New Critical followers. Since Brathwaite and Walcott consider themselves neither wholly a part of nor estranged from this mythical age of Eliot, they respond more easily to the complexities of Eliot. So while Eliot's reputation was probably as distinguished in the West Indies as it was in the West End of London, Brathwaite and Walcott do not feel overwhelmed or stifled by his example, as do many of their Anglo-American contemporaries. Since they are more detached from the prevailing Anglo-American notions of Eliot and his modernism, they are able to find in his legacy a more varied and accommodating poetics than most recent Anglo-American readers have been willing to recognize.

Accordingly, this study seeks neither to "recuperate" nor to "thrust aside" Eliot's modernism, but to reassess its useful features and changing significance in light of the complementary Caribbean modernisms offered by Brathwaite and Walcott. Such a reassessment broadens our understanding of modernism's discrepant cosmopolitanism and also begins to address the need, identified by Sanford Schwartz, to examine the "larger patterns" of Eliot's "international influence" ("T. S. Eliot" 253). While Eliot's cosmopolitanism has long been recognized—Delmore Schwartz declared him "the international hero" and "citizen of the world" as early as 1945 ("T. S. Eliot" 120, 127)—it is a cosmopolitanism that has been studied almost exclusively in terms of Eliot's allusive practice rather than in terms of his subsequent international influence. Even the best contemporary readers of Eliot have only reinforced this retrospective approach. Jewel Spears Brooker claims, for example, that Eliot is "inseparably linked" with "international modernism" (3) but then only cites his relationship to Marx, Nietzsche, Pater, Hegel, Yeats, Valéry, and Joyce as her evidence. In other words, we know a lot more about Eliot's debt to the comparative anthropology of Frazer's *Golden Bough* or to the religious teachings of the *Bhagavad-Gita* than we know about his significance for contemporary writers from Africa, Asia, or South America.[10] And what is true of the study of Eliot is even more true of the study of modernism in general. For instance, Malcolm Bradbury and James McFarlane claim that their influential study of modernism has a daring international perspective even as they justify limiting it to European writers (11–16). It is time to reconsider Eliot and modernism as exclusively European, time to understand modernism as a discrepant cosmopolitan literary movement.

There is, of course, a rich irony in this reshaping of modernism by postcolonial writers, for European modernism itself develops, at least in part, in response to the influence and demise of European colonial empires. Consider, for example, how many of the distinctive innovations of European modernism—Eliot's structural use of fertility myths, Matisse's shockingly brilliant colors, Picasso's cubist dislocations, and Stravinsky's dissonance and asymmetrical rhythms, to name a few—were deeply influenced by the non-European cultural forms being brought back to Paris and London by colonial anthropologists, ethnographers, missionaries, and administrators. Or consider how, as Edward Said contends, European modernists responded to the demise of the empire "with a desperate attempt at a new inclusiveness," creating new, "encyclopedic" forms that substituted "art and its creations for the once-possible synthesis of the world empires" (189). These modernist strategies of "making it new" by making it exotic and of substituting aesthetic for political domination clearly implicate European modernism in the cultural imperialism of its age, but these strategies do not irrevocably bind all of modernism's aesthetic innovations to colonialism's ideology. Subsequent postcolonial writers have transformed these strategies into different forms of innovation and inclusiveness that bring together the cultural fragments left by colonialism. It is certainly true that modernism was shaped in part by colonialism, but it is equally true, and less recognized, that modernism has developed, and been changed by, postcolonial writers. "A huge and remarkable adjustment in perspective and understanding is required," Said states, "to take account of the contribution to modernism of decolonization, resistance culture, and the literature of opposition to imperialism" (242). Forces of colonialism shaped modernism's initial vision, but leading postcolonial writers are reshaping its contemporary expression.

Indeed, the irony of Eliot's relationship to the empire and to Brathwaite and Walcott is particularly acute. Even before Eliot traveled to the Caribbean, he had already proclaimed the problems of Caribbean culture "insoluble," describing the Caribbean as a place in which "several uprooted peoples have been haphazardly mixed" and concluding that "any positive or excellent development of culture" in the West Indies would be a "miracle" (*Notes* 63). Eliot was a better poet than he was a cultural prophet, and he would have been surprised to learn not only that such a "miracle" has occurred in the work of Brathwaite, Walcott, Louise Bennett, Lorna Goodison, George Lamming, Wilson Harris, V. S. Naipaul, and others but also that some of these writers recast his modernist ideas and techniques to achieve this "miracle." These compelling incongruities demand a more nuanced understanding of Eliot and of his modernism.

The complementarity of Eliot's modernism tends to get lost in all but the most subtle of contemporary readings of his work, but it is critical to recognize it in order to understand how Brathwaite and Walcott could find his ideas and techniques useful in constructing their own poetics. Eliot's complementarity is both a poetic method and a habit of thought that brings together seemingly contradictory ideas as congruent parts of contingent wholes. In his poetry, his philosophy, and his criticism Eliot rejects the either-or logic of exclusion for the both-and logic of complementarity; his goal is to widen the circles of comparison to form new unities. For instance, Eliot conceives of tradition, not as a struggle between the past and the present, between the community and the individual, between continuity and originality, but as a collocation of the past and present, of the community and the individual, and of continuity and originality in a new contingent whole. He knows that these new wholes are only conventions, that they can never be fully grasped from a single perspective, and that they always remain open to change, but he believes that they remain important as the means by which we shape perceptions of reality into meaningful patterns.

Jeffrey Perl describes Eliot's complementarity as a form of ambivalence, a deep "skepticism about the belief in antithetical beliefs" in which the comprehending of opposites implies a "rudimentary consensus" (*Skepticism* 43, 48). This consensus is not a new synthesis that furthers the progress of some Hegelian dialectic but a glimpse of the contingent conventions that makes human communication and community possible. Perl convincingly argues that Eliot develops his understanding of the self-contradictory nature of human existence through his reading of F. H. Bradley and Buddhism. He also shows how this ambivalence explains, at least in part, Eliot's conversion to Anglicanism, a form of Christianity that asserts an authority of consensus through listening to a multitude of voices. Perl contends that, paradoxically, Eliot's skepticism and relativism deepen his commitment to the conventions of tradition, language, poetry, and religion as contingent ways to hold together the opposites of experience. In other words, Eliot employs a variety of contextual, conventional, and perspectival arguments to represent conventions of meaning as both groundless and significant, both philosophically untenable and pragmatically indispensable, both products of skepticism and tenets of faith.

Jewel Spears Brooker deepens our understanding of Eliot's complementarity or ambivalence when she characterizes it as a method of "mastery and escape" (1). She contends that Eliot "masters" the contradictions of the past not to "escape from" them to a new synthesis but to "escape *to* a broader perspective," a perspective that holds more and more of these contradictions together (2). It is a method that liberates writers from the potential tyranny of past conventions by authorizing them to reconfigure those conventions in newly inclusive and self-consciously contingent ways (2). It is a method that continues to uphold the making of meaning but evades making any single meaning conclusive. Brooker concludes that this complementarity or ambivalence is a defining characteristic of Eliot and other modernists, writers who "move forward by spiraling back and reconfiguring the past" and lose nothing en route (2).

Eliot recognizes the challenge of holding opposing positions simultaneously, claiming that it is "so difficult that I am not sure I grasp it myself except in flashes, or that I comprehend all of its implications" (*Christianity* 103). The task is even more difficult for Eliot's readers, for they tend to understand Eliot's complexity by affirming one position or the other. However, as Perl and Brooker show, this desire to identify Eliot's conclusive stand on any issue misses the larger point of his method. He is more interested in dissolving either-or choices than in resolving them, more interested in making diversity and unity concomitant forces in his poetics than in making them opposing ones. Walcott, in particular, recognizes this feature of Eliot's work. He praises the "inherent contradictions" in the "poetic process," claiming that in Eliot's work "the contradiction, . . . the opposite direction is much more fascinating than the one you're taking. . . . Eliot is wonderful like that" (Walcott, "Conversation" [Smith] 194–95).

It is not too surprising, then, to discover that Brathwaite and Walcott find this modernist dialectic of "mastery and escape" an attractive strategy to recast to create their complementary Caribbean poetics. The postcolonial and multicultural nature of their Caribbean experience makes them at least as sensitive to the historical, religious, linguistic, and cultural contradictions of modernity. Indeed, as Edouard Glissant suggests, the Caribbean has been so "driven by the daring adventure of modernity" that cultural "parochialism" is no longer a viable option; instead, Caribbean artists must develop a "cross-cultural poetics" or a "poetics of relating" that embraces the region's diversity (*Caribbean Discourse* 140, 146; *Poetics of Relation* 23–35). Brathwaite and Walcott are also aware of the danger of arriving at historical or cultural synthesis through the logic of binary distinctions because they recognize that logic as the epistemological method of colonialism. Yet, they aspire to create a vision of cultural wholeness that holds together the contradictions of life without relying on coercion, that offers a sense of common cultural identity without demanding a single cultural identity, that satisfies the human need to be both one and many. Brathwaite calls this method of complementarity *creolization,* while Walcott favors the term *mimicry.* Understanding the differences between these theories involves employing the method of complementarity itself, for the poetics of Brathwaite and Walcott should be viewed as concomitant rather than opposing theories. It is a view that honors their individual contributions to shaping a New World poetics without glossing over the depth of their ideological disagreements, that recognizes their methods as parallel without claiming their purposes as congruent, and that respects their different poetic practices as discrepant cosmopolitan modernisms.

Brathwaite versus Walcott

Brathwaite and Walcott are more often opposed than aligned in discussions of Caribbean poetry, a pattern that they seemed to encourage early in their careers. In March 1965 Brathwaite and Walcott participated in a seminar entitled "West Indian Poetry, a Search for Voices," sponsored by the Extra-Mural Department of the University of the West Indies. According to Mervyn Morris, Brathwaite challenged Walcott about the accessibility of his poetry to a general West Indian audience ("Walcott" 177–78). In elaborating his point, Brathwaite made a distinction between his "folk" poetry and Walcott's "humanist" poetry, between a "public" poetry that addresses the communal concerns of the Caribbean and a "private" poetry that addresses individual concerns that are more transcultural. Morris does not record Walcott's response at the seminar; however, in subsequent interviews Walcott denies Brathwaite's characterization as an illegitimate class distinction.[11] Indeed, while he rarely responds to Brathwaite by name, Walcott's seminal essays of the earlier seventies are consistently focused on attacking the integrity of this idea of a Caribbean "folk" poetics.[12]

Critics of Caribbean poetry quickly picked up on this binary distinction and proliferated its manifestations. For example, Bruce King contends that "Walcott's transformation of foreign models and Brathwaite's claim to speak for the folk are the two poles between which a national art moves according to the temperament of its practitioners and the intellectual fashions of the time" (*New English Literatures* 139). Even more recently, June Bobb repeats the tired critical dichotomy of the early seventies: "While Brathwaite's muse celebrates community, Walcott's muse celebrates the individual" (34). Brathwaite and Walcott came to represent a series of oppositions within Caribbean poetry: Afrocentric/Eurocentric, public/private, historical/ahistorical, black/mulatto, authentic/hybrid, popular culture/high culture, political/psychological, protesting/quietist, oral/written, and experimental/formalist. And then critics began to choose either Brathwaite ("It is therefore quite clear that the Caribbean needs Edward Brathwaite and has absolutely no place for Derek Walcott" ["How Far" 100]) or Walcott ("Walcott, as a craftsman, towers far above Brathwaite" [Ismond 221]) as their representative Caribbean poet. Even when a fine critic such as J. Edward Chamberlin recognizes that this "opposition between Walcott and Brathwaite . . . has skewed discussion of each," he still contributes little to our understanding of the relationship between these two leading Caribbean poets (154–55). As Gordon Collier asserts, when we move beyond the easy opposition of Brathwaite and Walcott, "two complementary and far from antagonistic bodies of fine poetry remain . . . neither can be fully understood without the other" (104).[13] Discrepant cosmopolitan modernism considers Brathwaite's creolization and Walcott's mimicry as different but complementary expressions of a modernist ambivalence in the Caribbean; it is an approach that recognizes the distinct contributions of each of them to the poetics both of the region and of the language.

Brathwaite's Creolization—"To See the Fragments/Whole"

Brathwaite's theory of creolization is often cited but rarely given the critical attention it deserves.[14] As Eliot's poetics of complementarity develops out of his dissertation on Bradley and is elaborated in his literary essays, Brathwaite's poetics of creolization originates in his doctoral dissertation, later published as *The Development of Creole Society in Jamaica, 1770–*

1820 (1971), and is amplified in his subsequent literary and cultural criticism. Indeed, Brathwaite's *Contradictory Omens* (1974) summarizes concisely his theory and begins to suggest its aesthetic applications.[15] He defines creolization as a dialectical process of acculturation and interculturation that has produced a series of fragmented and contingent cultural norms in the Caribbean. In Brathwaite's model, *acculturation* refers to the colonial process whereby the subordinated African cultures conformed to the norms of the dominant European cultures through the power of force and the prestige of example. *Interculturation* is the reciprocal activity whereby the subordinated African cultures influence European cultural norms through their "unplanned, unstructured but osmotic relationship" (*Contradictory Omens* 6). To his credit, then, Brathwaite defines creolization in a way that recognizes both the hierarchical relationships among cultures in the Caribbean and the reciprocal undermining of those hierarchies through cultural intermixing. In other words, more so than other theories of creolization (hybridity, liminality, rhizomes, chutnification, or *métissage*),[16] Brathwaite's theory underscores the historical inequality of cultural power in the region as he affirms the possibility of cultural cross-fertilization.

Moreover, Brathwaite does not limit his discussion to a historical analysis of creolization; he also considers it to be a model of the aesthetic response to this history. He worries that acculturation has produced too much aesthetic "mimicry" in the Caribbean, too many writers uncritically imitating European culture for prestige or advancement. He does not condemn this imitation completely—he recognizes it as an essential part of the creolization process—but he wants to shift the focus to the innovative creations that contribute to interculturation. Indeed, he rejects defining creolization on the basis of any "either/or distinction," claiming that it is not a choice between mimicry and authenticity but "both imitation (acculturation) and native creation ('indigenization')" that leads to interculturation (16). In true modernist fashion, then, Brathwaite describes his creolization as a poetics of "creative ambivalence," a poetic method that seeks to hold together the contradictory forces of acculturation and interculturation (16).

To this point, Brathwaite's creolization follows a logic similar to those of Eliot's complementarity and Walcott's mimicry. However, Brathwaite concludes that the unique history of colonization in the Caribbean has interrupted the process of creolization and that a poetics of creolization must address this interruption. For example, he claims that the cultural practices of African slaves were more likely to survive in submerged forms in the Caribbean because the plantation system of absentee landownership tended to impose European cultural norms from afar rather than as immediate conventions. As a result, these African cultural practices became part of a Maroon experience that resisted acculturation and interrupted the process of interculturation (62–63). In addition, Brathwaite contends that the need for labor after Emancipation "slowed/halted/altered" creolization by initiating East Indian and Chinese immigration to the region (6). While the acculturating force of European culture remains dominant after Emancipation, the introduction of these new "subordinated" cultures leads to "lateral" creolization. As each "lateral" culture seeks to establish its dominance vis-à-vis other subordinated cultures, the process of interculturation is further frustrated. Accordingly, Brathwaite concludes that the process of creolization in the Caribbean is "incomplete" because of this "interruption/disruption of the process of interculturation" by the Maroon experience of the African slaves and the subsequent lateral creolization among African, East Indian, Chinese, and other subordinated cultures (63).

Brathwaite's theory of "incomplete" creolization is a useful diagnosis of the complexity of the cultural history in the Caribbean, but it is his aesthetic prescription for that complexity that sets his theory apart. Others, including Walcott, would agree that Caribbean colonization affected the process of interculturation in unique ways, but they typically advocate a more hybrid, liminal, or multicultural aesthetic, a poetics of creative ambivalence that would intentionally seek to represent and encourage more interculturation. Brathwaite, however, concludes that he can best advance Caribbean cultural unity by fully recovering and articulating the Maroon experience of the Afro-Caribbean folk culture. He defines this Maroon experience as the slaves' capacity to preserve the essence of their African cultural identity despite the brutality of colonization through a strategy of withdrawing, disguising, and submerging the self.[17] He implies that this submerged identity must be recovered before the process of creolization can continue toward establishing a new cultural unity in the region. In other words, he contributes to creolization best by recovering and expressing the Maroon experience of his Afro-Caribbean cultural heritage.

In *Contradictory Omens* (1974), creolization is central to Brathwaite's poetics and *maronage* is offered only as a tentative corollary. In subsequent essays, he reverses this emphasis and develops the concept of maronage with more specificity. In particular, he coins the term *nam* to identify the cultural essence that survives in the Maroon experience.[18] Literally, he defines it as the "disguise of man; his utter soul, cultural fundament and atomic core" ("Caribbean Culture" 53).[19] Etymologically, he identifies *nam* as a transcultural word for "root or core or spirit" and associates it with man ("man backwards") and with name ("even if you lose your *name* . . . your nam(e) . . . you cannot lose your *nam*") (36–37). Figuratively, he represents nam as the submerged presence of Caliban's mother, Sycorax, in his life (35). In each of these definitions Brathwaite affirms his growing convictions that people are defined by a historical and cultural essence and that the writer's task is to articulate that essence. In *Contradictory Omens* the Caribbean writer articulates the Maroon experience so that interculturation can continue and the process of creolization can be completed; in these subsequent essays, completing creolization seems more allusive, and articulating nam, more urgent. Indeed, Brathwaite has asserted that "interculturation . . . is not the final answer" because "no matter how intimate the symbiosis, there remains the residual nam which, at moments of crisis, has the ability to re-activate itself" ("World Order Models" 63).

Accordingly, Brathwaite's poetic theory employs contradictory notions of cultural identity. In his theory of creolization the fluidity of cultural identity seems to be not only a given but also an ideal to bring about cultural unity: given a chance to run its course, interculturation will bring about a unified sense of the Caribbean self. However, he goes on to contend that this process of creolization can only be completed by recovering the irreducible core of the diverse cultural identities in the Caribbean, a poetics of nam that relies on an essentialist understanding of the self and community. Surprisingly, Brathwaite's critics comment only sparingly on this contradiction, so they do not recognize how his modernist sense of complementarity changes over time.[20] In his poetics of creolization Brathwaite advocates recovering the diverse cultural traditions of the region and holding them together in a creative ambivalence. He describes the goal for this creolization in standard modernist terms: "to see the fragments/whole" (*Contradictory Omens* 7). However, in his later emphasis on nam he seems to limit the effort of his creative ambivalence "to see the fragments/whole" to the Afro-Caribbean community.

As Dash and others have observed, there are conceptual problems with this limitation.[21] When Brathwaite talks about the ambivalence within creolization, he recognizes the influence of interculturation among European, African, East Indian, Chinese, and other cultures in the Caribbean; however, when he discusses the Caribbean writer's need to recover nam to complete creolization, he speaks almost exclusively in terms of recovering an Afro-Caribbean nam. While some Afro-Caribbean writers may resonate with this goal, it excludes the aspiration of writers who associate themselves with other cultural traditions. Certainly, if there is such a thing as nam, there must also be an East Indian nam, a Chinese nam, and other interethnic nams that need to be articulated for creolization to be completed in the Caribbean; however, Brathwaite remains silent about these possibilities. In addition, he does not explain the relationship between nam and racial, ethnic, geographical, or political sources of identity, so the parameters of his concept are unclear. Why relate nam to an African rather than a Yoruba, Ibo, or Ashanti sense of identity? What are the internam possibilities for interethnic people? In short, Brathwaite develops the concept of nam to reconfigure the colonial past in order to create a vibrant Afro-Caribbean identity in the present; however, he has been hesitant to encourage the recovery of other cultural identities in the region. It is a hesitancy that originates from his admirable attention to the inequality of cultures in the region, but it is a hesitancy that also calls into question his commitment to creolization as the ultimate method of complementarity to imagine a new Caribbean self, a question that persists throughout his career.

Walcott's Mimicry—"Everything Is Mere Repetition"

Even though Walcott and Brathwaite are often contrasted and even though Walcott's poetics of mimicry has been thoughtfully discussed, most prominently by Rei Terada, surprisingly little effort has been made to compare Walcott's theory of mimicry with Brathwaite's concept of creolization.[22] It is important to make this comparison, not only to complicate the facile distinctions between Walcott's "mulatto" and Brathwaite's "folk" poetics, but also to understand how these theories reflect their discrepant cosmopolitan modernisms. Walcott's mimicry and Brathwaite's creolization employ similar methods to understand and represent the diverse cultural resources of the Caribbean, but they differ in their choices of sources to emphasize. More importantly, while Brathwaite believes that the process of creolization depends on the recovery and articulation of nam, Walcott develops his theory of mimicry on the absence of origins and the contingency of identity.

Even though Walcott is less systematic in his theoretical writing than either Eliot or Brathwaite, John Thieme rightly suggests that he is "arguably the finest prose stylist the anglophone Caribbean has yet produced" and that his essays still remain "seriously neglected" by his readers (199). Walcott develops his theory of mimicry primarily through three essays written in the early 1970s and then reiterates and revises it in his Nobel lecture in 1992.[23] In these essays he avoids simple definitions and indulges freely in contradictions, but he repeats themes and illustrations frequently enough that they eventually coalesce into the tenets of an aesthetic theory: he conceives of mimicry as the necessary, creative, trenchant, unifying, and ephemeral poetics of the New World.

Mimicry is necessary in the New World because human beings create cultures through imitation: "Everything is mere repetition" ("Culture" 54). As Terada rightly contends, Walcott characterizes this imitation as mimicry rather than mimesis to underscore the absence of origins in the New World (1). Mimicry connotes a representation of a representation in a series of representations, whereas mimesis implies a representation of reality, a representation that assumes an authentic cultural origin. In his theory of creolization Brathwaite identifies mimicry with acculturation (an illegitimate or excessive imitation of the European cultural norm) and authenticity with interculturation (the strategic undermining of the dominant culture through contact with the authentic expressions of the subdominant cultures). Brathwaite aspires to hold this mimicry and authenticity together in creative ambivalence. Walcott claims that there is only mimicry. In Walcott's view, there are no core cultural identities, only the representation of other representations. "Cultures can only be created," Walcott contends, "out of this knowledge of nothing" ("Culture" 57).

To this point, then, the difference between creolization and mimicry is primarily epistemological. Brathwaite claims that a writer can know and articulate a distinct cultural identity, whereas Walcott contends that the absence of this cultural essence requires the writer to create a cultural identity from nothing but repetitive imitation. However, ideological differences also underlie this distinction. Brathwaite recognizes the diversity of cultural influences that contribute to creolization in the Caribbean, but he also asserts that the historical inequality among these cultures has impaired the capacity of some to influence the Caribbean way of life. Indeed, he develops the concept of nam almost exclusively in terms of an Afro-Caribbean cultural identity in part to address the historical neglect of the Afro-Caribbean cultural connection.[24]

In contrast, Walcott has little patience, particularly in his earlier essays, for recounting the historical inequality among cultures in the region because he cannot recover or change that history. As he polemically asserts, "Amnesia is the true history of the New World" because it is "not the pressure of the past which torments great poets but the weight of the present" ("Muse" 4). His theory of mimicry assumes that the representations of all cultural forms are equally derivative and therefore equally permissible. Indeed, he reiterates throughout his essays that the ideal New World writer would be able to mimic the full diversity of cultural forms in the region: "Maturity is the assimilation of the features of every ancestor" (2).[25] In practice, however, he is more reluctant, particularly earlier in his career, to encourage or practice the mimicking of cultural representations associated with Africa, calling such practices a "degeneration of technique" that "hides itself in originality" (19). When he seeks to justify this reluctance, Walcott typically makes an epistemological claim about language. He contends that the African languages are not sufficiently present in the region to enable the poet to mimic African cultural forms.

However, Walcott's reluctance to mimic African representations also reflects his deep ideological antipathy toward the influence of the Black Power movement in the Caribbean. Retrospectively, he associates this antipathy with his split with Brathwaite: "There was a time, particularly at the peak of the Black Power movement, when the division between Edward Brathwaite and myself became almost political" (Walcott, "Conversation" [Smith] 189). What he feared in the Black Power movement was "the narrowing down of everything to a kind of an idea called heritage, and heritage, being particularly black, emphatically black in the Caribbean, which I consider to be very narrow-minded since, obviously, the presence of the Indian and the Chinese makes that idea of heritage [more complex]" (189).[26] Walcott's argument is a bit disingenuous, for he refers to Indian and Chinese sources of culture only rarely in his own work. His real struggle with Brathwaite over the years has been over the relative weight to be given to African and European cultural forms in a Caribbean poetics.[27] As they have grown older, Brathwaite's interest in establishing an Afro-Caribbean cultural tradition has intensified, whereas Walcott's antipathy to African cultural sources has lessened, to the point that they now occupy a prominent position alongside his European, American, and Caribbean cultural allusions.

So, while in principle Brathwaite's creolization and Walcott's mimicry both recognize the region's multicultural influences, in practice the two writers initially disagree sharply about Africa's cultural influence in the region. For Brathwaite, recovering and articulating nam becomes the means to achieve equality for the historically neglected Afro-Caribbean culture and to further the process of creolization. For Walcott, such an approach is epistemologically mistaken and ideologically suspect; instead, he advocates the New World writer's mimicking all of the available cultural traditions until he or she masters them. He does not fully satisfy this rhetoric of pluralism in his poetry or recognize the ideological choices involved in this strategy; instead, he asserts that this mastery will enable the writer to create a new cultural tradition that unifies the diversity of the region and informs a new collective sense of identity.

For Walcott, mimicry is not only necessary but also creative. Indeed, he describes mimicry's creativity as a necessary result of the region's history. When artists in the New World recognize their separation from the Old World, recognize their "loss of history," what becomes "necessary is imagination, imagination as necessity, as invention" ("Culture" 53). Accordingly, he believes that mimicry is more than "mere imitation"; it is also an "act of the imagination" that creates something new (55). The artist takes the Old World (Asian, African, or European) cultural forms, repeats them in the different geographical and cultural context of the New World, and makes a new representation that combines and supersedes its sources. The art of Carnival serves as his example of this creative mimicry: the steel drum and calypso "originated in imitation" of the xylophone and the group chant, but they "ended in invention" as they became distinctly New World art forms (55).

This creativity within mimicry also explains how Walcott conceives of his aesthetic as a trenchant critique of earlier cultural representations of the region—what Tejumola Olaniyan describes as the "coherent deformation" of Walcott's poetics (*Scars* 114). By repeating, mastering, and redeploying these earlier representations, the New World writer gains control over and can change their meaning. Walcott's Crusoe is not just a figure of European expansion and Enlightenment rationality; he also embodies the existential loneliness and pragmatic creativity of people forcibly transported to the New World. Walcott's New World poet is a "second Adam" who enjoys the same "elemental privilege of naming a new world" but who exercises this privilege only after the fall of colonialism and slavery. His Adam knows the evil that has brought him to this paradise, so "the apples of [his] second Eden have the tartness of experience" ("Muse" 5). Walcott's Caliban is not just an "enraged pupil" but a poet whose speeches "are equal in their elemental power to those of his tutor" ("Muse" 4). Whereas Brathwaite seeks to reverse a prevailing cultural hierarchy by elevating the profile and influence of Afro-Caribbean cultural resources, Walcott aspires to disassemble the hierarchy by mastering its representations and reorienting their significance. Brathwaite risks oversimplifying the cultural complexity of the region to sharpen his resistance to its historical inequalities and to recover the submerged Afro-Caribbean communal identity. Walcott risks masking those historical inequalities to imagine a new, interethnic cultural community. Brathwaite recovers nam; Walcott renames Adam. They agree that a poetics should aspire after the modernist goal of offering a unifying vision of cultural wholeness for the region, but they disagree about the particulars of that vision.

Through repeated allusions to religious ceremonies and rituals, Walcott suggests that literature offers this unifying vision in a way analogous to religious practice. Indeed, Bruce King claims that "Walcott may be one of the few remaining religious poets" (*Derek Walcott: A Caribbean Life* 40), and Paula Burnett argues persuasively that "Walcott's writing is . . . both mimetic of a culture of faith and a counterdiscourse to a generally growing lack of faith" (110). In "Twilight" Walcott contends that his drama emerges from the street theater of the Salvation Army and the black mass of the Christmas pantomimes, two opposing forms of religious popular drama that seek to convert their audience into participants in the drama in order to change their perceptions of reality (21–22). In "Muse" he asserts that his aesthetic of mimicry merely repeats the resistance strategy of the slave who understood experientially the "Christian rituals of a whipped, tortured and murdered redeemer" and who converted to Christianity to wrest "God from his captor" (11). Finally, in keeping with the broadening of his cultural references later in his career, in his Nobel lecture he offers two "epiphanies" as models for his art: East Indian children participating in the Hindu religious drama of Ramleela in Trinidad and Afro-Caribbean children attending a Christian church service in Saint Lucia. They are exemplary for him because "they believed in what they were playing, in the sacredness of the text;" they exhibit the "delight of conviction, not loss" *(Antilles)*. Walcott suggests that poetry asks for a similar faith in the sacredness of the text, a belief that words should and can inspire hope in the community's future rather than despair, revenge, or guilt about the community's past. Just as religious practices emerge from people's faith, he imagines his aesthetic of mimicry as the "painful, new, laborious uttering that comes out of belief, not out of doubt" ("Culture" 57). Just as religious practices define a communal identity by encouraging people to participate in common rituals, he aspires after a poetry that mimics the rituals of literature in such as a way as to contribute to the making of a common New World identity. Just as religious practices renew hope through ritually recognizing historical experiences of suffering, he aspires to recast poetic rituals in order to imagine an ideal interethnic New World community emerging from the anguished historical experience of colonialism. As Burnett suggests, Walcott's "faith in art is still astonishing and beautiful" (103).

This sacralizing of poetry's social function is not without its risks, particularly in the Caribbean, where religious discourse and practice were an integral part of colonial oppression. By equating his poetic mimicry of European cultural forms with the forced conversions of African slaves to Christianity, Walcott risks devaluing the religious and cultural trauma of colonization. He responds pragmatically: the slaves convert to survive, and the poet conforms to the conventions of poetry as a matter of necessity. However, he also suggests a more compelling rationale for this analogy. Walcott cites Eliot in claiming that "the culture of a people" is the "incarnation of its religion" (Eliot, *Notes* 28, quoted in "Muse" 8). His poetic recasting of religious discourse, then, is an integral part of representing the culture of the Caribbean. Indeed, he is not alone in employing this strategy. As Silvio Torres-Saillant contends, "The pervasive concern with the sacred in Caribbean texts corresponds to the decisive role played by religion in the human experience of the region" (88).

Walcott's final claim for his poetics of mimicry is that it best captures the ephemerality that does and should characterize New World art. He praises the "built-in obsolescence" of Carnival, a celebration of creativity in which the sculptures, costumes, and songs become "valueless" at "midnight on Shrove Tuesday" ("Culture" 55). He also admires the "waste" of the annual Ramleela drama, a ceremony in which the people construct an elaborate bamboo effigy of a Hindu god that is consumed by fire at the end of the drama. He links the ephemerality of the effigy with a practice of mimicry—"the point of such a sacrifice being its repetition"—and claims that this deliberate transience is the means by which cultures can perpetually renew themselves—"the point of destruction being renewal through fire" *(Antilles)*. This sense of art as a ritual of impermanence completes the logic of Walcott's poetics of mimicry. Walcott believes that if mimicry is to avoid viewing itself as the "exclusive" or "authentic" cultural practice of the region, it must self-consciously recognize the contingency of its own practice. Mimicry should celebrate the creative act of imitation without demanding that its artifacts become the norm of future imitation.

Complementary Caribbean Modernisms

Brathwaite's creolization and Walcott's mimicry express complementary visions for a Caribbean or New World modernism. Brathwaite's creolization reshapes modernism's ambivalence to recognize and express the historical inequalities that emerge from the contradictory forces of acculturation and interculturation in the region. Walcott repeats the strategy of modernism's ambivalence by mimicking the available fragments of "Old World" cultures to imagine a new, multicultural ideal for the region. Caribbean modernism needs the sharpness of Brathwaite's critique of colonialism's cultural legacy without the exclusivity of his poetics of nam. It also needs the breadth of Walcott's multicultural ideals without unduly homogenizing the cultural diversity in the region. The method of modernism affirms the collocating of these two writers to conceive of a broader unity that holds them together.

Some may question this characterization of Brathwaite and Walcott in particular and Caribbean poetics in general as modernist. For example, Paul Breslin argues that "Walcott is poised on the cusp between a modernistic aesthetic" that seeks to "salvage some sort of artistic order" and a "postmodern one that accepts brokenness and disorder as the way things are" (7). Rei Terada goes even further when she suggests that the "cultural and linguistic displacement" of Walcott's mimicry could be considered a "hallmark of Postmodern literature" (213). And Brathwaite himself describes the textual experiments of his Sycorax video-style as "post-modem" ("Newstead" 658). In addition, Antonio Benítez-Rojo and Glissant have independently developed compelling theories of Caribbean poetics that rely on such postmodern concepts as chaos theory and a rhizomatic sense of identity.[28] Attributes of Eliot's, Brathwaite's, and Walcott's work, such as contingency of identity, the emphasis on cultural absence, and making language visible, could fairly be characterized as postmodern, but the general thrust of their work is best described as modernist because it still aspires to create a provisional sense of cultural order or wholeness out of a multiplicity of cultural sources. These writers recognize difference and fragmentation, but they seek to shape these differences and fragments into larger patterns of cultural meaning. And as Sanford Schwartz rightly suggests, the line between modernism and postmodernism is more flexible than is often acknowledged, so "the rereading of modernism from a postmodern perspective . . . introduce[s] a more variegated understanding of modernist enterprise . . . and prompt[s] the claim that modernism (or certain elements of modernism) may be more postmodern than we ordinarily assume" ("Postmodernity of Modernism" 10).

The aesthetic, epistemological, and ideological differences between Eliot's ambivalence, Brathwaite's creolization, and Walcott's mimicry are sharp enough that one could also reasonably question whether they are really complementary modernisms or radically different poetics. Modernism offers the most satisfying category for explaining the relationships between these writers because it identifies some common questions to which all of them feel compelled to respond. How does tradition function in twentieth-century literature? What is the relationship between poetry and speech in the contemporary context of multiple languages and dialects? How does the twentieth-century writer fulfill his or her social obligation and contribute to cultural wholeness? The poets in this study offer discrepant answers to these questions, but the asking of these common questions suggests a shared method. It is to these questions that we turn next.

2 "Not Borrowers, But Bearers of a Tradition"

In a letter to Mary Hutchinson in July 1919 the young Eliot claims that he had "started on a long subject which I have not now either time or energy to carry out" (*Letters* 316). Although physically worn out from the demands of his marriage, his work, and his poetry, he finds the time and energy to transform the sketchy ideas of this letter into the magisterial pronouncements of "Tradition and the Individual Talent." In this essay Eliot boldly claims that creating art in the modern world depends on recovering a proper understanding of tradition. Tradition is not the "blind or timid adherence" to the past but a recognition "not only of the pastness of the past, but of its presence," an awareness of the simultaneity of influence among works of art (14). He reconceives tradition not only to revitalize an apparently exhausted European culture but also to claim authority for his own poetic practice as part of that tradition. He so successfully combines these public and personal motivations that this essay has become a defining document of modernism and of his own career.[1]

However, the letter to Mary Hutchinson also suggests another motive for his attempt to recover a concept of tradition. He asks her to "remember that I am *metic*—a foreigner, and that I *want* to understand you, and all that background and tradition of you" (*Letters* 318). In ancient Greece the metic was an alien allowed to reside in the city because of a special skill but never granted full rights as a citizen. It is a rare and illuminating self-description, for the usually impervious Eliot admits to his own anxious liminality as an American poet trying to succeed in London. Pound had convinced him (and tried to convince his parents) that he should not return to America because his poetic skill needed to be recognized and advanced by the metropole.[2] In claiming this classical status as his own, Eliot affirms Pound's assessment but recognizes that it comes with an inescapable sense of estrangement. The metic possesses an enduring skill but not a permanent home. For the young Eliot, constructing a tradition becomes a way to respond to this alienation.

Eliot's expatriate experience in London is not unique. Indeed, self-imposed exile was almost a prerequisite for becoming a modernist writer at the beginning of the twentieth century, not only for Eliot and the younger Pound in London but also for Hemingway, Stein, and Fitzgerald in Paris, H.D. in London and Zurich, and Joyce in Trieste, Zurich, and Paris. This status of exile is represented in modernism as both painful and empowering to the artistic consciousness, as both a fragmenting separation from cultural origins and an enabling vantage point to represent more comprehensively the familiar and the foreign as a both discrepant and cosmopolitan experience.

Exile also defines the experience of many contemporary postmodern writers. However, as Aijaz Ahmad contends, postmodern writers seem less ambivalent in their response: "The terrors of High Modernism at the prospect of inner fragmentation and social disconnection have now been stripped, in . . . postmodernism, of their tragic edge, pushing that experience of loss, instead in a celebratory direction" (129). The theme of exile also dominates Caribbean literature, but the prevailing response is more typically modernist in its ambivalence.[3] It is a response that for Brathwaite emerges from his own experience. When he went to Cambridge as a student, he expected to be received as a "citizen of the world," in part because he knew *The Waste Land* and *Macbeth* by heart. He quickly learned, however, that memorizing Eliot and Shakespeare did not give him the right to become a denizen either in the poetry magazines of Cambridge or in the expatriate Caribbean writers' community of London (*Barabajan Poems* 57–63). After graduation he accepted his status as a "West Indian, rootless man of the world" and applied for jobs around the globe ("Timehri" 33). Hired to teach in Ghana, he ended up spending a decade in West Africa. It is through this experience that Brathwaite recognizes more deeply the connections between African and Caribbean culture, which encourages him to develop his insurgent Afro-Caribbean folk tradition. Eliot had left St. Louis and Boston for London in order to become "European";[4] Brathwaite leaves Barbados and travels through England and Ghana in order to see himself as Afro-Caribbean. These ambivalent experiences of exile in England and Ghana give Brathwaite the perspective to begin to recover the Caribbean as his cultural home.

Unlike Brathwaite and most other Caribbean writers of their generation, Walcott spent all but a year of his early career in the Caribbean.[5] Even though he does not himself undergo the classic metic experience, Walcott transposes this theme to reflect on the coerced migrations of colonialism. Through slavery, criminal deportation, indentured servitude, or economic necessity most of the inhabitants of the Caribbean were forcibly uprooted from their cultural "homes" and arrived in the New World, in Walcott's figurative language, as "castaways."[6] The task of these New World "castaways," however, parallels that of Old World metics. They must employ their skills to construct a tradition that transforms the results of these colonial encounters into a satisfying cultural home. In Walcott's New World each person is a "craftsman and castaway," a creator as well as a casualty of his or her history ("Crusoe's Island," *Collected Poems* 69). Walcott creates from his castaway experiences an ironic New World classical tradition to define his cultural home.

Of course, qualitative differences of race and class exist between Eliot's experience of emigrating to England as a relatively well-off, white, Harvard-educated young man and Brathwaite's exile experience in England and Ghana or Walcott's imaginative exile and cultural estrangement. Even so, Brathwaite and Walcott find Eliot's modernist sense of tradition useful to recast because it offers a way for them to construct new unities from the fragments of their colonized cultures. Whether described as metics, rootless men, or castaways, these poets share an anxiety about the perceived inferiority and disintegration of their cultural heritages, and it spurs them to transform and reorder the concept of tradition. These discrepant cosmopolitan modernisms converge in this need to construct a tradition as a cultural home.

Critics tend to overlook the colonial anxiety in Eliot's idea of tradition because of the rhetorical confidence of his prose style and the success of his critical opinions. Indeed, "Tradition and the Individual Talent" is often decried as the ur-text for inaugurating a monolithic, Eurocentric literary canon. Henry Louis Gates Jr. speaks for many when he writes that "the Western literary tradition . . . has been defined since Eliot as a more-or-less closed set of works" (*Loose Canons* 44). However, we should separate the success of Eliot's opinions about individual authors—his canon—from the comparative method that guides his understanding of tradition. Of course, he contributed to defining a particular literary canon (Donne in, Milton out; Dante in, Wordsworth out; Tourneur's *Revenger's Tragedy* in, Shakespeare's *Hamlet* out), but it was primarily his New Critical successors who hermetically sealed this list as *the* canon in Anglo-American universities.[7] Eliot himself conceives of tradition as anything but closed; he views it as a contingent, ideal order that participants construct and revise by making relative comparisons among their predecessors. When a new work arrives, "the *whole* existing order must be, if ever so slightly altered" ("Tradition and the Individual Talent" 15). In addition, while Eliot equates tradition with the "mind of Europe," he subsequently recognizes that traditions form along multiple national, regional, or linguistic lines.[8] Moreover, his poetic practice in *The Waste Land,* with its allusions to comparative anthropology and Indic traditions, explicitly critiques the limits of a Eurocentric tradition. We should therefore resist the urge to dismiss too easily Eliot's conception of tradition as a fixed canon. As Brathwaite and Walcott realize, it is both more complicated and more useful than is often recognized.

Even when critics credit the contingency of Eliot's concept of tradition, they often still condemn it. For example, Terry Eagleton agrees that "Eliot's 'tradition' is a labile, self-transformative organism extended in space and time, constantly reorganised in the present," yet he finds that it can only advance an "authoritarian cultural ideology" (147). Other critics reject any gesture by writers to establish new unities. Consider John Guillory, who argues that any appeal to tradition reflects a worn-out "longing for consensus, for the metaphysics of the same," when we should instead be trying to understand "what it means that 'difference' has become our central critical category" (194–95). What is striking, then, about the counterexample of Walcott and Brathwaite is that they choose to appropriate and renew Eliot's sense of tradition in order not only to transform the cultural legacy of one of the most authoritarian of ideologies—colonialism—but also to imagine new lines of consensus, however provisional, among their broadly heterogeneous cultural communities. It is an anomaly that reverses current critical shibboleths, for Brathwaite and Walcott recognize difference but still aspire after consensus; they see tradition as an enabling practice, not as a limiting authority.

Again, critics of Caribbean literature have led the way in helping us to see the empowering flexibility of Eliot's concept of tradition. Laurence Breiner was the first to suggest that examining Brathwaite's and Walcott's work could help to revise "American theorizing about tradition" ("Tradition" 1). He contends that Brathwaite and Walcott shift their definition of tradition, so it is "not, as for Eliot. . . , a body of work, but a function, a place in society . . . the 'Western' poet is responsible to his predecessors, but the [Caribbean poet] is responsible to his community" (6).[9] Breiner rightly emphasizes the social function of the poet in the Caribbean, but he is too quick to conflate that social function with tradition and to neglect Eliot's own comments on the poet's social function. A poet's relationship to tradition and society are related but separate issues in these poets' thinking.[10] Breiner has also identified the Anglo-American tendency to see Eliot as the "authoritative theorist" of tradition, a poet "whose works enact allusive homage to the Great Tradition," but he rightly encourages us to "historicize" Eliot in order to see the "desperate *bricolage*" of a poem like *The Waste Land* and recognize it, as Brathwaite and Walcott do, as a "very American—very creole—poem" (*An Introduction* 202–3).

In addition, it is important to note that Brathwaite and Walcott are not the only Caribbean writers who have reworked the concept of tradition with Eliot in mind. Wilson Harris, the Guyanese writer and contemporary of Brathwaite and Walcott, has written extensively throughout his career about the West Indian writer's relationship to tradition, and, as King claims, "if Wilson Harris has any direct forebear it is T. S. Eliot with his mediations on time and tradition" (*New English Literatures* 109). Harris serves as a useful counterpoint in this chapter as we look at the reworking of the concept of tradition by Walcott and Brathwaite.

Of course, there are also Anglo-American critics less hostile to Eliot who would join with these Caribbean critics and writers and recognize "Tradition and the Individual Talent" as a defining document of modernism. Hugh Kenner calls it Eliot's "most influential single essay" (11). Jewel Spears Brooker suggests that Eliot's concept of tradition is one of the ideas that make the modern world possible for art (111). Timothy Materer simply calls this essay "the classic statement of Eliot's critical theory" (51). The influence of Eliot's essay is not, however, limited to studies of European modernism, for it has proven useful to writers from around the world. Instead, we should follow the lead of Edward Said, who opens *Culture and Imperialism* by citing Eliot's "Tradition and the Individual Talent." He suggests that Eliot's essay is "particularly suggestive" in understanding the "privileged role of culture in the modern imperial experience" (5). Said's critical instinct is correct, but he does not follow through to examine the influence of Eliot's ideas on any particular writer. In fact, Eliot's essay has been well received by postcolonial writers because his arguments resonate with their colonial experience of fragmentation and aesthetic aspirations for cultural wholeness. Examining how Walcott and Brathwaite recast Eliot's concept of tradition deepens our appreciation for these changing but complementary manifestations of modernism as a cosmopolitan literary movement.

Tradition Cannot Be Inherited

Early in his essay, Eliot betrays his colonial anxiety by claiming that tradition "cannot be inherited" but must be obtained "by great labour" ("Tradition and the Individual Talent" 14). Only an American, according to W. H. Auden, could make this claim, for only an American would feel that the "whole responsibility for contemporary poetry has fallen upon his shoulders" (366). However, Eliot is claiming not only a responsibility but a right. As an American, Eliot stands out of the direct line of descent under the logic of tradition as cultural legacy. So he shifts from the metaphor of inheritance to that of labor, and tradition becomes property that a poet acquires not by blood but by hard work. As long as Eliot mixes his labor with a tradition, he establishes his rights to it; tradition passes not by the English Statute of Wills but by the U.S. Homestead Act. With this shift, Eliot ensures that the accident of being born in St. Louis will not impede his claim on the "whole literature of Europe" ("Tradition and the Individual Talent" 14). Moreover, if traditions are limited not by rules of inheritance but by the efforts of the poet, he is not limited only to European literature but can freely mix other traditions in the labor of his art; he can have both Augustine and Buddha speak about sensuality in *The Waste Land*. For Eliot, tradition becomes a temporally contingent but structurally coherent matrix through which he constructs, compares, and evaluates the relations between participants in a cultural practice.

Eliot also develops this concept of tradition as an alternative heuristic to a positivist narrative of historical progress, an alternative that eliminates a shared modernist and postcolonial anxiety about being belated. On the one hand, Eliot believed that to be true to his age, his poetry must reflect the cultural fragmentation of modern life, which could no longer affirm a sense of historical progress. On the other hand, he believed that to be true to his convictions about art, his poetry must also embody some ordering principle to suggest the possibility of cultural wholeness. This dilemma of creating a poetry of fragmented order is central to the modernist project.

Eliot responds by redefining tradition to recognize temporal succession but not to be controlled by it. He contends that an artist's "significance . . . is the appreciation of his relation to the dead poets and artists," but he refuses to privilege the past or the present; instead, he claims that a tradition always has a "simultaneous existence and composes a simultaneous order" (15). In other words, tradition refuses to equate temporal priority with literary authority; instead, relative comparisons are made "in which two things are measured by each other" (15). A tradition forms a coherent order at any one time; but time passes, so a tradition is always subject to change. In Eliot's words, "The existing order is complete before the new work arrives; for order to persist after the supervention of novelty, the *whole* existing order must be, if ever so slightly, altered; and so the relations, proportions, values of each work of art toward the whole are readjusted" (15). With this concept of tradition, then, Eliot affirms that a contingent order exists among works of art that can be culturally empowering for the new writer without affirming the worn-out narratives of linear, historical progress. Walcott and Brathwaite are drawn to Eliot's distinction between tradition and history in part because of the Caribbean colonial experience. They also desire to find and represent the order of their cultural home without having to rely on the narratives of historical progress that had so often been used to ignore or repress Caribbean cultural life.

The relativity of Eliot's preference for this comparative approach is also reflected in his praise of the "mythical method" of Joyce and Yeats, a corollary concept of tradition that Eliot shapes through his criticism ("*Ulysses,* Order, and Myth" 177). Eliot suggests that these modernist writers have found a new way of using myth to manipulate "a continuous parallel between contemporaneity and antiquity" and that this comparative method has become "a way of controlling, of ordering, of giving a shape and a significance to the immense panorama of futility and anarchy which is contemporary history" (177). Again, having grown up with colonialism's particular "futility and anarchy," Brathwaite and Walcott readily accept Eliot's cultural diagnosis and proposed artistic cure and translate his concepts into an art that reflects their New World experiences.

Eliot's comparative sense of tradition and myth arises in part from his interest in the methods of the comparative anthropology of his day, not just Frazer and Weston but Lévy-Bruhl, Gilbert Murray, and Jane Harrison.[11] Eliot hints at this interest in "Tradition and the Individual Talent" itself when he describes the changes in a tradition as "a development which abandons nothing *en route,* which does not superannuate either Shakespeare, or Homer, or the rock drawing of the Magdalenian draughtsmen" (16). This list of examples illustrates how tradition and anthropology converge in Eliot's imagination: both modes of thought employ a common comparative method. Indeed, he suggests that the findings of anthropology should be the beginning of a writer's tradition. Eliot expresses this desire most clearly in an uncollected review of Native American literature written contemporaneously with "Tradition and the Individual Talent."[12] He writes: "Primitive art and poetry can even, through the studies and experiments of the artist or poet, revivify the contemporary activities. The maxim, Return to the Sources, is a good one. More intelligibly put, it is that the poet should know everything that has been accomplished in poetry (accomplished, not merely produced) since its beginnings in order to know what he is doing himself" ("War-Paint"). Eliot's statement is a classic example of modernism's appropriation of the "primitive" to enhance the "civilized," an appropriation repeated by the likes of Lawrence, Pound, Picasso, Stravinsky, and others.

Modernism's appropriation of these "primitive" cultures was made possible, of course, only by the complicit role of anthropology in the colonizing efforts of Europe. Accordingly, Eliot and these earlier anthropologists have been fairly criticized for replicating this imperial approach with respect to cultural matters.[13] The civilized anthropologist or poet studies the cultural and artistic practices of primitive peoples to benefit the metropolitan culture. Even though this approach is so closely associated with Europe's imperial process, Walcott and Brathwaite still choose to recast it. Indeed, they confront the even more daunting task of creating poetry that represents both the fragmented reality of their postcolonial and multicultural society and an aesthetic order that points toward a possible cultural wholeness for a region split by geographical, linguistic, ethnic, and political differences.

Eliot's ideas about tradition, myth, and comparative anthropology are so well known in their European modernist context that they have become the critical clichés of introductory lectures; however, examining how these ideas have migrated to the Caribbean fulfills modernism's guiding principle to "make it new." Moreover, while European modernism is often criticized today as hopelessly authoritarian in its ideology, Walcott and Brathwaite redeploy Eliot's method for new ideological purposes, implicitly separating ideology and aesthetics in a way that challenges current critical paradigms. Their example is particularly instructive, for they recast Eliot's method with complementary but discrepant ideological emphases. These subtle differences broaden our understanding of the ways in which central ideas of modernism are being renewed to make poetry possible in the New World.

A Tradition Broken and Re-created

Employing the trope of inheritance to speak of tradition is even more troubling in the New World because colonialism forcibly cut cultural and familial ties between generations. Walcott underscores this brokenness in reflecting on Eliot's understanding of tradition. For example, in an interview he qualifies Eliot's claim that tradition reflects an "unbroken arc" between Homer and the present by contending that in the New World tradition is more accurately described as an arc "broken and re-created"

(Walcott, "Reflections Before and After Carnival" 41–42).[14] He returns to this trope in his Nobel lecture when he compares his Antilles tradition to a shattered but restored vase, suggesting that "the love that reassembles the fragments is stronger than that love which took its symmetry for granted when it was whole" *(Antilles)*. Eliot is one who takes for granted the wholeness of tradition, but Walcott offers greater praise to New World writers who cannot make this assumption because of colonialism but who still aspire to create cultural wholeness from cultural fragmentation. Walcott's project of "restoration" does not conceal the pain of brokenness—the "cracked heirlooms" show their "white scars"—but he holds that this restored tradition is greater than its original sources because it takes a greater amount of imaginative energy to bring together the fragments in the New World than to reorder the whole in the Old World.

While Walcott focuses on the brokenness rather than the wholeness of his New World tradition, he affirms Eliot's notion that the simultaneity of tradition is a superior way to conceive of art and culture than the linearity of historical progress. Indeed, as Paula Burnett suggests, Walcott's "Muse of History" has "clear echoes of T. S. Eliot's . . . 'mythical method'" in its emphasis on synchronicity (98). Like Eliot, Walcott rejects "the vision of progress" as "the rational madness of history as sequential time" ("Muse" 6); instead, he claims that what the true "revolutionary" poets "repeat to the New World is its simultaneity with the Old," by which he means equality (2). The "responsibility of tradition" in the New World is not a recovery of "Europe as a nourishing museum" nor a "magnifi[cation] of Africa," but a recognition that the New World tradition must be "alert, alive, simultaneous" to amalgamate its broken traditions into a new contemporary whole (7). For both Eliot and Walcott, then, the "simultaneity" of tradition undermines the commonplace idea that temporal priority means literary authority. They both believe that the new work of art has the capacity to change the significance of the old. And both believe that this change comes through mastering the tradition by imitation rather than resisting it by rejection. Eliot argues that the "best" and "most individual parts" of a writer will be those "in which the dead poets, his ancestors, assert their immortality most vigorously" ("Tradition and the Individual Talent" 14). Similarly, Walcott claims that the "only valid tradition" is the "common genius" of great poets, poets who "have no wish to be different, no time to be original, [whose] originality emerges only when they have absorbed all the poetry which they have read, entire" ("Muse" 25). As Eliot's poet travels through the wasteland of modern culture to unify its fragments, Walcott suggests that the New World poet is a cosmopolitan "wanderer, the man who moves through the ruins of great civilizations . . . carrying entire cultures in his head, bitter perhaps, but unencumbered" (3).

Their views are similar but not identical, and Walcott's parenthetical "bitter perhaps" suggests a crucial distinction. Eliot attributes the fragmentation of modern English culture to a "dissociation of sensibility" that occurred *within* English culture in the seventeenth century ("Metaphysical Poets" 288). Walcott's New World poet is "bitter perhaps" because he can more readily identify colonialism as an *external* cause of cultural fragmentation in the region. Walcott does not want this identification to turn into a claim of revenge or guilt, but he does see it as permeating the tone of a New World tradition. "The common experience of the New World," he contends "is colonialism" ("Muse" 1). Walcott accepts Eliot's concept of tradition as useful even as he inflects it with his own Caribbean experience.

This difference emerges even more clearly in the different tropes that they employ to describe tradition. Eliot imagines tradition as a sort of literary and mobile Stonehenge: "the existing *monuments* form an ideal order," but that order changes when "the new work arrives" ("Tradition and the Individual Talent" 15, emphasis added).[15] Walcott's tropes incorporate this sense of tradition as temporal and spatial, but they also reflect the importance of an oral tradition and the different perspectives of colonialism in the region. In the New World, he contends, "the mode is simple, the response open-ended so that each new poet can add his lines to the form, a process very much like weaving. . . . There is no beginning but no end. The new poet enters a flux and withdraws, as the weaver continues the pattern, hand to hand and mouth to mouth, as the rock-pile convict passes the sledge" ("Muse" 12). Temporally, the weaver passes his own shuttle or the convict hands along the hammer in a particular sequential practice. Structurally, however, it is the pattern on the loom or the pile of rocks that is more important, for it reflects the collective practice among the weavers or convicts. Walcott follows Eliot's modernist strategy in spatializing time and in recognizing the multiplicity of participants in a tradition, but again he does more. Combining textile and prison similes, Walcott suggests that tradition is served in situations both of privileged cooperation and of coerced necessity. Accordingly, it is not enough to characterize Walcott's theory of tradition, as Tejumola Olaniyan does, as merely an "assenting modification" rather than a "dissenting criticism" of the Western tradition ("Derek Walcott" 201) because Walcott does recognize and implicitly resist the bitter taste of coercion that is part of that tradition and colonialism.

Paradoxically, however, this fragmenting of traditions by colonialism does not make Walcott resentful but actually emboldens him to claim his right to all of them. He contends that every New World castaway experiences that colonial "moment of surrender and claim, dispossession and possession" of tradition, but "the issue is the claim" ("Culture" 54). In other words, he reverses the illegitimacy of the colonial practices that broke cultural and familial ties by boldly asserting his right to re-create their legacy. This legacy includes not only the colonial education that taught him to love the language and literature of English as his "natural inheritance" but also the forced migrations that combined the cultures of the world with the physical beauty of the Caribbean archipelago ("Muse" 25). Accordingly, Walcott concludes that "Classicists" are more useful than "radical" writers for creating a decolonized but whole New World tradition because they know that "maturity is the assimilation of the features of every ancestor" (1). So, while he refuses to equate modernist form with colonial ideology, he also questions linking too quickly "radical" forms with a liberating postcolonial ideology.

Walcott had not reached this assimilating maturity in his poetry when he made this claim in the early 1970s. While he openly acknowledges the diversity of Caribbean culture in these critical essays, his earlier poetry more often relies on the specific cultural resource of Europe rather than those of Africa or Asia. Similarly, it tends to draw more on elite literary texts than on popular or oral forms of culture for its allusions and techniques. Indeed, the distance between Walcott's multicultural rhetoric and his poetic practice is one of his greatest challenges early in his career. In defense of this gap, he suggests that Indian and Asian cultural resources are too far outside of his own personal experience to be used effectively in his poetry.[16] His early resistance to African sources is, however, more prominent and deserves more attention.

First, he links tradition to the development of a written language and its poetic conventions and concludes that the only written languages widely available in the region are European. Perse and Césaire are part of the same tradition in his mind because they both contribute to "the tidal advance of the metropolitan language" ("Muse" 15). Similarly, he contends that "the degeneration of technique" in New World poetry, by which he means an ignoring of English poetic conventions, emerges from a "rejection of language" (19–20). Accordingly, he resists any appeal to African cultural forms without any real access to African languages.[17]

Second, he makes a modernist, even Eliotic anthropological distinction between writers who have an atavistic interest in the past and those who have a contemporaneous one. Eliot encourages artists to study "primitive" art only to "revivify the contemporary activities," not to recover some "mystical insight" or "artistic feeling" ("War-Paint"). Similarly, Walcott criticizes "epic" poets in the Caribbean who look "to anthropology, to a catalogue of forgotten gods, to midden fragments, artifacts, and the unfinished phrases of a dead speech" to create an "artificial past" ("Muse" 8). He praises instead the anthropological imaginations of Denis Williams, Ted Hughes, and Samuel Beckett because they represent the common "displaced, searching psyche of the modern man" repeating that "pre-Adamic" and "pre-histor[ic]" need to burrow "into the origins of life" (24). The distinction is subtle but important. He sees the "epic" poets as trying to recover the actual artifacts and languages of a particular cultural past; they are archaeologists and linguists in search of an Africa that he believes has been forever lost in the New World. In contrast, he affirms an anthropological imagination that recognizes the ancient human impulse to name the world anew and restates that impulse in contemporary poetic language. Walcott modifies these views of African cultural resources later in his career, and these modifications affect how he represents the New World tradition. But these modifications are the subject of chapter 4. For now it is sufficient to recognize that he conceives of tradition as a simultaneous and contingent order among writers who are from different cultural backgrounds but share a common metropolitan language. He concludes that the great New World writers perpetuate the "common genius" of a language as their "only valid tradition" (25).

A Tradition Submerged and Recovered

Brathwaite also appropriates Eliot to conceive of a New World tradition, but his insurgent Afro-Caribbean folk tradition differs noticeably from Walcott's ironic New World classicism. The contrast between the ways Brathwaite and Walcott appropriate Eliot is a fascinating and instructive example of intertextuality, for it shows not only how the method of Eliot's modernism could be adapted to develop these complementary New World modernist poetics but also the different points of ideological emphasis offered by Walcott and Brathwaite.

From the beginning of his critical work, Brathwaite defines the need for a Caribbean tradition in explicitly Eliotic terms: "The «individual talent» [cannot] maintain a meaningful flow of work without reference to his society and its tradition" ("Roots" 37). He attributes the lack of a tradition in the Caribbean to West Indian writers' being "unable" to "commit" to "any one position or viewpoint" about their society (37). Accordingly, while he has a similar objective for establishing a tradition—creating a matrix of texts that gives a sense of cultural coherence to his practice as a poet—he is more anxious to orient his tradition around a particular viewpoint. He achieves this goal by narrowing the ethnic and class focus of his tradition as he simultaneously expands the range of cultural "texts" available as resources to establish that tradition. So while Walcott imagines an elite, literate, New World tradition existing among Whitman, Perse, Césaire, Borges and Neruda, Brathwaite conceives of popular, oral, Afro-Caribbean folk tradition that includes musicians such as the jazz artist John Coltrane or the calypso singer Mighty Sparrow, gods such as Ogun and Legba, and folk heroes such as Sam Sharpe or Nanny. Brathwaite even claims Eliot as part of what he describes as this "little tradition," claiming that he considers him to be primarily a "folk" poet (quoted in Rohlehr, *Pathfinder* 67).[18] Clearly there is a difference in emphasis between Walcott's "great tradition" of literature and Brathwaite's "little tradition" of popular culture, but as Breiner rightly suggests, the "values of the two traditions were of much less interest than the exploration of the West Indian's relations to the two of them" (*An Introduction* 11).

When Brathwaite recalls listening to Eliot's voice, he remembers hearing the "«riddims» of St. Louis," rhythms that he associates with jazz, with Africa, and with a resistance to the "establishment" ("History of the Voice" 286n34). The next chapter explores in depth how Brathwaite reinterprets Eliot's poetics of speech, but this linking of Eliot and jazz is important here because jazz is the trope through which Brathwaite creolizes Eliot's concept of tradition and the individual talent. Brathwaite argues that Caribbean artists should follow the example of jazz soloists, who improvise in relationship to the ensemble's general theme, creating a music that is an "expression not only of the individual artists. . . , but of the *group* of which the artists are a part" ("Jazz" 57). This improvisation can sound chaotic, an accurate representation of cultural fragmentation, but jazz is a trope for Brathwaite's Caribbean tradition because "the chaos is always resolved in order" (58). This trope does more than just cleverly parallel Eliot's ideas. Brathwaite identifies jazz with the hybridity of the Caribbean situation—it "is played in an Africanized manner on European instruments"—but he also associates it with a "mainly . . . Negro" and a primarily "folk" experience: it is the "archetype" of "New World creative protest" (61–63). The metaphor of jazz conveys Brathwaite's commitment to create an insurgent Afro-Caribbean folk tradition, but it is a misreading of this essay to conclude, as Glyne Griffith does, that this recasting of the modernist principle of tradition makes Brathwaite "anti-Modernist" (76).[19] The aesthetic principle is not necessarily aligned with a particular content or ideological position.

Brathwaite turns to jazz not only to creolize Eliot's concept of tradition but also to distinguish his Caribbean understanding of the anthropological imagination from Eliot's. Brathwaite describes jazz as a "living, active" folk form in contrast to earlier modernists' "mainly cerebral" and overly "conscious neo-primitivism" ("Jazz" 57). Brathwaite agrees with Eliot that the anthropological imagination "makes it possible to leap our discontinuities and connect our fragments," but he reorients that principle by relocating it to his Caribbean cultural context (*Wars of Respect* 6). In his autobiographical essay "Timehri" (1973) he begins by identifying "rootlessness" as the most common feature of West Indian life and imagination; he describes it, appropriating another one of Eliot's famous phrases, as the Caribbean "dissociation of the sensibility . . . of art from the act of living" (30). Again, while Eliot sees this dissociation as emerging from within English culture, Brathwaite clearly identifies colonialism as the cause in the Caribbean. In particular, he claims that unique circumstances of colonialism in the region—the complex relations among multiple imperial and colonized cultures—frustrated the process of creolization until "it simply fragmented itself" into a series of different "sociocultural orientations" (30).[20] As a result, Caribbean artists are born with the "ideal" but not the "perceived and inherited reality" of cultural "wholeness," a problem that his generation of writers must "transcend and heal" (30). In a move similar to Walcott's, Brathwaite transposes the dilemma of modernist art—the dilemma of simultaneously representing fragmentation and order—into the even more complex cultural context of the Caribbean.

At this point Brathwaite turns from a theoretical to an autobiographical account of this challenge to recover a sense of cultural wholeness from which to develop a tradition. He says that after graduating from Cambridge he accepted the disillusionment, exile, and rootlessness of being West Indian: "I applied for work in London, Cambridge, Ceylon, New Delhi, Cairo, Kano, Khartoum, Sierra Leone, Carcassonne, a monastery in Jerusalem. I was a West Indian, rootless man of the world. I could go, belong, everywhere on the world-wide globe. I ended up in a village in Ghana. It was my beginning" (33). The echo of Eliot's *East Coker* is conscious. Just as a mature Eliot returns to the English village from which his ancestor left for the New World, Brathwaite sees his return to Africa as a return to his ancestral home. It is a telling parallel. Andrew Eliot immigrates from East Coker to America in 1669. Some 250 years later his famous descendant can confidently return to the same village only because the social stability of England and the United States enables the recording of accurate genealogies and the geographical permanence of small villages. Of course, the practices of slavery and colonization frustrate a commensurate certainty for Brathwaite, yet he still claims the equivalent right to return and work with the resources of an ancestral home as a way to renew a contemporary cultural tradition. Brathwaite alludes to this older Eliot looking for his cultural and familial roots because he believes that Caribbean writers must reestablish similar connections with their cultural pasts before they can begin to create a unified Caribbean tradition in the present. So even though he remains a rootless West Indian in Ghana, Brathwaite experiences a sense of cultural wholeness there that prepares him to respond to the Caribbean "dissociation of the sensibility." He leaves Ghana "no longer a lonely individual talent" but with a "mind now linking Atlantic and ancestor, homeland and heartland. . . . The connection between my lived but unheeded non-middle-class boyhood and its great tradition on the eastern mainland had been made" (34). Passages such as these confirm Dash's observation that "Eliot is as important to Brathwaite's creative imagination as the overwhelming moment of revelation in the African experience" ("Edward Brathwaite" 221).

It is a remarkable example of literary appropriation, for Brathwaite transvalues Eliot's ideas and life to offer an Afro-Caribbean folk alternative both to Eliot's European-oriented tradition and to Walcott's ironic New World classicism. Eliot conceives of tradition primarily as an expression of the "mind of Europe" ("Tradition and the Individual Talent" 16). Brathwaite parallels Eliot's ideas, but he reorients the hemispheric allegiance; he accesses the "great tradition" in Africa through the "folk" forms of culture in the Caribbean because he conceives of "*the two traditions [as] interdependent*" (Redfield 70–71, quoted in Brathwaite, *Folk Culture* 35). And unlike Walcott, Brathwaite refuses to accept the broken traditions of colonialism with a bitter thanks; instead, he seeks to recognize the wholeness of the African past as the basis for establishing a Caribbean folk tradition in the present. Brathwaite distinguishes himself from Walcott by damning him with faint praise, describing Walcott as the "brilliant exception" who seeks to convert "his heritage into a classical tradition" but who achieves only "individual" rather than "communal" wholeness ("Timehri" 34). Walcott's ideal West Indian artist is a jack-of-all-traditions; Brathwaite's is a thorough archaeologist of an Afro-Caribbean tradition.

Indeed, Brathwaite describes the contemporary West Indian artist's need to develop this anthropological imagination by means of a specific archaeological example from the New World. He alludes to Aubrey Williams, the Guyanese painter who lived with Warraou Indians and who could "actually *see*" the prehistoric art of the Amerindians—the "*timehri:* rock signs, paintings, petrogylphs" (40). Again, the echoes of Eliot are conscious and instructive. Just as Eliot refers generally to the "rock drawing of the Magdalenian draughtsmen" as the origin of the European cultural tradition ("Tradition and the Individual Talent" 16), Brathwaite cites the *timehri* as a "living source" from which Williams could recover an Amerindian cultural origin ("Timehri" 41). Eliot contends that the modern artist must be "more *primitive,* as well as more civilized, than his contemporaries" ("Tarr" 106), and Brathwaite praises Williams as "a modern artist working in an ancient form" and "an ancient artist working in a modern form" ("Timehri" 41). Eliot believes that this anthropological imagination enables the modern artist to develop a perception "not only of the pastness of the past, but of its presence" ("Tradition and the Individual Talent" 14). Brathwaite argues that the Caribbean artist's "recognition of an ancestral relationship with the . . . aboriginal culture involves" not only a "journey into the past" but a simultaneous "movement of possession into present and future" ("Timehri" 42). For Brathwaite that "aboriginal culture" is Africa. So whereas Eliot tacitly accepts the imperial distinction between the civilized and the primitive, Brathwaite rejects this distinction as an extension of colonialism's ideology. Whereas Eliot is open to anthropological information about any "primitive" culture, Brathwaite seeks to recover specific evidence of the ancestral relationship between Africa and the Caribbean in order to restore a sense of cultural wholeness for the Afro-Caribbean folk. Again, we see in Brathwaite another Caribbean writer adapting Eliot's modernist methods to achieve very different ideological ends, different not just from Eliot's aims but also from Walcott's.

Walcott recognizes the challenges of Brathwaite's folk tradition early on, and he responds by questioning the integrity of its empirical, class, and racial claims. Empirically, he doubts whether the contemporary Caribbean artist can recover enough evidence to reconnect the Caribbean to Africa in any meaningful way. Instead, he claims that the slaves "courageously yielded" their "history" and that the "true African" is the one "who does not need to proclaim it" ("Muse" 9, 21). With respect to class, he speaks of the "treason" of the intellectual "who masks his education and privilege behind a fake exoticism of poverty and the pastoral," an implicit attack on the Cambridge-educated Brathwaite advocating a folk tradition (19). With respect to race, he characterizes a "revolutionary" folk tradition as "pure black Afro-Aryanism" and the "decor of African tourism" (19, 21).

Walcott's critiques are trenchant but not conclusive, for Brathwaite's insurgent folk tradition collocates a different but equally cogent set of cultural fragments. Brathwaite's poet still moves through the ruins of great civilizations, but he recovers Yoruba, not Greek remains; he renews interest in an Ashanti, not an English, renaissance; he reclaims the limbo dance, not the tarot cards.

At about the same time, Wilson Harris offers glimpses of a vision of tradition that seems to mediate between Walcott and Brathwaite. On the one hand, Harris stresses, with Walcott, that tradition is not "dogma . . . entirely dormant and passive" but "inherently active at all times," and in the great writers it is this "living open tradition which realizes itself in an enduring capacity associated with the obscure human person" ("Tradition and the West Indian Novel" 46, 36). And similar to Walcott, Harris cites an eclectic group of writers as conveying "intimations" of this living tradition, including classical writers such as Dante, modernist writers such as Proust, Joyce, and Faulkner, and postcolonial writers such as the Australians Patrick White and Hal Porter, the Canadian Malcolm Lowry, and the Nigerian Amos Tutuola (35–36). On the other hand, Harris also recognizes, with Brathwaite, the importance of the folk tradition for the West Indian writer. He cites the limbo dance and the dance of possession in Haitian vodun as "gateways" between Africa and the Caribbean ("History, Fable, and Myth" 158–59). These cultural practices do not offer a "total recall of an African past"; instead they "translate and accommodate African and other legacies within a new architecture of cultures" (158). Moreover, Harris recognizes, as does Brathwaite, that the power relationship must be addressed in recasting a tradition, but he is more dialectical in his approach. He asserts that "the making of tradition anew" involves "a creative unravelling and re-creative redress of ruling majorities and ruled minorities," but he also claims that this process happens "vice versa" ("Making of Tradition" 92–93). Harris is more suggestive than systematic or straightforward in articulating his views of tradition, so the influence of his ideas is perhaps more muted. However, his work at least offers the possibility of a New World tradition that collocates the cultural resources emphasized by both Walcott and Brathwaite, and it is a possibility that emerges again out of the influence of the comparative method of Eliot's modernism.

In the early seventies Brathwaite and Walcott offer competing visions of a decolonized Caribbean tradition that would have been more compelling if less diametrically opposed. Brathwaite's insurgent Afro-Caribbean folk tradition vigorously resists the existing cultural hierarchies of colonialism, but its class and racial allegiances seem much too narrow to reflect the cultural diversity of the region. The multicultural rhetoric of Walcott's ironic New World classicism reflects this diversity promisingly, but his poetic practice relies too heavily on classical Western cultural resources to match that rhetoric. In particular, they offer opposing views of the role of Africa's cultural influence on the Caribbean tradition: for Brathwaite, the tradition is defined primarily by recognizing Africa's influence, while for Walcott, it has already been irrevocably shaped by the loss of Africa's influence. They share modernism's comparative methodology, but they use it for different ends. They modify these initial positions later in their careers, as discussed in chapter 4, but first let us consider how these initial views of tradition shape their adaptation of specific modernist poetic practices.

Enacting a Tradition, Practicing a Poetry

While Walcott and Brathwaite vigorously recast Eliot's concept of tradition in their critical essays, the full value of this recasting is best seen in the way it animates their vibrant poetic practices. Prosodically, each of them transmutes the poetic line to enact the rhythm and tone of his tradition, and each transforms the poetic speaker to stress the different cultural perspectives that contribute to his tradition. Again, Eliot serves as a model, for his experiment with Tiresias in *The Waste Land* offers a new way to represent the surface fragmentation of experience and the underlying order of art. Walcott's Crusoe and Brathwaite's Tom transpose Eliot's experiment into a Caribbean context and thus reorient the shape of cosmopolitan modernism to imagine new national, regional, and hemispheric traditions. Comparing Walcott's "Crusoe's Journal" with Brathwaite's "Ogun" allows the complementary features of Walcott's ironic New World classicism and Brathwaite's insurgent folk tradition to emerge more clearly.[21]

These features emerge first at the level of prosodic technique. Walcott writes "Crusoe's Journal" in alternating lines of regular iambic pentameter and iambic trimeter. It is a conventional form that may seem unremarkable except that the poem is set in one of Walcott's favorite liminal spaces, a beach. Slowly one begins to feel the undulating regularity of his poetic lines, conveying the regular cadence of waves rolling on a shore. "Like those plain iron tools" that Crusoe salvages "from shipwreck" to make the island his kingdom, conventional prosodic devices of a "Western" tradition are redeployed by Walcott to convey the unique rhythm of his island culture. Consider also the regularity of his stanzaic form. He divides the poem into three verse paragraphs, each of which is divided into three grammatical units. Writing a postcolonial triptych in words about the slaves' conversion to Christianity, Walcott suggests through his trinitarian form what he makes explicit in the poem's argument. He mimics the "Western" tradition, not as a debased performance of homage, but as a claim to control and transform influential cultural symbols:

> parroting our master's
> style and voice, we make his language ours,
> converted cannibals
> we learn with him to eat the flesh of Christ.
> ("Crusoe's Journal," *Collected Poems* 93)

With characteristic irony, Walcott shows that converting *to* a religious and linguistic tradition can also be a conversion *of* that tradition for new purposes. As he argues in prose, "The slave converted himself, he changed weapons, spiritual weapons, and as he adapted his master's religion, he also adapted his language, and it is here that . . . our poetic tradition begins" ("Muse" 12–13). For Walcott, this strategy of "conversion" is the best way available to create a New World tradition that resists the cultural legacy of colonialism because the "convert" is in control of the master's forms and can wield them for his or her own ends.

Brathwaite's poetic technique suggests the more oppositional approach of his "jazz" tradition. Like "Crusoe's Journal," Brathwaite's "Ogun" falls into three sections: the first ten stanzas establish the persona, his great-uncle Bobby O'Neale, as a poor and slightly disabled carpenter; the middle three stanzas explain why he is poor; and the final ten stanzas describe his secret life as a sculptor. Despite this structural similarity, the difference in rhythmic regularity between these two poems strikes the reader immediately. As he suggests in "History of the Voice," Brathwaite wants to "break out of the entire pentametric model . . . to move into a system that more closely and intimately approaches [the Caribbean] experience" (265). This difference has led some critics to conclude too hastily that "Walcott, as a craftsman, towers far above Brathwaite" (Ismond 221). However, such critics fail to see Brathwaite's craft in relation to his conception of jazz as a trope for the Afro-Caribbean folk tradition. Consider, for example, Brathwaite's description of his uncle walking across the shop floor:

> He was knock-knee'd, flat-
> footed and his clip clop sandals slapped across the concrete

flooring of his little shop where canefield mulemen and a fleet
of Bedford lorry drivers dropped in to scratch themselves and talk.

There was no shock of wood, no beam
of light mahogany his saw teeth couldn't handle.
("Ogun," *Arrivants* 242)

He uses strong, repeated stresses and alliteration ("knock-knee'd," "flat-footed," "clip clop," and "sandals slapped") to syncopate the first two lines in jazz fashion, then he uses irregularly placed rhymes and near rhymes ("concrete"-"fleet"-"teeth," "knock"-"shock," and "clop"-"shop"-"dropped") to echo this beat in subsequent lines. The rhythm of these lines illustrates the impairment and resistance of Brathwaite's folk tradition. For him, the normal walking meter of iambic pentameter cannot describe the carpenter's physical and cultural disability, a disability arising from the crippling effects of colonial exploitation. However, his uncle does not submit, and the broken rhythm of his walk testifies to that dogged resistance. Brathwaite's poetic line embodies this resistance by skillfully breaking with the conventional rhythms of English poetry. For him, Caribbean poetry must "break down the pentameter," not just master it, to create a decolonized literary tradition ("History of the Voice" 271).

This difference between Walcott's "mastering" and Brathwaite's "breaking" the colonizer's conventions is not limited to the rhythms of the poetic line. Each of them chooses a central persona and has him undergo a series of transformations in order to embody his sense of the defining features of tradition in the region. Eliot, again, serves as an instructive example of this strategy for both of them. In a famous footnote to *The Waste Land* Eliot explains Tiresias's role in the poem: "Tiresias, although a mere spectator and not indeed a 'character,' is yet the most important personage in the poem, uniting all the rest. Just as the one-eyed merchant, seller of currants, melts into the Phoenician Sailor, and the latter is not wholly distinct from Ferdinand Prince of Naples, so all the women are one woman, and the two sexes meet in Tiresias. What Tiresias *sees,* in fact, is the substance of the poem" (52). While Eliot's critics have long fought about the significance of this footnote in interpreting *The Waste Land,*[22] it does succinctly summarize one of Eliot's modernist poetic innovations. Unlike earlier poetic personae, Tiresias does not function as a single controlling consciousness in *The Waste Land;* instead, he serves as a conditional point of stasis through which the multiple perspectives in the poem surface, momentarily cohere, and quickly dissipate. As Michael Levenson so aptly puts it, "Tiresias is . . . an intermittent phenomenon in the poem, a *subsequent* phenomenon, emerging out of other characters" (*A Genealogy* 191). So, for example, when Eliot claims that "the two sexes meet in Tiresias," he asks us to accumulate the perspectives of the couples in the poem: the hyacinth girl and her suitor, the husband and his neurasthenic wife, Lil and Albert, the typist and the clerk, and Elizabeth and Leicester. "Uniting all the rest," Tiresias does not merely juxtapose these different perspectives; he amalgamates them into a broader and more comprehensive whole. This whole remains contingent, for the method of the poem suggests that experience is always open to new contexts, to new points of view, to wider perspectives. Yet meaning still exists, for the multiple perspectives overlap through Tiresias. In other words, Tiresias serves the same hermeneutic function within the logic of the poem as tradition serves within the logic of Eliot's critical theory: he is an organizing principle through which to compare possible relations between texts and to construct new shared yet contingent meanings. Tiresias literally personifies the comparative method that makes Eliot's modernism distinctive.[23]

Indeed, the pseudoscholarship of Eliot's footnotes in general reinforces this comparative approach: he introduces more than one-third of them with the signal *Cf.* (*The Waste Land, Complete Poems* 50–55). Some of these notes ask the reader to compare the poem with other works of literature, religion, and anthropology, while others ask for comparisons of lines within the poem. Eliot's insistent intertextuality is demanding. Readers are expected to relate the popular music of "that Shakespeherian rag" with the canonical lyrics of Shakespeare's Ariel song, to "collocate" the wisdom of Buddha and Augustine, to recognize the parallels between "the journey to Emmaus, the approach to the Chapel Perilous, and the present decay of eastern Europe" (55). These demands are rewarding, however, because they teach the reader to appreciate both the surface fragmentation and the underlying order of the poem. They demand, in other words, that the reader also develop an Eliotic sense of tradition, that the reader participate in collocating the different perspectives to imagine a new, more comprehensive whole.

Reconfiguring the significance of Western canonical characters is a common strategy of postcolonial writers.[24] In particular, reworking Shakespeare's characters from *The Tempest* has become a paradigm of postcolonial cultural resistance.[25] In the Caribbean, for example, George Lamming recasts the hierarchal relationships between Prospero, Caliban, and Ariel in his autobiographical criticism *(The Pleasures of Exile)* and in his fiction *(Natives of My Person)*, and Aimé Césaire has transformed Caliban into a figure of wounded dignity in *Une tempête*. Indeed, this strategy of reconfiguration extends beyond Shakespeare—Jean Rhys retells Bertha Rochester's story in *Wide Sargasso Sea*—and beyond Caribbean writers—the South African J. M. Coetzee introduces a woman to narrate anew the lives of Robinson Crusoe and Friday in *Foe,* and the Australian Peter Carey reinvents the characters of Dickens's *Great Expectations* in *Jack Maggs.*

Even though these fictional and dramatic reconfigurations are varied in their subject matter, they are fairly standard in their strategy. The postcolonial novelist or playwright focuses on an oppressed character maligned in the canonical work—Caliban, Bertha, Friday, or Magwitch—and retells the story from, or at least in sympathy with, that character's perspective. While this "rewriting" of canonical Western characters is an important postcolonial strategy, it also tends to be limited by the prevailing realist expectations about character in postcolonial narratives. The novelist or dramatist rightly recuperates the oppressed character, but this recuperated character is expected to have a single, coherent identity. It is a reasonable expectation given that colonial powers denied, both in their practice and in their books, the human identity of the Calibans, Fridays, and Berthas in the world; however, it is an expectation that makes it difficult, if not impossible, to represent the contingency and complexity of contemporary New World identities. As Wilson Harris contends, it is "one of the ironic things with West Indians of my generation that they may conceive of themselves in the most radical political light but their approach to art and literature is one which consolidates the most conventional and documentary techniques in the novel" ("Tradition and the West Indian Novel" 45).

Harris strives admirably to overcome these realistic expectations through his modernist fiction. Poets, on the other hand, particularly modernist poets after Eliot, are relatively free from such realist expectations, so it is easier for them to create a central "personage" who "melts into" and "is not wholly distinct" from a variety of other figures in the poem. Indeed, a modernist poetics seems better suited to representing the "plural masks" that Harris suggests characterize the West Indian experience and identity ("Quetzalcoatl" 185). Accordingly, in reworking the example of Eliot's Tiresias, Walcott and Brathwaite create poetic personae that move beyond the simple, binary reconfigurations of Western canonical characters so often found in postcolonial fiction, illustrating not only the advantage of poetry as a form of postcolonial discourse but also the differences between Walcott's and Brathwaite's complementary understandings of Caribbean cultural tradition and identity.

While Walcott seems to make the more obstreperous choice in selecting

Crusoe rather than Friday as his representative New World figure, however, many critics tend to view the choice as merely representing Walcott's pragmatism. For example, Stewart Brown suggests that choosing Crusoe enables Walcott to assume a public role as a poet, a role to help people make a home of the Caribbean after the "shipwreck" of colonization ("Between me and thee" 212). Similarly, Breiner argues that Walcott's Crusoe is the "patron saint" of "*bricolage,*" of ingeniously using what is at hand to create a world (*An Introduction* 200). Certainly Walcott chooses Crusoe because of the pragmatism of Defoe's character, but his choice also suggests a "more subversive strategy" (Burnett 118). As John Thieme argues, "Instead of contrasting or inverting the assumed hierarchies of the colonial text, Walcott creates a multiplicity of Crusoes who collectively dismantle the very idea of hierarchical positioning" (78). It is also a multiplicity that represents a modernist collocating of perspectives, which suggests a more comprehensive understanding of the New World tradition.

Consider how Walcott justifies his choice of Crusoe in his essay "The Figure of Crusoe" (1965), a justification that closely follows the logic of Eliot's explanatory footnote but recasts the cultural context: "I have, as you have heard, summoned the figure of Crusoe. It is not the Crusoe you recognize. I have compared him to Proteus, that mythological figure who changes shapes according to what we need him to be" (35). Eliot selects Tiresias as a modernist archetype of cultural exhaustion because he is mutable, wise, and weary of life. Walcott's Crusoe/Proteus also changes shape and speaks wisely, but Walcott chooses him for his oceanic origins, his exuberant energy, and his reluctant disclosures. By alluding to the multiple personae in this poem as "our ocean's Proteus," Walcott foregrounds again the geography of his island culture, a geography in which the ocean dominates the individual and collective imagination, and he suggests that people in the Caribbean must struggle vigorously with the changing and contradictory figures of their tradition to achieve wisdom ("Crusoe's Journal," *Collected Poems* 93). For the younger Walcott, cultural wholeness will come not through connecting to an alternative "great" tradition in Africa, à la Brathwaite, but through taking hold of characters in the "Western" tradition and reconstituting them.[26] He goes on to list the "catalogue" of "shapes" merging in "Crusoe's Journal": "My Crusoe, then, is Adam, Christopher Columbus, God, a missionary, a beachcomber, and his interpreter, Daniel Defoe" ("Figure" 35).

This catalogue helps to untangle the multiple and shifting perspectives contained in the poem. Eliot and his modernist cohorts saw themselves as inheriting an exhausted tradition and sought to make it new. In contrast, Walcott claims to be "at the beginning, rather than at the end, of a tradition," so he creates a representative New World persona that unites characters who initiate traditions (Walcott, "Art of Poetry" 106). For instance, he claims *Robinson Crusoe* as "our first book" because it is one of the first books set in the New World and because it is usually accepted as the first novel in the English language. Bringing together various generic traditions—history, romance, spiritual autobiography, sermon, criminal biography, personal journal—into a new imaginative context, Daniel Defoe invents a literary form that both initiates and reflects a larger cultural shift from an agrarian, aristocratic, and communal society to a mercantile, democratic, and individualistic modern society. While Walcott does not aspire to create a new generic form in this poem, he is equally ambitious about the cultural role of his work to inaugurate a shift from the Old World writing about the New to the New World writing about itself, a shift that he implies corresponds to the formal devolution of European empires. He speaks of the "powerful elation" that his generation of West Indian writers felt in having the "privilege of writing about places and people for the first time" (105).

Of course, this appropriation of Defoe is not innocent, a fact Walcott recognizes by identifying "our first book" as also "our profane Genesis" ("Crusoe's Journal," *Collected Poems* 94). He recognizes the racial and colonial myths perpetuated by Defoe's book but assiduously avoids evoking revenge or guilt by having Crusoe quickly become another archetypal genesis figure—Adam. Crusoe is "not wholly distinct" from Adam because they both have the power to name things for the first time, to speak

> that prose
> which, blessing some sea-rock, startles itself
> with poetry's surprise,
> ("Crusoe's Journal," *Collected Poems* 92)

As Rei Terada contends, prose becomes poetry because the denotative process of naming in a new world is necessarily metaphoric (160–61). This "extravagant naming" in the Caribbean redescribes the world by creating new, indigenous metaphors to identify this new landscape.

Walcott's transformations only grow bolder to reflect the creative power of this metaphoric naming. His Crusoe "melts into" Christopher Columbus because they are both European "discoverers" of the New World, one imaginatively through literature and the other actually through transatlantic exploration. Walcott, then, develops an elaborate and richly textured metaphor of baptism—the Christian ritual of naming—to depict the original "naming" of the Caribbean cultural tradition by these figures:

> like Christofer he bears
> in speech mnemonic as a missionary's
> the Word to savages,
> its shape an earthen, water-bearing vessel's
> whose sprinkling alters us
> into good Fridays who recite His praise,
> parroting our master's
> style and voice, we make his language ours,
> converted cannibals
> we learn with him to eat the flesh of Christ.
> (93)

Punning on the name Christofer (which literally, and for Walcott ironically, means "bearer of Christ"), Walcott suggests that this Crusoe/Columbus figure is also a missionary of European culture; he christens others as "savages" and imposes on them his rituals of language and religion. It is a baptism that involves violence—the shape of the baptismal font resembles the ships of the Middle Passage—but it is baptism that has forever altered (punning with *altar*) the savages into "good Fridays." The irony of this new name embodies his understanding of slaves' strategic response to this cultural baptism. They accept their role as suffering servants, but this role gives them more of a claim to be true representatives of Christ. In other words, they transvalue the significance of conversion to claim the power of the master's language and religion: they "wrested God from [their] captor" ("Muse" 11).

The power of this strategic acquiescence also explains how Walcott sees the relationship between Crusoe and Friday. It is in this section that he introduces for the first time in the poem the possibility of an opposition between characters rather than a conflating of them. He employs his pronouns carefully to distinguish between Crusoe/Columbus ("he") and the "good Fridays" ("us" and "we") ("Crusoe's Journal," *Collected Poems* 93). It is a small but telling way for Walcott to recognize the hierarchical relationship between master and slave and to identify himself with the slaves. However, he does not leave the relationship in opposition. The slaves expose the master's prejudices by ironically participating in another of his religious rituals—communion—"converted cannibals, we . . . eat the flesh of Christ" (93); at the same time, however, by participating in the ritual together Friday and Crusoe form a new identity as they re-create communion in the New World: "*we learn with him* to eat the flesh of Christ" (93, emphasis added). In other words, Walcott's representative persona accepts the coerced baptism of colonialism but also seeks to shape the new communion of independence of a New World Caribbean tradition and identity. "The Crusoe and Friday figures join in a composite identity," Breslin contends, because "their fusion enacts Walcott's belief that the integration of racial identities into a West Indian identity is the only viable alternative to debilitating fragmentation and angry obsession with past injustice" (105).

In the third verse paragraph, Crusoe becomes hermit figures "posing as naturalists / drunks, castaways, beachcombers" ("Crusoe's Journal," *Collected Poems* 94). It is an image repeated in his essay when he imagines Crusoe as "lonely man on a beach who has heaped a pile of dead bush [of tradition] . . . to make a bonfire. The bonfire may be purposeless. Or it may be a signal of his loneliness, his desperation, his isolation, his symbol of need for another" ("Figure" 34). The New World Caribbean writer brings together the debris of the Western tradition and sparks it with his imagination to create a fire that signals others to join his imagined community. The tradition is the fuel that is reconstituted through the power of the writer's imagination to overcome a very modernist sense of alienated loneliness. Indeed, it is a loneliness that Walcott suggests originates in God himself in the concluding lines of the poem where the persona is "hoarding such heresies as / God's loneliness moves in His smallest creatures" ("Crusoe's Journal," *Collected Poems* 94). Breslin suggests that these final lines could be attributed to God or to Crusoe, but again it is more in keeping with the rest of the poem to see them as a merging of these perspectives (111). This merging of perspectives also reflects the theological doctrine of *imago deo,* the doctrine that human beings are created in the likeness of God—a heresy in this context because Crusoe's need for others implies God's need for humans.

By having the figures of Defoe, Adam, Columbus, a missionary, Friday, a hermit, and God flow into and momentarily coalesce in Crusoe, Walcott transmutes their accepted cultural contexts and so reconceives their function in his tradition. As Walcott suggests in his essay, this multifaceted Crusoe becomes for "the West Indian poet . . . the metaphor of tradition and the individual talent" ("Figure" 34). Through this reordering, Walcott wants to create a tradition in which he can affirm both his love for the English language and its literature and his love for the Caribbean landscape and its people. Crusoe stands as a figure for the ambivalence of a colonial literary tradition, for he is a figure of both artistic ingenuity and violent exploitation: he creates tools to survive and then uses them to rule; he saves Friday and then enslaves him. Walcott sees the ambivalence of Crusoe's legacy as an unavoidable part of a Caribbean literary tradition. He responds by situating that legacy in new contexts, contexts that reflect his pragmatic perspective on how best to master that legacy to create an independent future by reorienting it:

> So from this house
> that faces nothing but the sea, his journals
> assume a household use;
> we learn to shape from them, where nothing was
> the language of a race,
> (94)

In *The Arrivants* Brathwaite also offers a literary figure—Harriet Beecher Stowe's Uncle Tom—as a central organizing persona. However, while Walcott boldly claims a catalog of figures from a literate, "Western" tradition, Brathwaite chooses this literary figure as a last resort: "When I came to write the poem called 'The Cabin' . . . I had been confronted for the first time with a slave cabin. . . . But when I tried to have someone living inside the cabin I could not find in my mind a Jamaican slave. . . . So I had to go back to the only slaves I knew, those in Harriet Beecher Stowe's *Uncle Tom's Cabin*" ("History, the Caribbean Writer, and *X-Self*" 37–38). Brathwaite's choice of Tom is more in keeping with the standard postcolonial narrative strategy of reconfiguring the marginalized Western character. However, as Eliot uses Tiresias and Walcott uses Crusoe, Brathwaite employs Tom in modernist fashion. As Kenneth Ramchand suggests, Tom is an "elastic figure" and "composite persona who has seen and suffered all that the race has suffered" (140). And as Louis James contends, this choice of Tom reflects Brathwaite's "insights into the 'viewpoints' within the work," for he is a stereotype from Stowe that Brathwaite "shatters and extends" to show a "human being related to him closer even than by blood, suffering, puzzled" ("Review" 38–39).

The multiple figures that merge in Tom reflect some of the differences between Brathwaite's more insurgent Afro-Caribbean folk tradition and Walcott's ironic New World classicism. So, for example, economic frustrations transform Tom into Shakespeare's "Tom of Bedlam":

> But with the winter I knew
> I was old. Poor
> Tom was cold.
> ("Didn't He Ramble," *Arrivants* 22)

But he responds to this frustration by melding with Haile Selassie I in rebellion

So burn the crops
raise flash car cities
I am Selassie

and Selassie God
(24)

Rather than a missionary's message of conversion, Tom preaches a lament in the voice of a Baptist preacher ("Tom") and for rebellion in the rhythms of "Brother Man the Rasta / Man" ("Wings of a Dove"). Where Walcott conflates Crusoe with Columbus, Brathwaite's Tom becomes an Amerindian testifying to Columbus's violence ("The Emigrants"). He even has Tom become figures as diverse as the jazz musician Charlie Parker ("Epilogue") and a caged leopard ("Anvil"). As this litany attests, Brathwaite uses Tom as a figure through whom to represent the coalescing of the oral, folk, African, and Amerindian cultural sources of the region.

In "Ogun" Tom merges with Brathwaite's great-uncle Bobby O'Neale. Whereas Walcott's Crusoe emerges from a mixture of classical and biblical figures (Proteus, Adam, and God), Brathwaite's Uncle Tom reflects the creolization of African and Christian cosmologies. As the title suggests, Uncle Tom "melts into" Ogun, the Yoruba and Afro-Caribbean divine craftsman, because of his work as a carpenter/sculptor. In addition, his impaired walk implies his transformation into Legba, the Dahomean and Haitian god who is the gateway to the spirit world. However, as a poor carpenter associated with Stowe's Christian novel, this Uncle Tom cannot be "wholly distinct" from Christ.[27] Whereas Walcott represents the slaves' conversion as a yielding of their own cosmology and a capturing of the master's God, Brathwaite suggests that the slaves suppressed but did not give up their belief in African gods when they converted to Christianity. Brathwaite's Tom does not accept that the coerced cultural baptism of colonialism eliminated the language and religious rituals of Africa.

Indeed, Brathwaite depicts the central action of "Ogun"—his uncle's secret carving of an African *mkissi,* or sacred sculpture—as a variation of the vodun ritual of possession, a ritual that Dash rightly claims is "central to Brathwaite's concept of the poet" because it reflects the poet's "superior vision" ("Edward Brathwaite" 223).[28] This poem also relies on one of Brathwaite's favorite early metaphors of identity, *roots,* to describe the relationship between the Caribbean folk artist and Africa.[29] His uncle's block of wood comes from a tree whose roots have long ago been severed, an apt image for the violent severing of cultural ties by the forced migrations of colonialism. However, as his uncle begins to work with this wood, his hands begin to

feel

how it had swelled and shivered, breathing air,
its weathered green burning to rings of time,

its contoured grain still tuned to roots and water.
("Ogun," *Arrivants* 243)

In other words, Brathwaite suggests that the evidence of Afro-Caribbean cultural origins is found in the material of Caribbean art itself, the cultural and linguistic practices of the folk. The Caribbean artist recovers these origins not only through patient and careful work with the material but also through an artistic vision of divine inspiration. As his uncle carves this wood, "a black rigid thunder he had never heard within his hammer / came stomping up the trunks" (243). Brathwaite associates this image of black lightning and thunder with Mabrak, which he describes as being possessed by the "visual imprint of the (blinding) face" of Shango ("Roger Mais" 80). In this ritual the individual worshipper "acts as a kind of lightning conductor for the gods" so that "the divine electrical charges become *grounded*" at the moment of "possession" (*Arrivants* 271). Brathwaite reworks this ritual so that the African gods "possess" his uncle as he sculpts; they assert their presence in Caribbean life through his art. Walcott's Friday strategically adopts Crusoe's religious rituals so that he can master and shape a New World tradition and identity. Brathwaite's uncle mystically participates in the Afro-Caribbean cultural ritual of possession, and it enables him to recover a distinctly African "nommo/name" (*Barabajan Poems* 155).

While Walcott's and Brathwaite's methods are complementary, their traditions are shaped by these diverging ideological commitments. Consider, for example, the different class commitments that emerge in a comparison of the representative personae of "Crusoe's Journal" and "Ogun." Walcott speaks of his New World Crusoe as living in an imagined second Eden, whereas Brathwaite presents his uncle as an ordinary craftsman who suffers simply, almost prosaically: "He was poor and most days he was hungry" ("Ogun," *Arrivants* 242). This uncle will never write poetry from a "beach house" but carves "within his shattered / Sunday shop" (243).

This uncle will never have the luxury of "hewing a prose" out of metaphoric wood; instead, he spends his weeks making actual chairs, tables, and coffins. Walcott's early poetry assumes a sophisticated, educated audience that can detect defiance in the boldness of his ironic reconfigurations of classical Western characters. In contrast, Brathwaite aligns cultural and economic decolonization in a much closer and more straightforward manner. Economically this simple carpenter cannot change the global markets where "imported cabinets" and "formica table tops . . . were what the world preferred," but artistically he can still protest the inequality by carving an "emerging woodwork image of his anger" (242). Brathwaite believes that even if his art cannot necessarily ensure social change, it should explicitly challenge injustice. As jazz becomes his metaphor for a Caribbean tradition of insurgency, his uncle's *mkissi* becomes an image that simultaneously reconnects the Caribbean with its African origins and protests the legacy of colonialism.

Even the way that these two poems conceive of the artistic task—Walcott's "Crusoe" writes and Brathwaite's uncle sculpts—reflects an epistemological difference between their traditions. Walcott sees writing as a way to recreate the significance of losing a past; his New World writers take Crusoe's journals and "learn to shape from them, where nothing was / the language of a race" ("Crusoe's Journal," *Collected Poems* 94). Brathwaite represents his uncle's carving as a way to recover a memory of the past's pain: he "explored its knotted hurts" ("Ogun," *Arrivants* 243). For the young Walcott, a poetic tradition depends on a shared written language, and colonization had left nothing but the metropolitan languages in which to construct a new tradition. Brathwaite, on the other hand, believes that the Caribbean artist can recover fragments of African culture in the social practices of common people—in the dance, the sermon, the religious ritual, the festival, and the wood sculpture. While Walcott ironically inhabits Crusoe's beach house in the Western tradition, Brathwaite seeks to preserve, even imaginatively recover, Tom's slave cabins and shattered workshops as the best way to construct a Caribbean tradition.

"Crusoe's Journal" and "Ogun" are exemplary of the poetic strategies that Walcott and Brathwaite employ in other of their poems written at this time. For example, when Walcott composes "Crusoe's Island," he again depicts his New World Crusoe as a conflation of figures from the English (Crusoe and Friday), biblical (Adam and God), and classical (Vulcan) traditions. He also compares poetry to religious ritual, although this time he is more pessimistic about the efficacy of art to bring about communion. Walcott sees "Friday's progeny" on their way to vespers and concludes that

> nothing I can learn
> From art or loneliness
> Can bless them as the bell's
> Transfiguring tongue can bless.
> ("Crusoe's Island," *Collected Poems* 72)

The church bell blesses by bringing different people together to affirm a common identity. He has lost faith in the teachings of the church ("I have lost sight of hell / of heaven"), and he fears that his faith in art will not be enough to form a similar community.

> My skill
> Is not enough,
> I am struck by this bell
> To the root.
> (71)

Whereas Brathwaite's uncle restores the roots of his diasporic identity by believing in his art, Walcott finds doubt at the root of his art. However, doubt is the only source of inspiration that he has left, so he prays that it will last throughout his life:

> may the mind
> Catch fire till it cleaves
> Its mould of clay at last.
> (71)

Again, Walcott accepts loss as the defining condition of the New World and affirms his capacity to create a tradition and identity from that loss.

Similarly, as Gordon Rohlehr argues, it is characteristic of Brathwaite's poetry that "the poet's ego is submerged in a multiplicity of voices, as the poetic word is democratized and all registers of speech allowed a privileged place" ("Dream Journeys" xi). For example, when he has the organizing persona of *The Arrivants* emerge as Caliban, he reconfigures this stock postcolonial character to recover the true significance of another Afro-Caribbean folk ritual, the limbo dance. The strategy is familiar. He redescribes a form of popular culture to show how it continues a historical practice of Afro-Caribbean cultural resistance. Brathwaite claims that this popular nightclub dance actually "originated [as] a necessary therapy after the experience of the cramped conditions between the slave-ship decks of the Middle Passage" (*Arrivants* 274). Since the normal means of cultural transmission—language and religion—have been so thoroughly suppressed by colonialism, Brathwaite is again drawn to a cultural practice—the physical performance of the limbo dance—as the most likely place to recover an Afro-Caribbean cultural connection. Indeed, he represents the limbo dance as yet another dramatization of the Afro-Caribbean ritual of possession. Caliban describes the limbo stick as the "silence" and "darkness" of slavery, a compelling image of the violence that dispossessed the slaves of their history ("Caliban," *Arrivants* 194). He dances under the stick to reverse imaginatively the journey of the Middle Passage and to recover an identity that lies beyond the silence and darkness of slavery. As he ascends on the other side of the stick, he experiences sound ("the drummers are praising me"), light ("sun coming up"), and finally possession:

> the dumb gods are raising me
>
> up
> up
> up
> . . . .
> hot
> slow
> step
>
> on the burning ground.
>
> (195)

For Brathwaite, this repossession of the cultural links between the Caribbean and African offers the most promising way to construct a decolonized tradition. As Caliban's insistent refrain suggests, Brathwaite entreats others to follow his example and

> *limbo*
> *limbo like me*
> *limbo*
> *limbo like me*
>
> (194)

Brathwaite even goes one step farther than Walcott in adapting Eliot's comparative method by providing his own glossaries, footnotes, appendixes, and other annotations to create the tradition in which his poetry should be read. For example, in the introductory paragraph to the glossary of

The Arrivants Brathwaite underscores the importance of the Afro-Caribbean religious ritual of "possession" to the trilogy by giving a brief explanation of it (271). He also establishes his poetry's relationship to the "folk" by contending that these "African-derived religions" are most often practiced by the "underprivileged and deprived masses of the population" (271). In fact, almost all of the terms in the glossary relate to African geographical references, African cultural practices, or African religious terms, a dominance that clearly points readers toward the traditions in which they should read his work. This practice of annotation continues through his second trilogy,[30] but it reaches its culmination in *Barabajan Poems,* in which his poetry is interlined with prose commentary by himself and other critics, in which he offers more than fifty footnotes, seven appendixes, and an index, and in which he even conducts a self-interview. As Rhonda Cobham perceptively suggests, Brathwaite's effort in *Barabajan Poems* "dramatizes the Sisyphean extremity of the postcolonial writer" because he has to create a "virtual archive" of personal and cultural references in order to "[invent] a literary tradition" (313). The modernist method of creating a text that recreates a tradition becomes a way to bring about cultural decolonization.

Poetry, Tradition, and Cultural Decolonization

As they grow older, Walcott and Brathwaite modify their views of tradition and alter the shifting personae that represent those traditions. While those modifications are examined in chapter 4, it is appropriate now to consider, at least preliminarily, the wider significance of their reworking of Eliot's modernist concept of tradition and shifting persona. Their reworking is significant not only because it illustrates postcolonial poetry's unique and too often neglected potential to contribute to cultural decolonization but also because it offers a more productive way to think about "canon" formation in general.

Poetry is not usually a genre favored by people interested in decolonizing the canon.[31] The formal, linguistic, and metaphoric complexities of poetry, particularly poetry that redeploys the technical innovations of modernism, do not easily conform to their expectations for postcolonial literature. Consider, for example, Georg Gugelberger's list of defining attributes of "Third World" literature: "[It] is bound to be always overtly political. . . . It tends to be allegorical and didactic. Formal aspects are not absent but they are clearly secondary. . . . It is a fighting literature which speaks against the traditional triad of oppression: gender, race, class. . . . [It] is generally a rejection of the West including its canonized literary models. . . . [It is] bilingual, even polyglot but in a meaningful way contrary to polyglot aspects of the Euro-American tradition" (515, 517–18). He suggests that reading, teaching, and writing about this literature is the only way to "decolonizing the canon" (520–21). The poetry of Walcott and Brathwaite exposes the glaring limitations of this approach. Walcott's protean Crusoe and Brathwaite's shifting Tom certainly reflect different ideological concerns, but these personae are not "always overtly political," "allegorical," or "didactic." Instead, they figuratively embody the complexity of the multiple cultural traditions and identities in the New World, a complexity that poetry is perhaps more equipped to convey because of the comprehensive logic of its figurative language. This comprehensive logic unites disparate ideas, objects, and people into new wholes and thus serves as a useful and important alternative to the binary logic of opposition that animates Gugelberger's understanding of postcolonial literature. Admittedly, Brathwaite's insurgent Afro-Caribbean folk tradition relies more frequently on the logic of opposition than does Walcott's ironic New World classicism, but he still recasts Eliot in ways that exemplify the promise of poetry. Indeed, both Brathwaite and Walcott reorient rather than "reject" Eliot's "formal" innovation because they consider poetic technique to be an integral rather than a "clearly secondary" part of their work. At a time when postcolonial literature is too often defined in simple political or sociological terms, Walcott and Brathwaite, at their best, exploit the generic strengths of poetry to create complementary visions of the overlapping and intertwining threads of a truly decolonized New World tradition.[32] And their skill justifies why poetry plays, as Breiner suggests, "an unusually prominent role in West Indian society" (*An Introduction* 13).

Their example does more, however, than elevate the unique strengths of poetry as a form of postcolonial literature; their reworking of Eliot also illustrates the strength of "tradition" as a concept to explain the relationship between cultural artifacts and cultural identities. The Anglo-American debate in this area has tended to cast this issue in terms of "defending" the Western canon to preserve a cultural identity or "opening" it up to reflect changing identities. The Caribbean experience of these poets and their approach to Eliot's modernism offer valuable strategies for rethinking the role of written and popular culture in forming collective identity. The religious connotations of canonicity imply that there is a cultural authority that has the power to establish a list of books and practices to advance a collective identity. As these poets use the term, tradition suggests that writers construct a contingent set of relations with their predecessors and their community to reorient a practice to serve a variety of collective identities. A canon is formed through the decision of a central cultural authority; traditions depend on the more diffuse agency of participants. A canon purports to settle finally the questions of a text's relative status; a tradition recognizes that questions of a text's value remain contingent and contested precisely because of the practice of subsequent participants. A canon aspires to offer a standard around which people form a single collective identity; a tradition recognizes that one person may associate with several different and overlapping identities.

Eliot, Walcott, and Brathwaite themselves exemplify how writers participate in overlapping and intertwining traditions and identities. Geopolitical boundaries offer one source of identification. Consider, for example, their national affiliations: Walcott claims to be a St. Lucian writer (Moyers); Brathwaite argues that the "core" of his work belongs in a Barbadian tradition (*Barabajan Poems* 23);[33] and Eliot is alternatively aligned with a distinctly English or American tradition.[34] They also align themselves with regional traditions: Walcott and Brathwaite speak of participating in a Caribbean tradition (Walcott, "Art of Poetry" 106; Brathwaite, *Barabajan Poems* 23), and Eliot calls for a "literature of Europe" ("Tradition and the Individual Talent" 15). Indeed, they even imagine broader hemispheric allegiances: Walcott talks of the "New World" tradition as everything created this side of an imaginary meridian in the Atlantic ("Culture" 6), and Brathwaite imagines a transatlantic community between Africa and the Caribbean ("Timehri" 33). Race serves as yet another marker to identify the contours of their traditions. Walcott describes himself as a "mulatto of style" ("Twilight" 9), Brathwaite accepts being described as a writer of the "African Diaspora" (*Barabajan Poems* 22), and Eliot distinguishes English, Irish, and American poetic traditions because of a "different rhythm in the blood" ("Tradition and the Practice of Poetry" 17). Finally, they turn to language as the most important way to define a tradition. Eliot contends that "literature is not primarily the matter of nationality, but of language; the traditions of the language, not the traditions of the nation or the race, are what first concern the writer" ("The Three Provincialities" 39). Walcott affirms that "language . . . is the empire, and great poets are not its vassals but its princes" ("Muse" 15). And Brathwaite develops his concept of nation language to identify the distinctiveness of his Afro-Caribbean tradition.

Of course, traditions and identities can be defined according to other categories—gender, class, religion—but the previous examples should suffice to show the overlapping and constructive nature of these categories.

The significance of a person's nationality, regional affiliation, racial identity, or linguistic aptitude is not inherent in the category itself but in how these categories are perceived and used. In fact, Caribbean writers such as Brathwaite and Walcott have probably done more to apprehend and represent the fluidity of these categories because of the overlapping and intertwining cultural histories represented in the region. Cultural traditions and collective identities do not have a metaphysical essence that must be protected or attacked but are constructed through the collective work of participants who see significant lines of affinity among texts and people. At their best, Walcott and Brathwaite transpose Eliot's concept of tradition in order to imagine new lines of affinity among the multiple cultural resources of the region.

Bereft of a single cultural center, do things necessarily fall apart? Has there been such a proliferation of traditions that there is no longer a way to imagine new cultural wholes? Are we left with irreconcilable difference as the defining characteristic of cultures in the late twentieth century? These poets respond with a resounding no, and this answer, more than anything else, defines their common modernism. Each of them recognizes the widespread fragmentation of his cultural milieu, but each also aspires to create a tradition that unites these fragments into new cultural wholes. These cultural wholes are not perfect or fixed, but they provide the contexts in which a writer's broader significance can be measured. As Henry Louis Gates Jr. asserts in advocating a pluralist understanding of tradition, a culture without a "center" is not necessarily a culture without "focus": "to read and write culture anew means additional demands for rigor and coherence, not emancipation from these things" (*Loose Canons* 119–20). As the diverse work of Eliot, Walcott, and Brathwaite clearly shows, this ideal of creating a culture anew by reordering its fragments is still most compellingly pursued by redeploying the poetic theories and strategies of modernism.

Bearers, Not Borrowers, of Tradition

Eliot's best-known statements about tradition appear in his collected and widely republished essay "Tradition and the Individual Talent."[35] The tone of this essay is magisterial and abstract, the tone of the confident philosopher-critic rather than of anxious metic. However, "Tradition and the Individual Talent" is not Eliot's only commentary on this topic. In an uncollected essay published simultaneously with "Tradition and the Individual Talent" and with his letter to Mary Hutchinson, Eliot speaks of the relationships between writers in a tradition in much more personal terms.

He talks of the "profound kinship," "personal intimacy," and even "passion" that exist between the practicing poet and his or her dead predecessors ("Reflections" 39). By "penetrat[ing] . . . the thick and dusty circumlocutions about his [predecessor's] reputation," the living poet gains the right to claim him as a "friend" (39). In their own ways, Walcott and Brathwaite have penetrated the accumulated layers of Eliot's reputation to reclaim him as a potential friend of Caribbean poetry. As Eliot describes it, the benefits of this friendship are "an introduction to the society in which our friend moved; we learn its origins and its endings; we are broadened. We do not imitate, we are changed; and our work is the work of the changed man; we have not borrowed, we have been quickened, and we become bearers of a tradition" (39).

A "metic" earns his right to citizenship in a tradition through hard work; "friends" establish a relationship through mutual appreciation that develops into fondness. It is a shift in tropes that it would be well to follow in thinking about the formation of cultural traditions, for friendship is worth more than citizenship, a claim of affection more compelling than a claim of right. As Walcott suggests at the end of "Crusoe's Journal," the desire to create is a desire to relate to others, a desire that he suggests even motivated God to create human beings. As his New World Crusoe composes poetry, he confirms the heresy that "God's loneliness moves in His smallest creatures" (*Collected Poems* 94). Moreover, as Eliot recognizes, true friendships transform the people involved: they "learn," "are broadened," and "are changed" by their relationships. Accordingly, this ideal of friendship captures the passionate generosity, engagement, and transformation that can occur among writers who set themselves in relation to one another, even among writers as different as Eliot, Walcott, and Brathwaite. Should readers not aspire to set themselves in a similar position vis-à-vis writers and each other? Should they not themselves learn, be broadened, and be changed by the experience of reading?

Finally, Eliot's trope of friendship is an appealing way to conceive of the equality among these writers. Brathwaite and Walcott are not merely derivative of Eliot—they do not merely borrow—but are animated by his example to become "bearers" of their own traditions. They are "bearers" both in having the responsibility of carrying on the practice of poetry (bearing a load) and in having the privilege of making that practice anew by representing their Caribbean experience (bearing as generative). It is an ideal that reiterates the modernist impulse to create continuities from chaos, to imagine a deeper order in the surface fragmentation, to restore wholeness from the experience of brokenness. It is also an ideal that these poets may be particularly equipped to fulfill because poets have the capacity, in Brathwaite's words, to make

> with their
>
> rhythms some-
> thing torn
>
> and new
> ("Jou'vert," *Arrivants* 270)

It is to these poetic rhythms that we turn next, for each of these writers conceives of poetry's relationship to speech as an integral part of its larger social function.

3 Listening to Eliot

Poetic Revolution and Common Speech

The kind of verse which began to be written about 1910 or so made the same break with tradition that we find in that of Wordsworth and Coleridge.

—T. S. Eliot, "The Last Twenty-five Years of English Poetry"

The mainstream poets who were moving from standard English to nation language were influenced basically, I think (again the models are important) by T. S. Eliot.

—Kamau Brathwaite, "History of the Voice"

Since our concern was speech, and speech impelled us.
To purify the dialect of the tribe

—T. S. Eliot, *Little Gidding*

In many islands, the West Indian poet is faced with a language which he hears but cannot write because there are no symbols for such a language. . . , so his function remains the old one of being filter and purifier, never losing the tone and strength of the common speech as he uses the hieroglyphs, symbols, or alphabet of the official one.

—Derek Walcott, "The Muse of History"

SOON AFTER Yeats's death Eliot recalled that he had learned "how much the Irish way of speech is needed to bring out the beauties of Irish poetry" by listening to Yeats read aloud ("The Music of Poetry" 31–32). Similarly, Brathwaite and Walcott both recall listening to Eliot reading his poetry as a formative event in their careers. However, whereas Eliot had to emigrate to London, meet Pound, and be introduced to Yeats before he could learn this lesson about poetry's relationship to speech, Brathwaite and Walcott heard Eliot through the technology of the phonograph. Brathwaite remembers the poetic "breakthrough" that came from hearing "Eliot's actual voice—or rather his recorded voice, property of the British Council (Barbados)—reading «Preludes», «The love song of J. Alfred Prufrock», *The Waste Land,* and later the *Four Quartets*" ("History of the Voice" 286n34). And Walcott lists "the Eliot recordings of the *Four Quartets*" as one of his most significant memories from adolescence ("Leaving School" 31). It is a suggestive example of cosmopolitan poetic exchange, for it illustrates how the audio technology of the twentieth century has reoriented poetic influence, not only by expanding greatly the number of people who could hear the poet's spoken voice but also by inspiring new ways to conceive of the relationship between poetry and speech. The audio recording inscribes a text to produce actual sound; it is a writing that can echo accurately the inflections of the spoken word; it is a medium that brings together the graphic and oral elements of language in a new equivalence. For Brathwaite and Walcott, listening to Eliot's voice is as formative as reading his texts in developing their own understanding of poetry's relationship to speech. And as Laurence Breiner suggests, "the fundamental question" of Caribbean poetry is "what language do West Indians speak, and how do we get it on paper?" (*An Introduction* 164).[1]

Indeed, for Brathwaite, Walcott, and other Caribbean writers this question of poetic language is as important and as vexed as the question of tradition. If language is the home of being, as Martin Heidegger evocatively suggests, then the poet's choice and use of language can fundamentally shape personal and communal identity (193). Clearly, Caribbean colonial history has made this question more difficult for writers from the region: the indigenous languages of the Arawaks, Caribs, and others have been all but destroyed; the Creoles heard on the street are mixtures of African and European languages that have little standardized orthography and still suffer from the social stigma of being considered "broken" dialects; the Asian languages Chinese and Hindi have also influenced the various Creoles but have not become multiethnic languages in the region; and the standard forms of European languages still carry the taint of colonial oppression.[2] Walcott and Brathwaite offer different answers to this question: Walcott is more apt to inflect Standard English with English and French Creole diction or accent and to work within the written conventions of traditional poetry, whereas Brathwaite is more keenly concerned with representing English Creole, or nation language, by experimenting with written conventions. Again, however, these choices are better viewed along a continuum rather than in opposition, for each of them constructs different, partial but complementary linguistic homes to house Caribbean Anglophone identity. And, again, it is striking how they arrive at their divergent answers through rereading Eliot's modernism differently, illustrating again the vibrancy of modernism's discrepant cosmopolitan influence. But most importantly, perhaps, the divergent answers and imaginative work of these New World poets is renewing and extending the capacity of the English language to convey new rhythms, idioms, vocabularies, and experiences. As Mervyn Morris playfully asserts in his essay on language and West Indian literature, a common identity arises out of this distinctive speech: "All the same, is English we speaking" ("Is English We Speaking" 14).

Receiving Eliot in the Caribbean

Brathwaite and Walcott both recall hearing Eliot read poems on the phonograph, and what each recalls him reading reveals a lot about that writer's own answers to the question of poetry's relationship to speech. Brathwaite primarily remembers Eliot reading his earlier works, "Prufrock" and *The Waste Land,* works in which Eliot mimics different urban dialects to revolutionize modern poetry with the colloquial idioms of contemporary speech. Eliot's poetic use of dialect speech encourages Brathwaite to develop his own nation-language poetry. In contrast, Walcott remembers Eliot's voice from *Four Quartets,* a poem in which Eliot echoes Mallarmé's poetic concern "to purify the dialect of the tribe" (*Little Gidding, Complete Poems* 141). The older Eliot conceives of poetry as "refining" ordinary speech to make it a more perfect linguistic medium. Walcott agrees that poetry "filters" or "purifies" speech, but says that it does this by amalgamating rather than refining dialects, by mixing rather than purging vernaculars. Walcott has a concern with speech, in other words, that impels him to fuse the dialects of the tribes.

Eliot invites this disparate reception of his career. In "The Music of Poetry" (1942) he speaks of the "cyclical movement" of poetry, a movement that alternates between periods of poetic "revolution," which announce themselves as "a return to common speech," and periods of poetic "purification," in which "the followers of a revolution develop the new poetic idiom. . . ; they polish or perfect it" (31). He argues that the last twenty years had been a revolutionary "period of search[ing] for a modern poetic idiom" but that poetry was then moving into a new period of developing the "musical possibilities of an established convention" of speech (35). It is a literary history of modernism that quite consciously coincides with his own career, the poetic revolution beginning with the publication of *The Waste Land* (1922) and the period of purification initiated by *Little Gidding* (1942).

Eliot's critical self-aggrandizement is well known,[3] but the distinction he makes here raises an interesting question about the complementary poetic "revolutions" of Brathwaite and Walcott. Brathwaite makes the seemingly obvious choice of transposing and extending the ideas and practices of the younger, more "revolutionary" Eliot. Walcott, on the other hand, boldly modifies the ideas of the older, more conservative Eliot, the Eliot who describes the desire to "live in a state of perpetual revolution" as a form of poetic and cultural pathology, a "craving for continual novelty of diction and metric [that is] unwholesome" (35). The conservative origin of Eliot's idea might seem to taint Walcott's appropriation of it, but it is a part of Walcott's genius to revise the ideological implications of other writers' ideas to achieve his own purposes. For Walcott, an allusion is never tantamount to an endorsement.

This debate about poetry's relationship to speech is not, of course, new. It has important precedents in the English tradition (the debate between Wordsworth and Coleridge being Eliot's implied *locus classicus*) and analogues in other postcolonial literatures. While the younger Eliot denounced romanticism as part of his strategy to initiate a modernist poetic revolution, the older Eliot admits that "the kind of verse which began to be written about 1910 or so made the same break with tradition that we find in that of Wordsworth and Coleridge" ("The Last Twenty-five Years" 9). Eliot conflates the positions of Wordsworth and Coleridge here for simplicity, but they take different positions on the issue of poetry's relationship to speech. Wordsworth makes the more revolutionary claim that poetry should adopt the "language really used by men . . . because such men hourly communicate with the best objects from which the best part of language is originally derived" ("Preface" 124). Ideologically, this claim emerges as part of his early interest in the radical egalitarian ideals of the French Revolution. Epistemologically, he claims that common speech is a superior linguistic medium because common people are in closer contact with the "best objects" of the natural world—their speech emerges from particular physical experiences. Coleridge worries that the material particularism of Wordsworth's poetics of speech will lead to excessive arbitrariness and provincialism: it places the "chief value on those things on which man DIFFERS from man" (*Biographia Literaria* 130). In response, Coleridge declares that poetry "is essentially ideal, that it avoids and excludes all accident; that its apparent individualities . . . must be representative of a class" (45). Accordingly, he argues that poetic language should not come from the "language really used by men" with all of its idiosyncrasies, but from the "*lingua communis,*" a language that "omits the peculiarities" (56) of a speaker's class, region, or educational achievement, a language that is "purified" (52).

Fascinatingly, the terms of this romantic debate get repeated and changed, not only in Eliot's distinction between modern poetry's "returning to" and then "purifying" common speech but also in the difference between Brathwaite's advocating a nation-language poetics and Walcott's pragmatically accepting Standard English as a *lingua communis* in the New World but inflecting it with the accent of West Indian speech. Similar to Wordsworth, Brathwaite wants to develop a poetry that advances a more egalitarian ideology and reconnects to the material reality of a folk experience. Similar to Coleridge, Walcott sees communal and linguistic fragmentation as a more pressing concern, so he aspires to create an ideal poetic language that unites disparate people into a single culture. While these debates are analogous in form, the Caribbean version is more ideologically charged because questions of language are so inextricably linked to questions of identity and to the legacy of colonialism in the region.

Indeed, this debate over language emerges in similar ways for other postcolonial writers.[4] Consider, for example, the debate between Chinua Achebe and Ngũgĩ wa Thiong'o concerning the proper language of African literature. Achebe takes a position similar to Walcott's. He pragmatically accepts English as a *lingua communis* of Anglophone African nations, but it is an English that African writers change through using it: they "[fashion] out an English which is at once universal and able to carry [their] peculiar experience" (100). English is a "universal" language, then, not because African writers have used it in a way that conforms to "standard" (i.e., Anglo-American) conventions but because they have transformed it to reflect the particularity of African speech and experience. English is a cosmopolitan language because of its discrepant representations. Ngũgĩ considers such a project illegitimate because he believes that the English language cannot adequately express African experience.[5] Interestingly, he too adapts Eliot's modernist language to make his argument. He contends that the colonial and neocolonial imposition of English caused a "dissociation of the sensibility" that led to "colonial alienation" (*Decolonizing the Mind* 17). The only way to "transcend colonial alienation" is to write in indigenous languages that reconnect African literature to the speech and experience of common people in Africa (28). He concludes that "African literature can only be written in African languages, that is, the languages of the African peasantry and working class, the major alliance of classes in each of our nationalities and the agency for the coming inevitable revolutionary break with neo-colonialism" (27). Accordingly, in its oppositional rhetoric, of class allegiance and materialist epistemology, Ngũgĩ's poetics of speech closely parallels Brathwaite's position, a convergence that has been too little studied given the closeness of their personal relationship.[6]

Comparing these pairs of postcolonial writers is illustrative but not conclusive, for colonialism affected speech differently in Africa and in the Caribbean. In African colonization, imperial languages were imposed as the official languages of government and education, but the colonized people usually continued to speak indigenous languages. The linguistic results of Caribbean colonization are more complex: the truly indigenous Amerindian languages were largely destroyed through genocide; the indigenous African languages of the slaves were violently suppressed but continued to exert an influence on the spoken languages of the region;[7] the "legal" successor to slavery, indentured labor, introduced new languages into the region, Hindi and Chinese being the most prominent; and the imperial languages English, French, Spanish, and Dutch overlapped more extensively in some islands because they were controlled by different colonial powers. Accordingly, African writers are more likely to be working in a primarily diglossic community, where the distinctions between imperial and indigenous languages are more clearly defined. Caribbean writers tend to work within a more polyglossic context, in which differences between indigenous, emigrant, and imperial languages are less obvious.[8]

Brathwaite and Walcott respond to this polygossia of language as they did to the multiple sources of tradition. In developing his theory and practice of nation language, Brathwaite risks simplifying the Caribbean linguistic situation in order to keep the colonial, linguistic, and political hierarchies of colonialism and neocolonialism clearly in view. By pragmatically accepting and inflecting Standard English, Walcott hazards masking these hierarchies in his attempt to master, and so dissemble, them. As Mervyn Morris suggests, they make complementary contributions to the development of the English language and literature. Walcott has tended to accomplish "distinguished work" by subtly creolizing "conventional mainstream criteria," whereas Brathwaite has "helped us to extend our recognition of excellence" to new forms of poetry ("Is English We Speaking" 2). The risks and rewards of these alternative poetic strategies are instructive not merely as new postcolonial theories of poetry's relationship to speech but also as means for rethinking the relationship between poetry, speech, and identity in a world in which more and more people speak English but speak it differently from one another.

It is a lesson that begins for both of them in listening to Eliot and that is refined in listening to each other.

"The Models Are Important": Finding Nation Language in Eliot's Use of Dialect

For the young Eliot, as for Wordsworth, poetry was in need of an infusion of common speech, not from Wordsworth's rustic life, but from the life of the office worker, the pub patron, and the jazz musician—the urban folk. The younger Eliot disparages romanticism in general and Wordsworth in particular,[9] but he approaches this question of poetry's relationship to speech with Wordsworthian assumptions about language. "Language in a healthy state," Eliot argues in his review of Swinburne, "presents the object, is so close to the object that they are one thing" ("Swinburne" 73). Indeed, he contends that the purpose of modern poetry should be to develop a language that arises from the physical experience of modern life, a language not merely from the heart but from "the cerebral cortex, the nervous system, and the digestive tract" ("Metaphysical Poets" 290). One of the ways that the younger Eliot conveys this physicality of language is by mimicking and juxtaposing different types of speech—"He do the police in different voices," as the draft title of *The Waste Land* suggests. It is a method that would revolutionize poetry's relation to speech in England, America, and throughout the Anglophone world. However, it is also a method about which Eliot is ambivalent because it reflects a cultural fragmentation, which he laments. In other words, he revolutionizes poetry with a modern colloquial idiom, but his methods mark the prevalence of linguistic alienation among all classes rather than celebrate, in Wordsworthian fashion, the authenticity of folk speech as an epistemologically and aesthetically superior form of language.

For his part, Brathwaite openly acknowledges the influence of Eliot's early methods and ideas on the development of nation-language poetry in the Caribbean. He argues that "the mainstream poets who were moving away from standard English to nation language were influenced basically, I think (again the models are important), by T. S. Eliot. What T. S. Eliot did for Caribbean poetry and Caribbean literature was to introduce the notion of the speaking voice, . . . that is what attracted us to Eliot" ("History of the Voice" 286–87). However, Brathwaite articulates a poetics of speech that is decidedly less ambivalent, both about the reason for linguistic alienation in the Caribbean—colonialism—and about the primacy of nation language as a means to respond to this alienation. It is a conceptual clarity that strengthens the power of his poetic critique of colonialism but that can also oversimplify the question of poetry's relationship to speech in the region.

For example, while he recognizes that a linguistic continuum exists in the Caribbean, he focuses almost exclusively on nation language because of its "revolutionary" potential (259–60, 265).[10] He defines *nation language* as the common Anglophone speech of the Afro-Caribbean folk, a definition that limits his poetic revolution by class and ethnic affiliations, elides the differences between Anglophone speakers from different islands such as Trinidad, Jamaica, or Barbados, and minimizes the potential influence of other imperial, Creole, or ancestral languages on nation language. However, he sacrifices these complexities in order to emphasize nation language as an alternative to Standard English. It may relate to English in its lexicon, but it "is not English in terms of its syntax. And English it certainly is not in terms of its rhythm and timbre, its own sound explosion. In its contours, it is not English" (265–66). By simplifying the issue to a choice between nation language and Standard English, Brathwaite mobilizes resistance to the prevailing colonial hierarchy of cultural value, a hierarchy that historically elevated the written word of the colonizer over the speech of ordinary West Indians. It is an important achievement. Indeed, Breiner even goes so far as to claim that publication of Braithwaite's *Arrivants* "is the single most *consequential* event in the history of West Indian poetry to date" because he showed to a wider audience how to make "entire poems speak nation language" (*An Introduction* 177).

What is striking is that Brathwaite recognizes the potential for writing in nation language by listening to Eliot. Indeed, he hears in "the phrasing of Eliot's poetry" the same "deep rhythmical and formal influence of Africa" that he hears in the best nation-language poetry ("Jazz" 74). Brathwaite's sensitive ear puts him decades ahead of critical readers of Eliot, for only in the past decade or so have critics such as Michael North, David Chinitz, and Ronald Schuchard begun to recognize the larger importance of Eliot's experiments with working-class and African American dialects and cultural forms.[11] Brathwaite hears the "riddims of St. Louis" in Eliot's voice and associates those rhythms with the jazz "dislocations of Bird, Dizzy, and Klook" ("History of the Voice" 286n34). Brathwaite is part of a group of writers that presciently reassesses Eliot's significance in terms of his strategic resistance of Standard English and his use of popular culture. It is a reassessment that Brathwaite exploits to claim Eliot as a "model" for his own experiments with nation-language poetry. And as Brathwaite himself says, "the models are important," so the nature of this intertextual relationship deserves more critical attention than it has so far received.

The people who recognize this relationship tend to criticize or defend the "originality" of Brathwaite's appropriation of Eliot, but they miss the more important distinction between Eliot's ambivalent and Brathwaite's adversarial poetics of speech.[12] Eliot "modernizes" poetic language by interjecting the speech of the class or racial other; however, he mimics these forms of speech ironically because he worries that in representing linguistic fragmentation he may also be contributing to it. Brathwaite "indigenizes" his poetic language by representing nation language as the speech of the Afro-Caribbean self. He is convinced that nation language resists the alienating power of Standard English and that it offers the most viable linguistic foundation on which to create a unified and decolonized cultural community. Ironically, then, Brathwaite takes Eliot's experiments to represent the linguistic and cultural fragmentation of modern Europe and transposes them to imagine nation language as a medium of linguistic and cultural unity in a postcolonial Caribbean. Even more ironically, the same Eliot who scoffed at the work of "colonial writers" because they had not "produced . . . a separate and distinct rhythm" is the Eliot who becomes Brathwaite's model for developing the distinct poetic "rhythm and timbre" of nation language ("Tradition and the Practice of Poetry" 16; "History of the Voice" 265). Eliot eventually steps back from his vernacular experiments and redirects his modernism toward a refining of the dialect of the tribe; however, he does not control the influence of those experiments as Brathwaite extends and transforms them to create his own Afro-Caribbean modernist poetics. Modernism has become a cosmopolitan aesthetic at least in part because its poetic strategies have survived despite, and even thrived against, the intentions of its first practitioners.

Class Ventriloquism

Eliot's claim to return poetry to modern speech rests in part on his successful class ventriloquism in "A Game of Chess." In particular, Eliot's mimicry of working-class speech in the pub scene serves as an illuminating example. As David Chinitz and Gregory Jay rightly assert, Eliot exhibits an affectionate ambivalence toward the speech and culture of the working class in this scene (Chinitz 243; Jay 236–37).[13] He respects it as an authentic expression of ordinary lives, but he also recoils from its unrefined and coarse physicality. It is an ambivalence that permeates the central sexual and linguistic tropes of this section. Eliot recognizes that love and language were the conventional ways for people to overcome their sense of alienated isolation, but he believes that the conditions of modern life now frustrate their fulfillment. Lil's body shows the physical effects of being sexually fertile and poor: she looks "so antique" because of "them pills I took, to bring it off," yet she still is admonished to make herself sexually attractive for her husband: "poor Albert . . . wants a good time, / And if you don't give it him, there's other's will" (*The Waste Land, Complete Poems* 41). Similarly, Eliot mimics Cockney dialect to underscore the aborted fecundity of lower-class gossip. The speaker exhibits great energy in telling Lil's story, but she is limited in her diction and repetitive in her narrative patterns. Indeed, Eliot uses the pub owner's refrain, "HURRY UP PLEASE ITS TIME," to suggest that this sexual and linguistic alienation portends the apocalyptic end of culture itself.

Sexual and linguistic alienation are not limited to the working class in "A Game of Chess." In the opening section Eliot conveys the horror of the upper-class women's disaffection by alluding to King Tereus's rape of Philomela, a sexual violence that can only be described through the vulgar onomatopoeia of "Jug jug" (40). In the middle section he represents the neurotic middle-class couple as speaking in Standard English, but they do not communicate ("Speak to me. Why do you never speak to me. Speak"). The husband dreams of escaping this relationship by going to the jazz hall, a place of sexual freedom that Eliot evokes through mimicking jazz rhythms:

> O O O O that Shakespeherian Rag—
> It's so elegant
> so intelligent
>
> (41)

However, the husband remains trapped in the routine of their marriage ("The hot water at ten. / And if it rains, a closed car at four"), and sex remains a meaningless game that merely fills the time before death ("we shall play a game of chess, / Pressing lidless eyes and waiting for a knock upon the door") (40–41). In moving adeptly through this social registry of linguistic and sexual alienation, Eliot renews poetic language with the speech of modern urban experience, but he also betrays an uncertainty about the larger social function of this poetic revolution.

Indeed, an exchange between Eliot and his wife, Vivien, in the margins of *The Waste Land* manuscript suggests the extent of his uncertainty about these experiments with dialect. Vivien suggests that he spell "something" with a final *k* instead of *g*, but he rejects the suggestion, claiming, "I want to avoid trying [to] show pronunciation by spelling" (*The Waste Land: A Facsimile* 13). The rest of the section, however, contradicts this statement, for he employs phonetic spellings and typographical variations to indicate not only the jazz inflection of "O O O O that Shakespeherian rag" but also the ominous tone of the pub owner's "HURRY UP PLEASE ITS TIME" and the slurred sound of the patrons' "Goonight" (15). While this inconsistency may seem slight, it reflects a deeper tension in Eliot's experiment with dialect. He modifies the conventions of spelling and typography to convey accurately the inflection of speech, but he also recognizes that these conventions are essential for intelligibility. Even as he mimics Cockney to renew modern poetry with common speech, he worries that he may actually contribute to the fragmentation of modern life by undermining linguistic conventions.

In "The Dust," Brathwaite recasts Eliot's pub scene to represent nation language as the working-class speech of the Caribbean and the best linguistic medium for Caribbean poetry. "The Dust" has long been praised by Caribbean critics as one of Brathwaite's finest nation-language poems; its representation of folk speech rhythms have variously been described as a "near perfect expression" (Pollard, "The Dust" 41), a "consummate achievement" (Morris, "Broken Ground" 23), and a "triumphant of *Rights of Passage*" (Rohlehr, *Pathfinder* 50). Even the reviewers who were more critical of Brathwaite's *Rights of Passage*[14] in general recognized the accomplishment of this poem. Edward Baugh claims that he knows of "no West Indian poet who has used dialect more subtly, probingly, or suggestively . . . to achieve at one and the same time poetry and authentic speech" as Brathwaite has done in "The Dust" ("Review" 67). And Walcott himself encourages people to "read and reread" it to recognize "how masterful a technician Mr. Brathwaite has become" ("Tribal Flutes" 44). The poem is rightly praised primarily for its verisimilitude of speech rhythms and patterns; however, these critics and reviewers have done relatively little to explain the significance of the poem's verisimilitude to Brathwaite's larger poetics, an explanation that is more readily made by contrasting it with the pub scene in Eliot's *The Waste Land.*

"The Dust" opens with a group of Barbadian folk women talking at the local village store. In contrast to the slurred farewells that conclude Eliot's pub scene—"Goonight Bill. Goonight Lou. Goonight May. Goonight"—the primary speaker of Brathwaite's poem, Olive, greets the other women with a friendly salutation:

Evenin' Miss
Evvy, Miss
Maisie, Miss
Maud. . . .
("The Dust," *Arrivants* 62)

The difference in communal life is felt immediately. Lil's friends gossip behind her back for their own amusement; Brathwaite's women exchange news and advice for their mutual benefit. Eliot's Lil takes pills from a back-street chemist for an abortion that ruins her health and fertility; Brathwaite's Olive recommends to Eveie an herbal remedy—"dat Miraculous Bush"—that restores her physical and sexual vitality.[15] Eliot presents Lil's story through the malicious monologue of her friend, whereas Brathwaite conveys the cooperative interplay of the individual and the village by representing this dialogue in the call-and-response form of a folk sermon. Eveie thanks Olive for her advice by mimicking a minister's call:

Then all uh kin say
an' uh say it agen:
we got to thank God
fuh small mercies.
(62)

And Olive answers by echoing the congregation's response:

Amen,
Eveie, chile,
Amen,
Eveie, chile

an' agen
I say is Amen.
(63)

The gossip in Eliot's pub underscores Lil's painful isolation in an alienating urban environment, whereas the folk wisdom and encouragement exchanged in Brathwaite's village store suggest the vitality of Barbadian communal life.

Brathwaite also employs a refrain—"Is de pestilence, man"—but he uses it to identify colonialism as the source of the Caribbean apocalypse. "De pestilence" manifests itself first in sick livestock and damaged crops, as evidence "that the Writin' Han' pun the Wall," to declare the destruction of the village (64–65). As Velma Pollard suggests, "Bible History and Oral History" come together to comment on the "now situation" (Pollard, "The Dust" 42). This biblical allusion triggers Olive's memory of the oral history of the volcanic eruption of Mount Pelee in Martinique in May 1902 (Rohlehr, *Pathfinder* 105). "De pestilence" reminds her of

> that story
> Gran' tell us 'bout May
> dust[.]
> ("The Dust," *Arrivants* 65)

a time when

> it black black black
> from that mountain back:
> in yuh face, in yuh food,
>
> in yuh eye. In fac',
> Granny say, in de broad
> day light, even de white
>
> o' she skylight went out.
> An' if you hear people shout!
> how they can't find the way
>
> how they isn't have shelter
> can't pray to no priest or no leader
> an' God gone an' darken the day!
> (66–67)

Figuratively, Brathwaite uses volcanic eruptions as a metaphor for the devastation of the slave trade. Both events abruptly kill people with little warning. Both events make people suffer in literal darkness, the volcano's ash blocking the sun and the slavers imprisoning people in the holds of their ships. Both events destroy the entire social, religious, and political structures of the village, leaving those who remain with little to reconstruct their speech or culture. Tonally, as Gordon Rohlehr suggests, Olive describes the volcanic eruption with more phonetically spelled words, more rhythmically regular lines, and more interwoven rhymes to suggest the sound of a communal folk lament (*Pathfinder* 106). Brathwaite contends that the writers who were influenced by Eliot "went on to create their own environmental expression" of his modernist poetics of speech, a goal that Brathwaite achieves with the central trope, rhythms, and diction of this passage ("History of the Voice" 286). With the pub owner's closing call, Eliot pessimistically warns of the eventual collapse of European culture from within. With Olive's refrain, Brathwaite identifies colonialism as the external threat to this village life, and he affirms the resilience of these folk women to preserve a speech and culture despite this threat. "It is this strength," as Velma Pollard contends, "that 'The Dust' illustrates . . . in the voice of the people it celebrates" ("The Dust" 47).

Brathwaite has justly received praise for the poetic ventriloquism of "The Dust." Morris describes it as "one of our finest poems in creole," and it certainly represents his ideal of the potential linguistic and cultural unity among the Afro-Caribbean folk despite the legacy of colonialism ("Overlapping Journeys" 127). However, Brathwaite also captures other nation-language voices in *Rights of Passage* that reflect the more fragmented reality of the postcolonial condition. For instance, he evokes the different generational responses to colonialism's injustice by contrasting Tom's voice of submissive lament ("Ease, / up Lord") and his children's violent curses:

> But to hell with this, nuncle!
> . . . .
>
> Cut the cake-
> walkin', man; bus'
> the crinoline off the white woman,
>
> man; be the black buttin' ram
> ("All God's Chillun," *Arrivants* 20–21)[16]

Brathwaite then evokes the depth of this younger generation's estrangement by mimicking other voices—the urban hipster who satirically repeats racist stereotypes to define himself

> I am a fuck-
> in' negro,
> man, hole
> in my head,
> brains in
> my belly;
> ("Folkways," *Arrivants* 30)

the Rastafarian who calls for a revolution

an' de poor dem
rise an' rage dem
("Wings of a Dove," *Arrivants* 45)

and the emigrants who are excluded from England's working-class community

The men who lever ale
in stuffy Woodbine pubs
don't like us much.
. . . .
So what to do, man?
Ban the Bomb? Bomb
the place down?
("The Emigrants," *Arrivants* 55–56)

In collocating these different disaffected voices, Brathwaite more closely echoes the tone of Eliot's ventriloquism in *The Waste Land,* but he still focuses the class and ethnic affiliation of his mimicry to better identify the decolonizing power of his poetics of speech.

The differences are instructive. Eliot juxtaposes a range of class dialects to mark the pervasive breakdown of European speech and culture, whereas Brathwaite employs a range of voices within a single class and ethnic identity, the Afro-Caribbean folk, to mobilize this class to resist colonialism's effects. Eliot is ambivalent about the ideological effects of poetic ventriloquism, so he tends to mimic voices more ironically. Brathwaite embraces nation language as the authentic speech of the folk, so he satirizes these voices only to criticize the degrading influence of colonialism. Eliot employs urban speech in a way that initiates a poetic revolution but that signifies a cultural demise. Brathwaite recognizes that nation language carries the scars of colonialism, but it remains for him the only language that can bring about poetic and cultural renewal in the region. By closely identifying nation language with the Afro-Caribbean folk, Brathwaite transforms Eliot's modernist poetics of speech into a more sharply edged poetic strategy of cultural unity and independence.

Racial Ventriloquism

Eliot does not limit his mimicry to the class distinctions of speech in London. As Michael North argues, he also engages in a modernist "pattern of rebellion through racial ventriloquism" (9). Shortly after publication of *The Waste Land,* Eliot turns from lyric poetry to compose a "jazz play," the fragments of which he would publish as *Sweeney Agonistes*.[17] This shift to drama does not, however, affect his views of poetry's relationship to speech: "The next form of drama will have to be a verse drama but in new verse forms . . . probably a new form will be devised out of colloquial speech" ("Introduction to *Savonarola*" xi). In *Sweeney Agonistes* he experiments with colloquial forms of speech from English and American popular culture to try to develop this new verse drama. It is an experiment that reflects Eliot's anthropological interests, for he aspires to create a modern drama that replicates what he understands to be the "original" or "primitive" function of art as religious ritual.[18] He wants to bring together poetry, music, dance, and ritual in a drama that invites the audience to participate and that creates a sense of genuine community. In other words, he sees this verse drama as a potential response to the alienated voices of *The Waste Land*.

Eliot looks to forms of popular culture—jazz and minstrelsy being particularly important for our purposes—as the most likely places to recognize this ritual function of art in the modern world. Even though Eliot eventually abandons *Sweeney Agonistes* unfinished, Brathwaite considers these cross-racial experiments with dialect to be a forerunner to his nation-language poetry. Indeed, Sweeney's line "I gotta use words when I talk to you" becomes a touchstone in Brathwaite's work,[19] for it signifies for him the ambivalence of resisting imperial English in the Caribbean context. Nation language resists "Standard" English in its rhythms, but it remains dependent on the lexical and graphical conventions of "Standard" English to maintain its intelligibility. Brathwaite eventually responds to this dependency by developing his Sycorax video-style to experiment with the graphic conventions of representing nation language; however, initially he builds on Eliot's tentative experiments with jazz and minstrelsy to develop his own distinctly Caribbean poetics of speech.

Eliot makes the rhythm of jazz conspicuously present in *Sweeney Agonistes* through his innovations in diction and dialogue. For instance, he relies heavily on American slang—not only words ("swell," "slick," "pinched," "gotta," "joint," and "gona") but also phrases ("all right" and "hit this town") and even solecisms ("you've got to know" and "did a girl in")—to evoke jazz's American cultural context. He also suggests the syncopated cadence of jazz in the accelerated exchange of the play's dialogue, in its pattern of repeating and developing a phrase, and in its use of rhyme. Consider, for example, this colloquy between Doris and Dusty.

DORIS: No it wouldn't do to be too nice to Pereira.
DUSTY: Now Sam's a gentleman through and through.
DORIS: I like Sam
DUSTY: *I* like Sam
Yes and Sam's a nice boy too.
He's a funny fellow
DORIS: He *is* a funny fellow
He's like a fellow once I knew.
He could make you laugh.
DUSTY: Sam can make you laugh:
Sam's all right
DORIS: But Pereira won't do.
(*Complete Poems* 75)

Structurally, this passage operates as a digressive counterpoint to the primary theme of this section of the play—why Pereira "won't do"—with Sam serving as a useful contrast. Sam's virtues are elaborated through a rapid repeating of short staccato phrases with italics marking subtle changes in intonation, an elaboration that itself follows a jazz pattern of repeating and improvising on the previous statement of the theme to give it a new inflection ("I like Sam / *I* like Sam" or "He's a funny fellow / He *is* a funny fellow"). This repetitive pattern breaks up the lyricism of the dialogue to the point that it begins to sound more like prose than poetry. Eliot is able to retain a poetic ordering of sound through his regular use of rhyme. While many of the lines in this passage are broken between the two speakers, every other line still ends with the same rhyme ("through," "too," "knew," "do"). In other words, rhyme serves as the bass rhythm for the improvisation in the dialogue. It is a rhythm that he intended to support in the production of the play by using "light drum taps to accentuate the beats" of the characters' speeches (quoted in Flanagan 82). David Chinitz concludes from examples such as this one that "every moment that he sounds 'like Eliot,' Eliot is alluding to jazz" (246), but he overstates the case. More accurately, jazz serves as a provisional model among several for Eliot's experiments to create a modernist poetics of speech.

Indeed, jazz is not even the only cross-racial experiment in *Sweeney Agonistes*, for Eliot also parodies the minstrel song "Under the Bamboo Tree" in a way that illustrates, as North argues, the "repetitive and disintegrative language of the whole fragment" (89).

Under the bamboo
Bamboo bamboo
Under the bamboo tree
Two live as one
One live as two
Two lived as three
Under the bam
Under the boo
Under the bamboo tree.
(81)

Eliot finds the idiom of this song attractive because sound, particularly repetitive sound, replaces sense as the organizing principle for choosing poetic diction.[20] Rhythm again is paramount as he seeks to elicit a physical response to his verse. At the end of the fragment Eliot recasts this method so that the seemingly comic association between "bam" and "boo" becomes the terrifying sounds of "a cream of a nightmare dream," the sounds of a phantasmagoric pursuit that he conveys as

Hoo ha ha
Hoo ha ha
Hoo
Hoo
Hoo
KNOCK KNOCK KNOCK
KNOCK KNOCK KNOCK
KNOCK
KNOCK
KNOCK
(85)

It is not an innovation for Eliot—he quotes minstrel songs in the draft of *The Waste Land* and uses "DA" in a similar fashion to represent what the thunder said—but he uses it more extensively in *Sweeney Agonistes* (*The Waste Land: A Facsimile* 5). Words are broken into their phonetic parts to accentuate the rhythmic rather than the semantic effect of speech.

"Poetry begins," Eliot contends, "with a savage beating a drum in a jungle, and it retains that essential of percussion and rhythm" (*Use of Poetry* 148).[21] In *Sweeney Agonistes* Eliot assumes that the rhythms of jazz and minstrelsy can revive modern poetry because they are in closer contact with the "primitive" origins of art. Eliot's experiments are shaped by his racial stereotypes, but they still produce powerful and innovative ways to reconnect poetry with common speech. Jazz inspires him to reclaim poetry's incantatory power by repeating and developing the tonal and semantic meaning of words or phrases. Minstrelsy offers him a way to restore poetry's visceral force by fracturing language into its phonetic parts. Both forms are performed before an active audience, so they serve as models for renewing poetry's function as public ritual. He conceives of the poet as the anthropologist of the oral artifact, investigating the rhythms of popular culture and speech to reconnect modern poetry with its origins in primitive society. "Primitive art and poetry can," he contends, "through the studies and experiments of the [civilized] artist or poet, revivify the contemporary activities" ("War-Paint" 1036).

When Brathwaite recasts and extends Eliot's experiments, he reverses the poetic and ideological ends. He finds the "civilized" art of Eliot's modernism to be an aid to recovering the origins of Caribbean "folk" poetry and to revivifying its contemporary practice. While many of Brathwaite's poems could be cited as examples,[22] "Wings of a Dove" offers a useful contrast to Eliot's *Sweeney Agonistes* because it seeks to reconnect his poetry to the revolutionary speech and musical rhythms of two important Afro-Caribbean cultural sources—Rastafarianism and Ska.

"Wings of a Dove" opens with a vivid description of the material poverty of its Rastafarian speaker in order to establish the connection between his speech and his physical condition.

> Brother Man the Rasta
> man, beard full of lichens
> brain full of lice
> watched the mice
> come up through the floor-
> boards of his down-
> town, shanty-town kitchen,
> and smiled.
>
> (*Arrivants* 42)

As Rohlehr notes, Brathwaite introduces two sounds in this passages that dominate the rest of the poem—the long *i* sound ("lichens," "lice," "mice," "smiled") and the diphthong *ou* ("down-town," "shanty-town") (*Pathfinder* 90). For Brathwaite, these sounds signify as much phonetically as semantically, the *i* registering a primal cry of pain and the *ou* evoking the drumbeat of resistance.[23] The sound of pain dominates the poem's opening paragraphs, with this *i* sound occurring in more than half of the lines.

Brother Man tries to blunt the pain by reaching "for his peace / and the pipe of his ganja," but the drug only intensifies his perception of alienation. It drives him into the streets, where he begins to hear the drums of the Ska dance[24] and to imagine rebellion:

> Down down
> white
> man, con
> man, brown
> man, down
> down full
> man, frown-
> ing fat
> man, that
> white black
> man that
> lives in
> the town.
> ("Wings of a Dove," *Arrivants* 43)

As Rohlehr suggests, Brother Man becomes in this passage the "history-filled and prophetic voice of a wider proletariat" by identifying an emerging class of rulers of various races in the West Indies ("white man, con man, brown man," and "white black man") who care more for money than for cultural rootedness ("Rehumanization" 176). As the ganja heightens Brother Man's perception of his pain, the sound of the drums increases his resolve to resist. Indeed, the drums induce an apocalyptic vision in which Brother Man sees himself as leading the poor to defeat their oppressors:

> we
> laugh
> dem, mock
> dem, stop
> dem, kill
> dem
> ("Wings of a Dove," *Arrivants* 43)

And then he calls them to return

> back
> to Af-
> rica.
> (43)

Similar to Eliot's method in *Sweeney Agonistes,* Brathwaite fractures speech into phonetically significant sounds in the context of popular cultural rituals. However, whereas Eliot believes that this recovering of the ritual function of poetry will lead directly to uniting a modern audience as a community, Brathwaite suggests that the Caribbean recovery of ritual must first incite a sweeping program of cultural decolonization before it can contribute to forming a community.

Brathwaite's revolutionary focus becomes clear in the third section of the poem, where he regularly repeats the nation-language word *dem* to convey the drums' insistent rhythm. He divides the section into three sentences, each sentence ending with a variation of the liturgical refrain "in the glory of the Lord." The first sentence suggests the capacity of the drums (and, by implication, a poetic imitation of those drums) to enable an audience to transcend the misery of everyday life:

> So beat dem drums
> dem, spread
>
> dem wings dem,
> watch dem fly
>
> dem, soar dem
> high dem,
>
> clear in the glory of the Lord.
> (44–45)

In these lines Brother Man recognizes and even indulges a bit the temptation of poetic transcendence. The incantatory rhythm of the drums so transports him that he momentarily forgets his material situation and dreams of a better world. Indeed, Morris argues that Brathwaite allows the "music rhythms" to "take charge" over the speech rhythms in this line ("soar dem / high dem" interrupting the normal Creole syntax of the previous part of the sentence) to suggest a moment of poetic transcendence ("Overlapping Journeys" 126). However, like his ganja, this rhythmic transcendence is an unsustainable high in the context of an exploitive economic system. Accordingly, in the second sentence Brother Man reminds his listeners of the material reality of Babylon, of the decadence and injustice of their neocolonial tourist economy.[25] While the cruise ships arrive "full o' silk dem / full o' food dem" and the planes land "full o' flash dem / full o' cash dem," the benefit of this wealth never reaches the lower classes of the community ("Wings of a Dove," *Arrivants* 45).

Combining the vision of the first sentence and the material reality of the second, in his concluding sentence Brother Man calls for an apocalyptic revolt that is both transcendent and immanent:

> when the flame dem
>
> from on high dem
> raze an' roar dem
>
> an' de poor dem
> rise an' rage dem
>
> in de glory of the Lord.
> (45)

In "Wings of a Dove" Brathwaite succeeds in bringing together Rastafarian speech, cultural practices, and ideology in a way that embodies his own, more oppositional Afro-Caribbean aesthetic. Brother Man starts from the material conditions of his poverty; escapes these conditions temporarily through the rituals of smoking ganja and listening to the drums; finds, however, that these rituals do not relieve but intensify his sense of the injustice about his material deprivation; and ends by looking forward to a day of judgment, a day when these intensified experiences of injustice will incite the oppressed to revolt against their oppressors, a day when

> de poor dem
> rise an' rage dem
>
> in de glory of the Lord.
> (45)

Similarly, Brathwaite aspires to compose a poetry that begins in the material conditions and speech of the folk experience, intensifies the folk experience of injustice through recovering its function as public ritual, and eventually inspires a revolt against the neocolonial structures of political and cultural power.

Baugh claims that poetry moves between the modes of the "sermon" and of the "ritual," of the discursive and of the rhythmic use of language, of the interpreting and of the enacting of meaning ("Poetry as Ritual" 7). He suggests that his "disquiet" with Brathwaite's work is "lessened when I feel the poem to be in the first place and over-archingly a ritual" (7–8). However, a poem such as "Wings of a Dove" suggests that Brathwaite truly succeeds when he brings together both sound and sense, both rhythm and rhetoric, both "sermon" and "ritual." The poem begins in the pain of an alienated cry and ends in the collective resolve of a drumbeat, sounds and rhythms that emerge from the Caribbean folk experience and are heightened by Brathwaite's enjambments and phonetic spellings. But the masterful speech rhythms of the poem also convey a Rastafarian worldview that is in keeping with the ideological commitments of the poem and the poet. Brathwaite may have been prompted to turn to nation-language poetry by Eliot's early experiments, but he transforms those initial promptings into vibrant Afro-Caribbean expressions of his own. He listens to Eliot but speaks as himself.

Critics have praised Eliot's ventriloquism as an important part of modernism's cultural breakthrough. One of the first, Delmore Schwartz, cites passages from "A Game of Chess" and *Sweeney Agonistes* as examples of the "purity and the exactness with which [Eliot] has listened to and quoted and recorded the speech of another human being" ("T. S. Eliot's Voice" 137). Henry Louis Gates Jr. points to *Sweeney Agonistes* as a model for using dialect because Eliot made "the American vulgar tongue contain the rhythms and idiom common to its slang uses at the time" (*Figures in Black* 289n17). Michael North goes so far as to suggest that Eliot's "linguistic mimicry and racial masquerade were not just shallow fads but strategies without which modernism could not have arisen" (i). While Eliot certainly deserves praise for these experiments to update poetry with modern colloquial speech, it is a praise that tends to obscure his own tentativeness about them. More often than not, he nullifies or undermines the more revolutionary aspects of these experiments: he cuts the allusions to minstrel songs in *The Waste Land*, rejects Vivien's suggestion to particularize the Cockney dialect through phonetic spelling; and abandons *Sweeney Agonistes* in the middle of composing it. Here again we see the distinct advantage of approaching these writers as part of a discrepant cosmopolitan modernist tradition. The partiality of Eliot's innovations becomes clear when one recognizes the breadth and brilliance of what Brathwaite accomplished with this poetics of speech. This discrepant approach still acknowledges the importance of Eliot's use of dialect, but less for its actual achievement and more for its inspiration of other poets, such as Brathwaite, to explore the meaning of the sound of speech in their own poetry.[26]

Brathwaite tends to ignore the ambivalence of Eliot's experiments with dialect because he is interested in appropriating a "revolutionary" poetic model. Or as Breiner argues, "Braithwaite, in effect, constructed for himself precisely the Eliot he chose to imitate" (*An Introduction* 204). However, this ambivalence leads Eliot to shift from revitalizing poetry by infusing it with common speech to purifying common speech through the refining power of poetry. It is this new modernist poetics of speech that Walcott finds so attractive.

From "Revolution" to "Purification": Eliot's Revised Poetics of Speech

When the familiar compound ghost declares in *Little Gidding* that the poets' "concern was speech, and speech impelled us / To purify the dialect of the tribe," he repeats what had already become a general principle in Eliot's later criticism.[27] Consider, for example, how Eliot uses this line from Mallarmé in the third Turnbull lecture, in January 1933:

> The important poets will be those who have taught the people speech; and the people had in every generation to be taught to speak: the function of the poet at every moment is to *make the inarticulate folk articulate;* and as the inarticulate folk is almost always mumbling the speech, become jargon, of its ancestors or of its newspaper editors, the new language is never learnt without a certain resistance, even resentment. *Donner un sens plus pur aux mots de la tribu,* Mallarmé said of Poe; and this purification of language is not so much a progress, as it is a perpetual return to the real. (*The Varieties* 289–90, emphasis added)

Eliot has completely flipped the orientation and the tone of his poetics of speech. He is now more concerned with how poetry can perfect the speech of the folk rather than with how the colloquial speech of the folk can renew poetry, that is, poetry as authoritative instruction, not as eclectic ventriloquism. Indeed, it is as if Eliot's model for the poet is now Henry Higgins instead of Sir James Frazer, the magisterial phonetician refining the speech of Lil and her friends into an ideal language instead of the oral anthropologist recovering the immediacy of their primitive speech to renew poetry.

However, as A. V. C. Schmidt has persuasively shown, Eliot does not appeal to Mallarmé here and elsewhere to advocate a return to the symbolist doctrine of *la poésie pure* (36–48), to the doctrine that poetry could so purify speech as to achieve the condition of music by having "nothing in view but itself" (Eliot, "From Poe to Valéry" 40). Instead, while Eliot agrees with *la poésie pure*'s "theoretical goal" of increasing people's "consciousness of language," he contends that "it is a goal that can never be reached, because . . . poetry is only poetry so long as it preserves some 'impurity' . . . so long as the subject matter is valued for its own sake" (39). Eliot is attracted to, but ultimately rejects, *la poésie pure* for the same reason that he curtails his experiments expressing jazz rhythms through dialogue or fracturing language into its phonetic parts. He values deeply poetry's capacity to use sound and rhythm to communicate meaning beyond conscious thought, but he will not completely abandon poetry's capacity to communicate in a rationally intelligible manner. In Baugh's terms, poetry cannot be exclusively "ritual"; it must also be "sermon." Accordingly, Eliot contends that the poet purifies speech into an ideal medium, not by representing it as pure sound, but by making it a more accurate medium for more people to articulate their experiences of life—"to teach people to speak," as he says in the Turnbull lecture. Or as he says of Dante, the poet should be a "scrupulous, painstaking and *conscious* practitioner of the *craft*" of poetry in order to develop, refine, extend, and intensify both the semantic and the aural aspect of speech, thus "making possible a much greater range of emotion and perception for other men, because he gives them the speech in which more can be expressed" ("What Dante Means to Me" 132, 134). Perfecting the conventions of poetry—perfecting the craft—becomes the means by which the poet purifies speech for the masses.

Eliot's shift can be understood as a move from a more Wordsworthian to a more Coleridgean explanation of poetry's relationship to speech. Whereas the younger Eliot imagines himself as part of a small vanguard of writers who can break the calcification of poetic language by infusing it with the speech of the urban folk, the older Eliot aspires to respond to, rather than merely represent, cultural and linguistic fragmentation. It is a broadening of his sense of the poet's social function. The poet who initiates a poetic revolution affects other poets; the poet who purifies the language affects "everybody who speaks that language, . . . whether they are poets, philosophers, statesmen or railway porters" (133). The poetry of his youth announces itself as a cacophony of individual voices—"He do the police in different voices"—whereas his later poetry claims to speak for a nation—"History is now and England," as he says in *Little Gidding*. It is a shift in keeping with his religious conversion: liturgy and sermons replace jazz and minstrelsy as models of "popular" culture that the poet can emulate to restore poetry's function as public ritual. Indeed, he moves from declaring the need for a poetic revolution to fearing its results: "We cannot, in literature, any more than in rest of life, live in a perpetual state of revolution," he contends toward the end of his career. "Poetry should help, not only to refine the language of the time, but to prevent it from changing too rapidly: a development of language at too great a speed would be a development in the sense of a progressive deterioration" ("Milton II" 160).

Some may see this shift in Eliot's poetics of speech as merely another example of his regrettable move to the right later in his career.[28] However, Walcott transforms it into a method to decolonize the language of Caribbean poetry: he aspires to collapse the distinction between idiomatic and imperial dialects by fusing them together. So whereas the older Eliot speaks of poetic purification as a refining of speech, Walcott purifies speech through the cross-contamination of dialects: the writer "dedicated to purifying the language of the tribe . . . is the mulatto of style" ("Twilight" 9). Ironically, then, this shift in Eliot's career serves as a singularly useful fulcrum to clarify the differences between Brathwaite's more trenchant and Walcott's more pragmatic poetics of speech. It also reveals the discrepant positions available on this issue within a more cosmopolitan understanding of modernism.

"A Language Which He Hears but Cannot Write": Fusing the Dialects of the Tribe

While other Caribbean poets wrote or performed dialect poetry before Brathwaite,[29] it is not until the convergence of the rise of the Black Power movement in the Caribbean and the publication and success of *The Arrivants* in the late sixties and early seventies that Walcott feels compelled to defend his own poetics of speech. In "The Muse of History" (1974) Walcott opens by questioning the revolutionary premise of "folk" poetry, the premise that writing in nation language is the exclusive way for a Caribbean poet to signify resistance to colonialism. In its place he offers his theory of cultural resistance through assimilation and mastery. He contends that when the "language of the torturer [is] mastered by the victim," it should be considered a "victory" rather than "servitude" (4).

Walcott then raises the Eliotic concern that Caribbean poets will in fact contribute to cultural fragmentation if they succeed in representing nation-language speech accurately. He claims that

> the West Indian poet is faced with a language which he hears but cannot write because there are not symbols for such a language and because the closer he brings hand and word to the precise inflections of the inner language and to the subtlest accuracies of his ear, the more chaotic his symbols will appear on the page, the smaller the regional dialect, the more eccentric his representation of it will become, so his function remains the old one of being *filter* and *purifier,* never losing the tone and strength of the common speech as he uses the hieroglyphs, symbols or alphabet of the official one. (13, emphasis added)

Walcott does not just echo Eliot's purifying rhetoric; he transforms it to emphasize the seriousness of linguistic fragmentation in the Caribbean. Eliot posits a natural "cyclical movement" in poetry to justify his shift from "updating" poetry to "purifying" speech, but Walcott asserts that violence of colonialism's linguistic legacy leaves the Caribbean poet with no choice but to become a "filter" and "purifier." In *The Waste Land* Eliot intuitively recognizes the tension between the graphic conventions of spelling and the accuracy of a poetic representation of speech. Walcott claims that this tension is so exacerbated in the Caribbean that true nation-language poetry would be unintelligible. Again, the confluence of these ideas is richly ironic. Eliot decides to purify the dialect of the tribe primarily to recover a sense of European cultural unity, whereas Walcott considers this poetic "filtering" to be the only viable means of forming a Caribbean *lingua communis* from the cultural fragmentation caused by European colonization.

Walcott also creolizes the sources of authority for this theory. Eliot appeals explicitly to Mallarmé and Dante (and implicitly to Coleridge) to illustrate his argument, but Walcott cites the French Caribbean writers Saint-John Perse and Aimé Césaire to support his claim.[30] In particular, Walcott finds Césaire useful because his "revolutionary" credentials are impeccable and yet his revolutionary poem *Cahier d'un retour au pays natal* is not written in dialect ("Muse" 13). He contends that this "great poem of Césaire could not be written in French Creole dialect because there are no words for some of its concepts, . . . and because even if they were suddenly found, they could not be visually expressed without the effort of an insane philologist" (15). It is a claim that likely emerges from his own experience of trying to translate Césaire's work into English (King, *Derek Walcott: A Caribbean Life* 236). And while Walcott may underestimate the metaphoric capacity of French Creole,[31] he uses Césaire's example to repeat his claim that Caribbean poetry cannot accurately represent the linguistic diversity of the region's dialects without unduly jeopardizing its intelligibility. Indeed, Césaire is exemplary because Walcott "hears" in his written imperial French the tone and rhythm of spoken French Creole. Walcott claims an analogous linguistic heritage—what he calls his "dual linguistic personality" of Saint Lucian patois and imperial English—and he aspires to a similar inflection of the English language with the melody of his "basic" speech, which is "tonally . . . patois" (Walcott, "Conversation" 29).[32] By infusing the official written language with the rhythms and tones of common speech, Walcott seeks to master the writing of the colonizer by having it echo the sound of the colonized.

By alluding to the older Eliot and by recasting the significance of Césaire, Walcott challenges Brathwaite's implicit claim that nation-language poetry is the only legitimate successor to the poetic revolutions of modernism and negritude.[33] It is a challenge that becomes personal, for Walcott criticizes the disparity between Brathwaite's nation-language poetry and his Cambridge education when he argues that it is hypocritical, or even worse, "academic," for the "educated and privileged poet . . . to write one way and speak another" ("Muse" 19). In contrast, Walcott argues that for his "poetry to be true, it had to be accurate, quietly accurate in terms of the sound of my own voice" and yet still be combined with the "strength of the root, the mass racial sensibility of expression" (Walcott, "An Interview" [Hirsch] 58–59). Walcott describes this fusing of the individual and communal speech as getting the "tone," "melody," or "accent" right in the rhythm and sound of a poem.[34] The poet achieves this goal, not by refining or endorsing dialects, but by fusing them and the standard language into a new whole:

> I can't create in pure Creole, French or English, for all sorts of reasons. You might be in a situation where accents differ within a small area, among people who all speak French Creole. The same applies to English Creole in the Caribbean. It is very difficult, in one sense, for a Trinidadian to understand a Jamaican, or for a Jamaican to understand a Barbadian, but since one considers the Caribbean—the English-speaking Caribbean—as a whole, as sharing one language with various contributory sources, one must try to find, using syntaxes from various dialects if necessary, one form that would be comprehensible not only to all the people in the region that speak in that tone of voice, but to people everywhere. It is like making an amalgam, a fusion, of all the dialects. (Walcott, "Reflections Before and After Carnival" 42–43)

Walcott never, of course, fuses "all the dialects" of the region, but he successfully rearticulates the theory of poetic purification to represent it as a unifying poetics of speech in the Caribbean. As Terada rightly suggests, "Creole is not simply an *instance* of Walcott's poetic language, but the *model* of poetic language aware of its own nature" (93).

The complementary nature of Brathwaite's and Walcott's poetics of speech takes shape from their alternative interpretations of modernism. Brathwaite hears the dialect speech of the younger Eliot's modernism and develops a poetics of speech that renews the revolutionary ideology of Césaire's negritude. Walcott hears the Creole inflections in Césaire's standard

French and recasts Eliot's theory of poetic purification as a method of cultural decolonization. The relative merits of these complementary poetics of speech are debated not only in terms of their prose but also in terms of their poetry. In particular, Walcott lyrically extends his critique of nation-language poetry in "Names" (1976), and Brathwaite responds to that critique in his "Nametracks" (1977). Indeed, names and naming become the figurative places of struggle between their discrepant modernist poetics of speech.

A Question of Names

Walcott publishes "Names" as part of *Sea Grapes* (1976). It is the first collection of lyrics that he publishes after defining and defending his poetics of speech in the pivotal essays "The Muse of History" (1973) and "The Caribbean: Culture or Mimicry?" (1974) and after exploring his own linguistic heritage in his autobiographical epic *Another Life* (1973). While critics have recognized "Names" as Walcott's lyrical apologia for his assimilating poetics of speech, none of them comment other than in passing on one of its most telling details, namely, its dedication, "for Edward Brathwaite" (305).[35] This neglect makes otherwise compelling readings of the poem incomplete, for these critics fail to recognize how Walcott's poem responds to the example of Brathwaite's nation-language poetry. Walcott divides "Names" into two sections. The first section rejects theoretically the premise that writing in nation language enables the poet to recover the origins of Afro-Caribbean culture; the second section illustrates specifically the method of his assimilating poetics of speech, a method in which the colonized pragmatically accepts, imaginatively uses, and ultimately masters the names of the colonizer.

In his poetics of speech Brathwaite traces the origins of nation language to the submerged presence of African ancestral languages in contemporary Caribbean culture, "the African aspect of our New World / Caribbean heritage" ("History of the Voice" 265). In contrast, Walcott questions this very concept of recovering linguistic origins or cultural essences. In "Names" he begins by asserting dispossession as the common experience of the Caribbean. It is a dispossession that Walcott characterizes as the loss of the cultural perspective embodied in a particular language and land:

> My race began as the sea began,
> with no nouns, and with no horizon,
> with pebbles under my tongue,
> with a different fix on the stars.
> ("Names," *Collected Poems* 305)

In addition, Walcott uses "race" to denote a broader Caribbean ethnic identity than does Brathwaite. Dispossession is a common experience not only for the African diaspora ("the bronzesmith from Benin") but also for the Indian and Chinese diaspora in the Caribbean ("the goldsmith from Benares / the stonecutter from Canton") (306). Walcott contends that it is impossible to recover the pure moment of cultural origin prior to the colonial period—"that moment / when the mind was halved by a horizon"—both because the Caribbean "race" has multiple "horizons" of origin and because each horizon is subjected to the contingency of time: each "horizon / sinks in the memory" (305).

Walcott recognizes that this loss of cultural origins threatens any collective sense of identity in the Caribbean; however, rather than engaging in what he sees as a futile project of cultural recovery, he claims the right to create a Caribbean cultural identity from this absence:

> A sea-eagle screams from the rock,
> and my race began like the osprey
> with that cry,
> that terrible vowel,
> that I!
>
> (306)

Terada notes that this interjection resembles a "human birth cry" (99), and Burnett suggests that it is a "primal utterance of self-consciousness" (21), but neither of them recognizes how Walcott's "I" of affirmation responds to Brathwaite's *i* of pain. As we saw in "Wings of a Dove," Brathwaite uses this sound to mark phonetically the atrocity of colonization, a tendency that Walcott criticizes as a limiting of poetic "language to phonetic pain, the groan of suffering, the curse of revenge" ("Muse" 3). Walcott suggests that this "terrible vowel" evokes both the pain of separation and the claim of identity, both the dispossession of a people from their speech and their landscape and the heroic self-will of a people who survived this dispossession to claim a new speech and landscape. Walcott aspires to create this new culture and language out of this loss of origins and with a recognition of its own contingency, a culture and language in which people have

> nothing in our hands
>
> but this stick
> to trace our names on the sand
> which the sea erased again, to our indifference.
> ("Names," *Collected Poems* 306)

For Walcott, naming is a provisional act of self-generation in the present rather than an authenticating act of recovery of the past. The Caribbean poet changes the present by recognizing the loss of cultural and linguistic origins as both painful and opportune, both a fact to be acknowledged and a myth to be revised.[36]

In the second part of the poem Walcott looks more specifically at the naming of Saint Lucia to illustrate his theory. He begins by underscoring the double-edged nature of the colonial naming of the island, a naming of the Saint Lucian landscape with French words that could have been motivated by either the colonizer's "nostalgia or irony" (306). When "little Versailles / meant plans for a pigsty," this naming appears to mock Saint Lucia as derivative and inconsequential in comparison with French monuments of civilization; however, these "belittling diminutives" also mock the colonizers' attempt to recreate France in Saint Lucia, their attempt to find

> names for the sour apples
> and green grapes
> of their exile.
> (*Collected Poems* 307)

More importantly, Walcott argues that these names have survived the bitterness of their colonial origin ("Their memory turned acid / but the names held") and have been transformed by the beauty of the Saint Lucian landscape ("Valencia glows / with the lanterns of oranges") and by the voices of the Saint Lucian people ("The African acquiesced, / repeated, and changed them") (307). Colonial nostalgia or irony may have motivated the naming of Saint Lucia, but the contemporary significance of these colonial names has been changed by the landscape of Saint Lucia and the speech of its people.

Indeed, Walcott identifies this pattern of assimilation—a pattern of acquiescence, repetition, and change—as the means for resisting the legacy of colonialism. The speaker of the poem says:

> Listen, my children, say:
> *moubain:* the hogplum,
> *cerise:* the wild cherry,
> *baie-la:* the bay,
> with the fresh green voices
> they were once themselves
> in the way the wind bends
> our natural inflections.
> (307)

The lesson is a simple one: French Creole and English are so juxtaposed in Saint Lucia that they are fusing into the rhythm of one language. The children will complete this fusion by repeating the names with their own "fresh green voices." Indeed, Walcott imagines that the breath of their spoken voices will bend the words of Standard English as the wind bends trees until the words conform to the people's "natural inflections" (307).[37]

The poem ends with the fresh voices of these children, who not only change the significance of old names through their new accents and references but also make new names through coining new metaphors. It is a scene of "colonial instruction," as Breslin suggests (116), in which the instructor asserts that the stars over Valencia's forest are "not Orion / not Betelgeuse" and asks the children, "What do they look like?" ("Names," *Collected Poems* 306). The children see the constellation as "fireflies caught in molasses" (308), which is not only an arresting figure of the ephemeral radiance of names caught in the semifluid conventions of a language but also, as Burnett points out, a figure that shows the "postcolonial project" of renaming the universe from the perspective of the local (42). Walcott contends that this propensity to create new metaphoric names is one of the poetic privileges of growing up in the Caribbean: it is a place where the "whole race [is] renaming something that had been named by someone else and giving that object its own metaphoric power" (Walcott, "An Interview" [Hirsch] 58). Accordingly, Walcott suggests that his poetics of "purifying" speech ultimately decolonizes the language best because it leads to new acts of creative naming that can be broadly shared. And he implies that poetry in general plays an instrumental role in a postcolonial culture because its facility with metaphor better represents the power of ordinary people to imagine new identities and communities.

Walcott's felicity with figuration can be hypnotic, so it is worth stepping back from his tropes to question the coherence of the poem's argument. In particular, the two sections of "Names" expose the recurring gap between the multicultural rhetoric of Walcott's speculations about poetic language and his actual practice. In the first section, Walcott recognizes linguistic and cultural dispossession as the common experience of the African, Indian, and Chinese diaspora in the Caribbean; however, in his poetic response to that dispossession in section 2 he imagines the children fusing only French Creole and English. This limited fusion makes sense in the linguistic context of Saint Lucia, but it falls short as a regional ideal. What about the accents of the children that speak an Indian- or Chinese-inflected English? Where do we hear their breaths bending the common language with their "natural inflections"? This gap is particularly egregious because Walcott is simultaneously claiming his aspiration to create an "amalgam, or fusion, of *all* the dialects" (Walcott, "Reflections Before and After Carnival" 42–43, emphasis added). Later in his career he is more careful to qualify his ability to fulfill this ideal, his self-conscious humility actually making the ideal itself more appealing.

Brathwaite responds to Walcott's position less directly but no less forcefully. Whereas Walcott asserts that the common experience of cultural loss necessitates the assimilating of the colonizer's speech, Brathwaite develops a theory of strategic essentialism, or *nam,* to reaffirm his commitment to nation language and to a more adversarial poetics of speech. For Walcott, languages, like names, are important but provisional markers of contingent identities; for Brathwaite, they preserve and convey the essence of individual and cultural identity. In "Names" Walcott calls for poetry to amalgamate and inflect the written language of the colonizers with the sound of the colonized. In "Nametracks" Brathwaite imagines a poetry that emerges from the oral speech and practice of the folk experience and that stands more in opposition, in both its sound and its written conventions, to the language of the colonizers.

A Question of Nam

Brathwaite uses nation language not to renew written English as an international medium in the Caribbean but to resist English as a colonizing cultural presence in the region, not to create a common interethnic Caribbean experience but to express the essence, or nam, of the Afro-Caribbean experience. Indeed, he contends that the collective identity of the Afro-Caribbean folk animates its common speech: "*Nam* is the heart of our *nation-language*" (*Mother Poem* 121n62). By developing this concept of nam Brathwaite questions the extent to which Afro-Caribbean culture was severed from its African origins and reasserts nation language as the best means to recognize these submerged connections as well as to resist their further repression. In the mid- to late 1970s, nam becomes the epistemological foundation of Brathwaite's nation-language poetics of speech. Even though some of Brathwaite's critics recognize, in Elaine Savory's words, that the "concept of *nam* is extremely important in relation to Brathwaite's writing" ("The Word" 24), they have spent surprisingly little time explaining the nature of that importance.[38]

Brathwaite has been redefining *nam* with slight alterations during the last two decades, so critics are not completely wrong when they stress the ambiguity of the term.[39] Breiner describes it as a "mysterious, multivalent concept" ("Edward Kamau Brathwaite" 20), and Rohlehr goes so far as to claim that it expresses the "fluidity of a New World sensibility" because it "means whatever he [Brathwaite] says it means"; ("Black Sycorax" 289). Nam is best understood, however, as Brathwaite's effort to revive and extend Césaire's concept of negritude for an Anglophone Caribbean context.[40] Brathwaite first "discovers" Césaire in the mid-1960s, when he considers translating *Cahier d'un retour au pays natal* into English (Brathwaite, "An Interview" 26). His wife, Doris Monica Brathwaite, actually completes a draft of her own translation of Césaire's work, which Brathwaite reads after completing *Rights of Passage* (26). From that point on, Césaire becomes an increasingly important influence in Brathwaite's work, a trend that Brathwaite himself acknowledges when he cites *Cahier* as the best "reference point" for understanding the method and intent of his *Barabajan Poems* (379).

Césaire's *Cahier* is arguably the most important poem in the literature of negritude, but his own understanding of that term is complicated and contradictory.[41] He coins the term *negritude* in the late 1930s in discussions with Léopold Senghor and Léon Damas about the ethnography of Leo Frobenius. While he seems to have initially defined it in biological terms, he later repudiates this definition and describes it in more cultural and historical terms: "I do not in the slightest believe in biological permanence, but I believe in culture. My negritude has a ground. It is a fact that there is a black culture: it is historical, there is nothing biological about it" (quoted in Arnold, *Modernism and Negritude* 37).[42] As A. James Arnold contends, it is to "Césaire's credit" that he makes this shift from a more biological to a more cultural understanding of negritude (38).

Brathwaite defines *nam* in keeping with Césaire's later understanding of negritude, for he too believes that the essence of collective and individual identity emerges from a common cultural, linguistic, and historical experience. He describes nam as "an essence, an indestructible culture-core, imparting to each group an identity" and as "yr own kernel . . . yr own sense and reality of incontro-vertible self" ("World Order Models" 36; *Barabajan Poems* 242–43). Brathwaite also follows Césaire in employing the roots trope to describe the relationship between identity and these conditions of history and culture. For instance, Césaire writes that "my negritude . . . takes root in the red flesh of the soil," and Brathwaite suggests that his "deepest strength . . . comes from his mother's mud, his culture's name, his nation language nam" (*Barabajan Poems* 260). Critics have increasingly questioned the propriety of defining a collective Caribbean identity in terms of this taproot metaphor. As Arnold argues, it fails to "imagine the nation . . . as something more inclusive than one's own ethnoclass" ("Caliban" 240).[43] Moreover, it seems dubious at best to imagine the conditions of history and culture as being as material and fixed as the earth. Negritude and nam are best understood as strategically essentialist concepts of identity that have been rhetorically useful in clarifying an Afro-Caribbean struggle for cultural decolonization but that do not fully reflect the interethnic multiplicity of the region.[44]

Brathwaite does, however, extend Césaire's initial insight by emphasizing the interrelatedness of nation language and nam, of speech and identity. As Glissant contends, "Brathwaite revives thirty years later Aimé Césaire's discourse, [but] he places it actually in a new context . . . the written becomes oral" (*Caribbean Discourse* 109). By inflecting Césaire's ideas with a sense of the oral, Brathwaite challenges both Walcott's interpretation of Césaire and his poetics of speech. What Walcott sees as Césaire's strength—his capacity to write in an imperial French that was inflected with the sound of French Creole—Brathwaite considers to be his prime weakness, a failure to break more completely from the textual conventions of the imperial language and develop a more distinctly Afro-Caribbean form of expression. Walcott eagerly appropriates Césaire's poetics of speech but only grudgingly recognizes the "necessity of negritude" (the title of his earlier essay on Césaire) as a principle of cultural decolonization.[45] Brathwaite affirms the centrality of Césaire's negritude by recasting it as nam, but he also explicitly ties this concept of identity to nation language as a distinct form of speech.

Brathwaite imagines a figurative etymology of *nam* that explains the relationships between nation language, Afro-Caribbean identity, and colonization. He contends that by suppressing ancestral languages, the colonizers sought to destroy the identity, or "name," of the colonized, but they were only able to "eat" the final *e*. Accordingly, even though the colonized people lost their "name," they retained their nam; they lost their public identity as expressed in their ancestral language, but they preserved the essence of that identity by submerging or disguising it through their use of nation language. Brathwaite even contends that the visual appearance of the word *nam* itself suggests how the African cultural essence was preserved through this strategy of subversive disguise. Nam is "man spelled . . . b(l)ackwards," and its "two intransigent consonants," *n* and *m,* protect the "alpha of our beginnings . . . like boulders" (*Barabajan Poems* 256, 241). It is an etymology that reflects the later typographical experiments of his Sycorax video-style, a style in which he tests the limits of making visible this relationship between nam and nation language and to which we will return at the end of this chapter. For now, it is sufficient to note that Brathwaite offers this imagined etymology as a metaphor for how an African cultural and linguistic presence could survive in the Caribbean despite colonization. Indeed, he is not satisfied with merely identifying the submerged presence of nam; he wants to restore this nam as the "name" of his community. In other words, nam becomes name only through developing nation language. It is poetic revolution that Brathwaite dramatizes in "Nametracks," a poem that responds in very pointed ways to Walcott's "Names."

Whenever Brathwaite discusses the relationship between nation language and nam, he invariably cites "Nametracks" as his illustrative example.[46] Indeed, Rohlehr claims that "Nametracks" is at the "core" of *Mother Poem* (1977), the first volume in his second trilogy, which includes *Sun Poem* (1982) and *X/Self* (1987) and which Brathwaite has revised and collectively published as *Ancestors* (2001) ("Black Sycorax" 280). In *The Arrivants* he focuses on the broad historical and cultural movements that have shaped Afro-Caribbean life; in the first two volumes of *Ancestors* he mythologizes his childhood experience in Barbados to make it representative of the development of the Afro-Caribbean poet. "Nametracks" serves as a good example of this approach, for it explores the Afro-Caribbean poet's relationship to speech by reconfiguring characters from Shakespeare's *Tempest* as players in the Barbadian childhood game "O'Grady says."[47] In other words, he recasts figures of the Western written tradition by placing them in the context of the Barbadian oral tradition of his youth. Brathwaite was taking something of a risk with this example, for the Prospero-Caliban trope was arguably already a cliché in Caribbean literature and theory by 1977,[48] and he himself had already used it once in the "Caliban" section of *Islands* (1969).[49] However, as Rohlehr suggests, Brathwaite's "unique invention" in "Nametracks" is highlighting Sycorax, Caliban's mother, to reorient the stock postcolonial conflict between Prospero and Caliban (279). Rohlehr does not, however, stress sufficiently the connection between Sycorax and nam. Brathwaite himself describes Sycorax as the one who teaches Caliban his "mother tongue" and who "still carries within herself, . . . in a submerged manner, the very essence of the native culture" ("Alternative View" 45, 44). She is, in other words, his personification of nam, the submerged presence of Africa as an alternative origin of Afro-Caribbean cultural identity and language.

Brathwaite organizes the poem around the premise that Caliban hears two competing voices in the game "O'Grady says"—the nation-language voice of his "mudda," Sycorax, and the colonizing Standard English voice of O'Grady/Prospero—as he struggles to develop his own speech and identity. The child/Caliban eventually finds the strength to resist the demands of Prospero/O'Grady by recognizing his collective identity (nam) and language (nation language) in his mother/Sycorax. It is a trope that implicitly challenges Walcott's vision of a cultural resistance through pragmatic acquiescence. Whereas Walcott represents Standard English and French Creole as partners in instructing the next generation, Brathwaite recognizes that all forms of speech are not equal. When Prospero/O'Grady commands the child/Caliban to speak Standard English instead of nation language, it is a command charged with a colonial history of using language for social control. It is only through the example and encouragement of his mother that Caliban finds a way to respond.

As with the women in "The Dust," Brathwaite represents Sycorax as a figure of authority and authenticity because of her close relationship to the physical environment. Caliban describes her as his

muh
muh
muh
me mudda
mud
black fat
soft fat man-
ure
("Nametracks," *Mother Poem* 56)

This figure of Sycorax as nourishing soil fits with Brathwaite's larger roots metaphor. Caliban is given life through Sycorax, and nam and nation language emerge from the historical and cultural experience of the Afro-Caribbean folk. Arnold justifiably questions the gender stereotypes that underlie Brathwaite's figure of Sycorax, claiming that "her role as an agent of cultural change . . . collapses into a purely natural function" ("Caliban" 240); however, this criticism should be tempered by Sycorax's more assertive role in this poem.

In the first three sections of the poem, Brathwaite establishes Sycorax as a formidable alternative to Prospero/O'Grady. She resists him herself ("spitt/in she curses upon him"); she challenges his authority ("[he] doan possess we at all"); and most importantly, she prepares her son for the game by revealing to him his nam:

ma ma *man*: she is tell muh

say *man*: she is tell muh
say *man*: she is tell muh

say *man*
say *manding*
say *mandingo*

(57)

Again, these lines show how Brathwaite tropes the relationship between speech and identity differently from Walcott. For Walcott, the contingency of individual and communal self-identification is best depicted as a form of ephemeral writing, a repeated tracing of "our names on the sand / which the sea erased" ("Names," *Collected Poems* 307). For Brathwaite, the naming process is an oral catechism in which the repetition leads not to an effacing but to a recovery of a nam(e) and identity *(man)* for the son, a language and identity that are deeply rooted in Africa *(mandingo)*. While Caliban does not yet fully recognize the significance of this name, he has been given the resources that will enable him to resist the domination of Prospero/O'Grady.

Indeed, in the middle sections of the poem the game begins in earnest as O'Grady seeks to control Caliban by suppressing his use of nation language.

ogrady says
say i
say i

not me
not man
not muddah

i

say
i
ogrady says
("Nametracks," *Mother Poem* 58)

By having O'Grady demand that Caliban say "i," Brathwaite implicitly responds to the individualism and optimism of Walcott's claim that "my race began" with "that terrible vowel, / that I" ("Names," *Collected Poems* 307). By linking that "terrible vowel" to O'Grady, Brathwaite suggests that Walcott's birth metaphor excessively romanticizes the capacity for self-creation, unduly minimizes the violence of colonialism, and narrowly construes speech as an individual rather than communal act. Of course, Brathwaite romanticizes the mother figure in a different way. Caliban must recover a nourishing relationship with his historical and cultural past, his "earth" mother Sycorax, to form his own decolonized identity. Brathwaite tempers this romanticism by representing the violence of colonialism, not as the sound of a painful birth, but as the sound of a cracking whip. Throughout the middle of the poem O'Grady demands that Caliban repeat alternatively the long vowel of pain ("say i") and the short vowel of violence ("say it," "say quick," "say stick," "say sick," "say wick," and "say whip"). Brathwaite describes this short *i* sound as conveying the "high-pitched whip-sound of the Europeans" ("History, the Caribbean Writer, and *X/Self*" 39). It is his way of linking phonetically the linguistic and physical violence of colonialism. As he writes, when "ogrady says / say / whip," he is also saying "say / *aei,*" for the loss of an ancestral language is as deeply felt as the pain from the whip used to suppress it.

Sycorax helps her son resist O'Grady by her example. She does not acquiesce, repeat, and change Prospero's speech; instead, she

> brek
> de word
> she eat it like cheese
> like curl'd milk
> like yellow bread
> ("Nametracks," *Mother Poem* 59)

Brathwaite's trope suggests that the experience of responding to the speech of the colonizer is both more violent and more contaminating than Walcott's pragmatic assimilation suggests. Sycorax disfigures rather than merely inflects the imperial language, and she is still left with the rancid taste of colonial injustice in her mouth.

Sycorax's resistance makes O'Grady increasingly desperate to establish his cultural dominance over her son. He attacks directly the link between language and identity:

> say name
> ogrady says
>
> not me
> not muh
> not mudda

drain
ograde says
say

name
(60–61)

In response to this threat, Sycorax reveals to her son the significance of his nam(e) in what Rohlehr rightly describes as Sycorax's "longest and most complicated speech" in the poem ("Black Sycorax" 287):

she lisper to me dat me name what me name
dat me name is me main an it am is me own an lion eye mane
dat whinner men tek you an ame, dem is nomminit diff'rent an nan
so mandingo she yessper you nam.
("Nametracks," *Mother Poem* 62)

The fluidity of the sound and the sense of the nation language in this passage pushes the limits of intelligibility. Rohlehr agrees that "meanings are approximate" in this passage, "except the most fundamental meaning of them all; Caliban's *nam*" ("Black Sycorax" 287). Inexplicably, however, Rohlehr does not go on to gloss the meaning of Caliban's nam, claiming that it is a "silent, secret and sacred pact" between mother and son and that it "means whatever he [Brathwaite] says it means" ("Black Sycorax" 287, 289). While the passage is ambiguous, its basic assertions are available. Sycorax initiates her son's cultural resurgence by affirming in her nation-language "yessper" the essence of his Afro-Caribbean identity ("nam"), an identity that has its origins in African language and identity ("mandingo") and that has survived despite O'Grady's cultural domination ("nomminit").[50] This affirmation enables the son to move from silently resisting to actively engaging O'Grady's linguistic domination through his own nation-language wordplay in the final sections of the poem.

When O'Grady again demands the repetition of the short *i* sound in the lines

so quick
says ogrady
say stick

says ogrady
("Nametracks," *Mother Poem* 63)

Caliban appropriates the sound as a recognition of his own pain and a declaration of nation language's superiority: "stick likkin an warrikin trix /

leff a crik in me nek an ogrady stick brek" (63). As Caliban begins to gain the upper hand in this verbal sparring, O'Grady loses control of his own speech and alternates frantically between Standard English and nation language, not, as Velma Pollard suggests, to "facilitate communication" ("Language" 70), but to coerce Caliban to conform to the colonial standard or to trick him into revealing his nam(e). Caliban parries these attempts with a confidence that comes from the self-knowledge of nam and from the self-sufficiency of nation language. As Rohlehr contends, O'Grady's "adoption of nation-language is . . . a sign that Sycorax has triumphed in her breaking of the word" ("Black Sycorax" 290). O'Grady eventually resorts to threats of actual physical violence in order to maintain his cultural dominance; he will "keel" Caliban if he cannot "nomminit" him ("Nametracks," *Mother Poem* 63–64). The threat has no effect. Caliban keeps his nam(e) secret—"but e nevver maim what me mudda me name"—because he knows that he has nothing else worth losing:

> *an me doan give a damn*
>
> *me back to me belly*
> *an me dun dead a'ready*
> (64)

The question of Caribbean speech and identity cannot be separated from the experience of colonial violence, but this violence does not determine the outcome. The poem ends with Caliban defiantly singing of the survival of his Afro-Caribbean cultural identity in nation language.

Brathwaite has rightly been praised as "the most uncompromising reproducer of speech among the major poets" in the Caribbean (Breiner, *An Introduction* 179). However, his poetics of speech relies on assumptions about language and identity that are vulnerable. While he may speak of nation language and nam in strategically rather than ontologically essentialist terms, his rhetoric still does not square easily with the linguistic and identitarian diversity of the Caribbean. He subsumes the region's myriad spoken dialects into the single category of "nation language" and blurs its different and overlapping communities of identity with the concept of nam. For example, he generally uses *nation language* to mean a language spoken by people of African descent from lower socioeconomic classes—the "folk"—a narrowing of the concept that seems unwarranted linguistically given the role of education and ethnic diversity in the shaping of a common English language in the Caribbean.[51] In addition, Brathwaite tends to use *nation language* and *nam* both to preserve and to elide the distinctions between forms of speech and identity on different islands.[52] In other words, he uses these terms sometimes to connote the language of a particular political entity—a Barbadian nation language or Jamaican nation language—and sometimes to refer to the language of a regional or racial entity—a Caribbean nation language or an Afro-Caribbean nation language.[53] It is a strategic ambiguity that enables Brathwaite to respond broadly to the difficult questions of defining the boundaries of a "*common* speech" in the Caribbean. He can use it to identify a common language for Barbados, with a population of several hundred thousand, as well as for the Caribbean region, with about 40 million people. He uses *nation language* to suggest the presence both of a Caribbean *lingua communis*—an idealized common language for the region—and of an indigenous language—a common language materially related to a specifically identified community of speakers.

These conceptual simplifications clarify the means by which he sees poetry contributing to cultural decolonization, but at the cost of not identifying the rich variety of spoken dialects and identities in the Caribbean, a variety that poetry could represent effectively because of its close attention to the relationship between sound and meaning. Moreover, as he experiments with textual conventions to express the distinct particularity of nation language, he stretches the limits of intelligibility even further and undermines his claim to be recovering a speech and identity that is truly common. Finally, while Brathwaite develops the concepts of nation language and nam to oppose colonialism's hierarchies of cultural value, he does not show how his poetics of speech relates to the material conditions of culture that he acknowledges support those hierarchies.

"Names" and "Nametracks" serve as compelling examples of the potential and the problems of Walcott's and Brathwaite's complementary poetics of speech at this midpoint in their careers. Walcott ingenuously makes poetry's capacity to "purify" speech part of a strategy of cultural decolonization, and he offers an attractive ideal for understanding speech and identity as creative, contingent, and nonessentialist concepts; however, he sets impossible expectations for his actual poetry by rhetorically claiming to fuse "all the dialects" in the region, and he too quickly assumes an easy assimilation of Standard English and other forms of speech, an assumption that tends to ignore how colonialism violently shaped, and continues to shape, the hierarchical relationships among languages in the New World.

Brathwaite's strengths correspond to Walcott's shortcomings, and vice versa. Brathwaite keeps the colonial hierarchy of speech clearly in view by opposing nation language and Standard English, and he imaginatively stretches poetic and typographical conventions to convey the robust speech and culture of Afro-Caribbean folk. However, the clarity of his poetics of resistance comes at the cost of simplifying and narrowing its focus. In short, both are working toward creating an independent poetics that simultaneously represents the particularity and the commonality of Caribbean speech and identity, and their shortcomings emerge from enthusiastically pursuing one of these goals at the expense of the other. What is needed is a poetics of speech that recognizes English as a cosmopolitan and discrepant language in the West Indies, cosmopolitan because it is spoken by people with a variety of ethnic and national identities and discrepant because they speak it differently not only from people from North America or England but also from people from Jamaica or Trinidad.

In the mid-1980s both poets return to this question of poetry's relationship to speech and again employ a common trope—poetry as carpentry—to develop their ideas. In "Letter Sycorax" (1987, 1992) Brathwaite represents Caliban as a visual and oral carpenter who uses the resources of the computer to design completely new textual and poetic conventions to represent nation language as orally and graphically distinct.[54] In "Cul de Sac Valley" (1987) Walcott imagines the poet as a carpenter framing quatrains, a recognizably conventional English stanzaic form, to suggest how even the most traditional of the colonizer's poetic and linguistic forms can still be transformed to represent the common speech in the Caribbean as different. Brathwaite's Sycorax video-style reflects his intensifying commitment to represent the particularity of nation language and nam as distinct from "Western" poetic and written conventions. In contrast, Walcott represents dialect speech more freely but still through "Western" written conventions in order to contribute to the sound of English as a cosmopolitan linguistic medium. The complementarity of Brathwaite's and Walcott's poetics of speech arose, in part, because they listened to different Eliots; it developed because they listened to each other; and it has deepened as they have chiseled out different sounds in their poetry workshops.

Poetic Carpentry: Working against and with Conventions

Brathwaite's experiments with Sycorax video-style emerge out of a series of traumatic events, the most important being the death of his wife in 1986.[55] He records his grief over her illness and death in *The Zea Mexican Diary;* however, it is a casual remark in the preface to his short story "Dream Chad" that best indicates the relationship between this grief and the development of his Sycorax video-style. He claims that his "Eagle Computer" was a "wonderful companion for me during & after the dark of my wife Zea Mexican's sudden unxpected & finally fatal illness" (*DreamStories* 48). This process of mourning leads to an aesthetic breakthrough, for learning to compose on the computer gives him greater control over how to represent nation language on the written page.[56] As he experiments with typefaces, fonts, and formats to convey the inflections of speech, he creates a poetic style in which the difference of his language and poetry is evident both to the eye and to the ear. These graphic experiments also daringly seek to expand poetry's ritual function, poetry as ritual not just liturgically through the rhythmic use of spoken words but also iconographically through the visual representation of language.

As Gordon Rohlehr and Stewart Brown have argued, Brathwaite's experiments with Sycorax video-style are more a continuation of his earlier techniques than a completely new direction (Rohlehr, "Dream Journeys" viii; Brown, "Writin" 129). Throughout his career Brathwaite has engaged in visual experimentation and syntactical "calibanisms," as he calls them—misspellings, fragmented words, broken lines, irregular use of periods, commas, dashes, and slashes, and unusual spacing—not only to resist the conventions of written Standard English but also to convey the "nuances, echoes, puns, rhymes and particular kinds of music" of nation language (Brown, "Writin" 129). Brathwaite does, however, consciously expand and intensify these visual experiments after the death of his wife. Brown suggests that these experiments emerge primarily from Brathwaite's commitment to "break and break away from the cultural constraints of English," but he also rightly traces the "modernist/formalist dimension" of Brathwaite's new style to the influence of Eliot's visual experiments to dislocate readers' expectations (128–29). Brathwaite's Sycorax video-style does makes Eliot's experiment seem conventional in comparison. Brathwaite will, for example, use several different fonts along with bold and italics on the same page, sometimes to suggest different tones of voice or different amplitudes but other times with no discernible purpose. He will also disrupt normal reading expectations by using right justification for a passage or placing text in a box or window frame. A page may also contain only a single word or no words, a picture, a highly stylized capital letter, or a combination of these things. Some of his words become almost unreadable because of the distortion of the visual representation. His irregular use of punctuation has also expanded to include brackets, asterisks, and question marks both within and between words (see fig. 1).

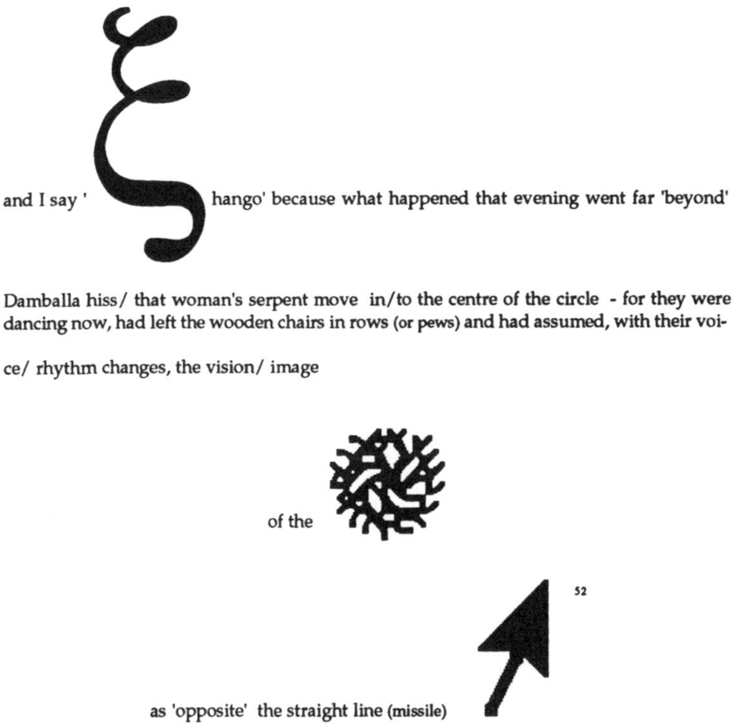

and I say ' hango' because what happened that evening went far 'beyond'

Damballa hiss/ that woman's serpent move in/to the centre of the circle - for they were dancing now, had left the wooden chairs in rows (or pews) and had assumed, with their voi-

ce/ rhythm changes, the vision/ image

of the

52

as 'opposite' the straight line (missile)

Fig. 1. Example of Sycorax video-style from Kamau Brathwaite's *Barabajan Poems, 1492–1992,* p. 187 (Courtesy of Kamau Brathwaite and Savacou Publications)

Brathwaite's experiments are innovative because they both resist the purported transparency of poetic language and suggest the unique orality of nation language. His resistance sets him apart from Walcott, for his Sycorax video-style makes the colonial conventions of poetry and language opaque: he wants to make his readers conscious that these conventions shape any representation before they try to look through them to the object of the representation. It is this expressiveness, however, that distinguishes Brathwaite from contemporary American postmodern poets engaged in similar experiments, poets such as Joanne Drucker, Charles Bernstein, and Susan Howe.[57] Brathwaite "visualizes" the language of his poetry not only to display how language itself works but also to suggest the sound of language as spoken by people in the Caribbean in general. He contends for poetry as writing and as voice, as what he calls "word-sculptures on the page" and "word-songs for the ear" (quoted in Rigby 708). Moreover, as Brown suggests, Brathwaite is less interested in the opacity of language for its own sake than in how his experiments with language better represent the cultural and linguistic aspirations of West Indians ("Writin" 130).

"Letter Sycorax" offers Brathwaite's *ars poetica* for this new poetics of speech even though it is limited in its typographical experiments because of the constraints of his publication.[58] It is the poem that recenters his poetics of speech following the loss of his wife. Visually, Brathwaite suggests the poem's importance by centering horizontally the words in each line and vertically the lines on most of the pages. Indeed, Brown suggests that this centering layout signals the resistance of Brathwaite's new poetics because it "visually rejects" the expectations of the conventional English poem ("Writin" 132). Thematically, he returns to the Sycorax-Caliban-Prospero motif as the poem's organizing narrative. Structurally, the poem is set up as a two-part letter from the poet/son/Caliban to his muse/mother/Sycorax, a structure that also echoes the personal mourning of a living husband writing to his dead wife.[59] In the first part Caliban offers Sycorax pragmatic reasons for appropriating the computer as Prospero's new writing technology; in the second part he explains how this technology reshapes his understanding of cultural decolonization.

Caliban begins by justifying his new method to Sycorax, by explaining

Why i cyaan nuse me hann & crawl
up de white like i use
to?
("Letter Sycorax," *MiddlePassages* 101)[60]

Initially, he claims that his borrowing of Prospero's technology reverses the historical experience of the colonizer's exploitation of the cultural inventions of the colonized. Sycorax is, however, less interested in the "**same ole story**" of binary opposition; instead, she wants to know how this new technology of writing advances his efforts to represent Afro-Caribbean nation language and culture. He responds by claiming a competency of the technology that leads to a new form of poetry:

yu know me cyaan
neither flat
foot pun de key

boards like
say
charlie chap dance/in

far
less touch
tappin/in like bo.

jangles

walk/in down chauncery
lane

yu hear/in me mwa?

but i
mwangles!
(102–3)

Even though Brathwaite's typing is not as proficient as Charlie Chaplin's dancing, he suggests that the computer enables him to emulate the physicality of the dancer's expression because it allows him to control the visual representation of nation language.[61] It enables him to represent, as Cynthia James argues, "the kinetic aspects" of poetry that the "griot has never been able to set to enduring print" ("Caliban in Y2K?" 359). By rhyming **bo.jangles** with **mwangles,** Brathwaite even suggests that this new means of representing speech, this dancing on the keyboard, enables him to simultaneously manage and mangle the writing of poetry.

In the second part of the poem Brathwaite suggests how the computer has reoriented his understanding of the poet's role in cultural independence. Brathwaite suggests that instead of the high-stakes and violent language game of "Nametracks," his Sycorax video-style is primarily about representing the speech of his community rather than about opposing O'Grady:

learn.

in prospero ling.
go

&
ting

not fe dem/not fe dem
de way caliban

done

but fe we
fe a-we

for nat one a we shd response if prospero get
curse
wid im own
curser

(106–7)

This passage completes Brathwaite's transposition of the Caliban trope. In Shakespeare's *Tempest* Miranda teaches Caliban to speak in the imperial language, and he responds by cursing her and her father. These curses debase the imperial language, but they reinforce Miranda's and Prospero's superior position because they do not change Caliban's material conditions. In "Nametracks" (1977) Sycorax replaces Miranda as the source of language for the Caribbean poet, but the poetics of speech is still represented as a binary struggle between Caliban and O'Grady/Prospero. In "Letter Sycorax" (1992) Caliban engages in these graphic experiments, not primarily to respond to Prospero, but to speak "**fe we**"—for the Afro-Caribbean folk. Cursing is now an inevitable but incidental part of the process because Caliban's new style distorts the oral and typographical conventions of the imperial speech; however, cursing no longer remains his primary purpose. As Brathwaite himself contends, this Caliban is not a "binary opposite of Prospero" but rather a "gateway to an alternative" ("An Interview" 16).[62]

This new approach is not without its ironies. In Brathwaite's earlier work he creolizes Caliban and poetic language by organizing his lyrics around forms of Afro-Caribbean popular culture (Carnival songs, limbo dances, childhood games). His experiments with Sycorax video-style, however, emerge out of a computer technology that is removed from the popular culture of the Afro-Caribbean folk. Elaine Savory may be right when she argues that redesigning "the intention of Euro-American technology" with "African-descended forms" is a "far more effective" means of cultural resistance and formation than "protest speeches" or "abstruse arguments," but she does not recognize the anomaly of Brathwaite's shift in emphasis ("Wordsongs" 751). Indeed, his rationale for Sycorax video-style seems closer to Walcott's poetics of mastery. He masters Prospero's technology to represent better the distinct features of Afro-Caribbean culture and nation language. The difference is that Brathwaite seeks to master technology in order to change poetry's conventions, whereas Walcott wants to control the ideological significance of poetry's existing conventions. The complementarity of their shifting positions is evident again.

What is more important, Brathwaite seems drawn to the computer because it enables him to emulate his model figure for the artist, the carpenter/sculptor. In "Ogun" Brathwaite offers the carpenter as a model for the Caribbean poet because the carpenter is literally "in touch" with his artistic medium—wood—and because this medium retains its essential character even after it has been severed from its roots. In "Letter Sycorax" he comes closer to realizing this poetic ideal because the computer gives him greater control over the physical representation of language. Indeed, he describes his composing as a form of sculpting:

Yet a sittin dung here in front a dis stone
face

eeee
lectrical mallet into me

fist

chipp/in dis poem onta dis tab.
let

chiss. ellin dark.
ness writin in light

(115)

By sitting **dung here** in front of **dis stone / face**, Brathwaite claims that his artistic method, even a method that employs Prospero's technology, emerges fundamentally from the material fertility (**dung**) of his island home (**stone**). This passage still recognizes the need for intense, even violent resistance to the colonialism of Standard English: the computer mouse is a **mallet** that he holds in his **fist** to sculpt the poem. However, the passage also reverses subtly the colonial trope of light and dark to suggest Africa as the source of light and colonialism as the source of darkness in the Caribbean. And what is perhaps most important, this sculpting of language extends the ritual function of his poetry: it is a ritual not only in its rhythmic repeating of words but also in its carving of visual images—poetry not only as liturgy or incantation but also as iconography or mkissi. In "Ogun" Brathwaite describes his great-uncle's carving as a *mkissi,* the BaKongo word for a sacred sculpture that protects or heals a person or community (*Barabajan Poems* 155, 393).[63] Now he conceives of Sycorax video-style as the means to create poems that are verbal *mkissis*.

The poem ends with Caliban telling his mother that this new method offers the means to establish both his individual and his cultural independence.[64] He says that **writin in light** makes him feel

like i is a some. is a some. is a some
body.

a X
pert or some

thing like moses or aaron or one a dem
dyaaam isra
light

&
mamma!

(115–16)

By comparing the writing of this poem in Sycorax video-style to the carving of the Ten Commandments in stone, Brathwaite makes clear the scope of his public ambition. He aspires to create a foundational cultural text and language for the African diaspora in the Caribbean, a text that will unite this diaspora to reclaim possession of its common spiritual and cultural African heritage. By alluding to both Moses and Aaron, he suggests that the poet contributes to freeing people from this cultural captivity by combining writing and speech, by assuming the role of the sculptor (Moses) and of spokesperson (Aaron), by developing his unique Sycorax video-style to represent visually the unique sound of nation language. And with his concluding exclamation Brathwaite suggests that Caliban can only fulfill this public role by staying in touch with the materiality of the Caribbean folk experience, by listening to the muse and addressee of his letter, by calling out for inspiration from his "**mamma!**"

Chapter 4 explores the relationship between Brathwaite's typographical experiments and his conception of the poet's public role; however, some preliminary assessment of the success of these experiments in relation to his poetics of speech is appropriate here. Some critics have been too enthusiastic in their praise. Elaine Savory, for example, suggests that "Brathwaite has stepped into a space in which orality, the book and the screen combine to project an immediate sense of cultural identity and linguistic freedom" ("Returning" 217). There is, however, too much interpretive work necessary in reading Sycorax video-style to assert such immediacy between this new style and either a collective sense of identity or a free expression of nation language. Stewart Brown is rightly more measured in his appraisal:

> If we accept that the Caribbean isles are indeed "full of noises" which formal, traditional English-as-text cannot adequately represent, it is clear that in the

> process of resisting the conventional pressures of the text in order to give voice to the noises of nation language on the page, Brathwaite's "writin in light" Sycorax video style *is* both a logical development of his own creative practice and another step on the road Caribbean poets have been treading . . . towards finding a means of accommodating the language of life as it sounded in the Caribbean and life of letters as they are printed on the page. ("Writin" 135)

Brown nicely captures the dual aspirations of Brathwaite's new style, the desire to resist the standard conventions of the written text and to give voice to the sound of nation language.

Brathwaite has come far closer to achieving the first goal than he has to achieving the second, for his Sycorax video-style clearly breaks with the "illusions of verisimilitude offered by more conventional forms of production" (Cobham 301). However, as Rohlehr suggests, Brathwaite's new style creates "an arbitrariness in the appearance of the text," an arbitrariness that makes it more difficult for Brathwaite to achieve his second goal, that of giving voice to the sound of nation language, because the reader has so little guidance to calibrate sign to sound ("Dream Journeys" viii).[65] How should one hear the tonal modulation in his changing of a font style? What is the inflection of a line that starts flush to the right margin? How does one relate the amplitude of sound to the font size? What is the tonal inflection of a picture or blank space? Sycorax video-style may well be analogous to a "musical score" that "demand[s] enunciation . . . on the part of the reader," as Brown suggests, but it has not yet established a system of conventions that would enable different readers to enunciate the texts in a way that would allow them to hear the common sound of nation language ("Writin" 134).[66] In other words, while Sycorax video-style effectively represents nation language as visually distinct from Prospero's language, it does not yet reliably convey the sound of Caliban's nation language as a common speech of the region. Indeed, the more Brathwaite strives to represent the particularity of nation language, the more he stretches the conventions of intelligibility and undermines the claim for nation language as a common speech.

Walcott anticipates the dilemma of Brathwaite's Sycorax video-style in his defense of his own purifying poetics of speech. He writes:

> In many islands, the West Indian poet is faced with a language which he hears but cannot write because there are no symbols for such a language and because the closer he brings hand and word to the precise inflections of the inner language and to the subtlest accuracies of his ear, the more chaotic his symbols will appear on the page, the smaller the regional dialect, *the more eccentric his*

> *representation of it will become,* so his function remains the old one of being filter and purifier, never losing the tone and strength of the common speech as he uses the hieroglyphs, symbols, or alphabet of the official one. ("Muse" 13, emphasis added)

In other words, Walcott does not accept what Stewart Brown asserts is Brathwaite's starting point in developing Sycorax video-style, the assumption that "formal, traditional English-as-text cannot adequately represent" the sound of the Caribbean speech ("Writin" 135). Indeed, Walcott assumes that the Caribbean writer must turn to the "official" language of Standard English as the only possible means to represent and communicate to a wide audience the "tone and strength of the common speech" of the region. Walcott's "Cul de Sac Valley" exemplifies his complementary poetic sculpting of speech because it redeploys the conventions of tradition poetry, as well as Standard English, in order to represent more freely "dialect" speech.

"Cul de Sac Valley" appears in the "Here" section of Walcott's *Arkansas Testament* (1987), a volume in which Walcott experiments with strict quatrains in more than half of the poems. In an interview, he says that he is drawn to these quatrains because he sees himself "as a carpenter, as one making frames, simply and well" and because he sees his poetry as a craft as "ritualistic as that of a carpenter putting down his plane and measuring his stanzas and setting them squarely" (Walcott, "Art of Poetry" 101). Edward Baugh suggests that "Walcott's sustained engagement with the quatrain" in this book reveals "his insistence on the notion of poetry as discipline, as a craft which one has to learn, and work at, and 'get right'" ("The Arkansas Testament" 124). Poetry's relationship to speech is a theme of many of the quatrain poems in this volume, which suggests that part of "getting it right" is the shaping or refining of speech through the discipline of poetry.[67]

Comparing Walcott's "Cul de Sac Valley" with Brathwaite's "Letter Sycorax" and "Ogun" reveals again the complementarity of their approaches to developing a poetics of speech. While the "folk" poet, Brathwaite, ironically turns to the computer as the muse for his experiments with Sycorax video-style, the "metropolitan" poet, Walcott, identifies a "folk" scene as his inspiration to rework traditional quatrains:

> A panel of sunrise
> on a hillside shop
> gave these stanzas
> their stilted shape.

If my craft is blest;
if this hand is as
accurate, as honest
as their carpenter's,

every frame, intent
on its angles, would
echo this settlement
of unpainted wood.
(*Arkansas Testament* 9)

The visual presentation of Walcott's quatrains contrasts immediately with the irregular text of Brathwaite's "Letter Sycorax." Brathwaite manipulates the conventions of the visual text to convey the distinctiveness of nation language, but Walcott refines the oral elements of his verse to conform to the typographical conventions of his poetic stanza. For instance, Walcott intentionally varies the metrical length of his lines to maintain the visual regularity of his stanza, whereas Brathwaite varies the visual appearance of his lines and stanzas to suggest the irregular meter of nation language. In addition, Walcott primarily chooses simple monosyllabic or disyllabic words from Standard English and spells them conventionally to speak for the village, whereas Brathwaite's Caliban speaks "fe a-we" through phonetically spelled words ("mwangles") and idiosyncratic punctuation ("bo. / jangles"). Brathwaite accentuates the difference of nation language with his new style; Walcott reaffirms the discipline of poetic conventions to fuse differences into a new unity.

In "Ogun" Brathwaite equates the making of window frames with the writing of traditional English verse because he sees both activities as reflecting the colonial alienation of the Caribbean carpenter and poet. Walcott takes this metaphor even more literally to reverse its significance and argue for the simple utility of poets' reusing conventional forms. Walcott contends that just as carpenters painstakingly learn the conventions of making windows level and square because such training ensures that the windows will function according to their purpose, poets must master the conventions of their craft to create useful poems. He does not advocate an easy or mechanical appropriating of form—there are no prefabricated or mass-produced poems in Walcott's cultural house—but an appropriating of form that shapes and is shaped by the material of poetry itself, by language. Like Brathwaite in "Ogun," Walcott represents this language as a "tree," but his poetic craftsman refines rather than accentuates the irregularities of his material.

Walcott suggests the nature of this refining by extending the carpentry trope. Just as the carpenter planes his wood to remove its knots and imperfections, the poet should purify the idiosyncrasies of Saint Lucian Creole:

as consonants scroll
off my shaving plane
in the fragrant Creole
of their native grain;

from a trestle bench
they'd curl at my foot,
C's, R's, with a French
or West African root

from a dialect throng-
ing, its leaves unread
yet light on the tongue
of their native road;
(9)

In this passage he affirms but qualifies his purifying poetics of speech. He still sees Creole as primarily an oral language—"its leaves unread / yet light on the tongue"—but he now attributes its distinct inflection to the influence not only of French but also of West African languages. While such recognition still does not fulfill the full scope of his multicultural ideal, it does reflect his growing willingness to acknowledge more explicitly the African sources of Caribbean culture and language. Even though the particulars of this speech still end up on the floor of his poetry workshop, he now aspires to retain the tone of that speech, the smell of that "fragrant Creole" permeating his poetic and textual conventions.

Walcott recognizes that this poetic refining of speech is open to criticism. When the poet/carpenter comes to complete his frame at the end of the first section, the trees themselves mock his aspiration to create a common language:

exhaling trees refresh
memory with their smell:
bois canot, bois campêche,

hissing: *What you wish*
from us will never be,
your words is English,
is a different tree.
(10)

Echoing Brathwaite's arguments, these trees claim an essential difference between Creole and Standard English, a difference that no amount of refining will bring together. For Walcott, this claim oversimplifies the complex relationship between speech, poetry, and identity in the Caribbean. He does not simply prefer "the mongrelized language of St. Lucia," as John Thieme suggests; instead, he values the poetic possibilities of bringing together spoken Creole and written Standard English, Creole invigorating the conventions of Standard English poetry with its unique oral rhythms and those written conventions giving artistic form, expression, and exposure to Creole (176). He develops a variety of overlapping tropes for the relationship between Creole speech and Standard English—the water cycle, a young schoolgirl, and the echoes in the Saint Lucian mountains—to suggest the contributions and limitations of each in representing Caribbean life.

Walcott opens the second section of "Cul de Sac Valley" by comparing the poetic refining of Creole speech to the water cycle. He suggests that Creole originates in people's experience of the landscape like the sound of water in a stream ("light gutturals begin" in the "rivulet's gravel" [*Arkansas Testament* 10]); then, as the speech evaporates into the air, it mixes with the common natural sounds of ordinary life (the "black vowel barking" of "a mongrel," the "grating squeak" of a worker's shovel, and the "blue smoke" of a charcoal fire [10–11]), what Rei Terada describes as the "Earth's dialect" (177); finally, it condenses again when the "crusted clouds open" and returns for use "in a rain barrel" (*Arkansas Testament* 11). It is a hydrologic trope of great ingenuity: just as water is purified and becomes visible through a process of filtration, evaporation, mixing, and condensation, Creole must be combined and distilled to make it "visible" in a Standard English written text; just as this purified water is collected for use in a rain barrel, the poet collects and arranges this distilled Creole for use in his artistic forms; and just as the water in this rain barrel "unwrinkles to glass," poetry abstracts from the irregularities of speech to serve its traditional function as a mirror of experience (11). It is not that Creole is both "spoken and written, audible and visible" so that it "writes itself," as Terada contends, but that it is distilled through the linguistic process and collected by the discipline of the poet (177).

Walcott then proliferates and intermingles his tropes for Creole speech. He personifies Creole as the "lime tree's daughter," and she "studies her face" in the water of the rain barrel as her mother braids her hair for school (*Arkansas Testament* 11). She may "meet the poet halfway by studying English," as Terada suggests, but at a cost (178). She cries at the sight of her reflection not only because her image is distorted by this mirror of refined speech but also because her braids distort her "natural" appearance. Just as the "government school" demands that girls weave their hair into recognized patterns, poetry requires a refining of speech to conform to its recognized conventions. This trope reiterates Walcott's general position that he must master the poetic conventions of the colonizer in order to advance cultural unity; however, he is now more willing to recognize the pain involved in braiding together the dialects of the region—the schoolgirl cries when

> her nape knot is
> pulled by her mother's
> comb;
>
> (11)

In the poem's third section the hills of Saint Lucia challenge the poet with "their stony question" about naming:

> "Can you call each range
> by its right name, aloud,
> while our features change
> between light and cloud?"
>
> (13)

The heart of this question probes the relationship between identity ("right name") and speech ("aloud"). Walcott poses this question so as to underscore the contingency of this relationship: the hills' "features change / between light and cloud," so one should expect that their names will also change through time (13). He even suggests that the Caribbean poet must be like the "woodsman" who

> relaxes
> to hear the sky split
> seconds after the axe's
> stroke
>
> (13)

because the people of the Caribbean have been severed from their linguistic and identitarian roots. Despite this experience of loss, they still create a vibrant language and identity through mimicry: the hills' "names fit their echo: Mahaut! / Forestière" (13).

This naming of the hills distinguishes Walcott's mimicry from Brathwaite's strategic essentialism. For Brathwaite, identity precedes speech:

nam animates and distinguishes nation language as a different form of speech spoken by a different people. For Walcott, speech and identity exist in a more reciprocal relationship: the speaker of the poem names the hills by imitating the echo created by trying to name the hills. This reciprocal echoing is dizzying, but it illustrates how Walcott has developed his concept of mimicry to include the orality of speech. He represents poetry's refining of speech not only with the visual trope of the rain barrel as a mirror reflecting the Creole schoolgirl's braids but also with this oral trope of the valley as an echo chamber repeating the poet's naming of the mountains. In both situations poetry records not a presence but an imitation, not an original image and sound but a reflection and echo, not a permanent and stable sense of Caribbean identity and speech but a derivative and contingent sense. Even though these artistic representations are derivative and contingent, Walcott contends that they still serve a useful public function and have real social effect: others repeat, conform to, and eventually change these names as they create and recreate their own sense of speech and identity. In other words, Walcott suggests that poetry instructs by self-consciously inviting others to engage in the practice of mimicry.

It is this lesson that concludes the poem. As the sun sets on the day, Walcott amalgamates his tropes of speech for a final time by comparing the schoolgirl to the poet. Just as the poet returns to his island home "from the rim of the world," the girl comes back to her "shack" in the village—"the tree returns / from her lessons, late" (14). She returns, however, as a student and as a teacher. As she sits and eats her "supper / of bread and fry-fish," the other "trees repeat her / darkening English" (15). Walcott represents this echoing as a validation of his poetic method. These trees are the same ones that initially scoffed at his refining of Creole, but now they speak in his "darkening English," an international English that has been modified by its encounter with Creole. At the beginning of the poem he aspires to create quatrains that

> would
> echo this settlement
> of unpainted wood
> (9)

an echo that he embeds in the line itself with his homonym rhyme, but he ultimately succeeds only if the people of the settlement accept his "darkening English" as an echo of their own speech and identity (15). To achieve this end amid the linguistic, identitarian, and cultural fragmentation of the New World, Walcott masters rather than "mwangles" the imposed conventions of Standard English poetry because he considers their "discipline" useful for infusing the sound of the region's dialects in his work yet maintain intelligibility. He transfigures that initial inspiration, the "panel of sunrise / on a hillside shop," into a public vision as the "door" of his poetry workshop "flings a panel of light / on the road" for others in the settlement to follow (15).

Selective Listening

Chapter 4 explores in more detail how Brathwaite and Walcott revise Eliot's ideas and practices to conceive of poetry's social function; however, first we should assess the results of their selective listening to Eliot not only in forming their own discrepant modernist poetics of speech but also in reforming our broader view of modernism as a cosmopolitan literary movement. When Brathwaite listens to Eliot, he hears the revolutionary voice of early modernism, a voice that challenges Standard English poetry with new types of speech and forms of popular culture. To his credit, Brathwaite transforms Eliot's tentative experiments into a compelling and comprehensive poetics of speech, a poetics that clearly asserts the distinctiveness of nation-language forms of popular culture in the Caribbean. In addition, his Sycorax video-style offers a fascinating, even if not a fully worked out, extension of early modernist textual experiments and of his own poetics of speech, for it seeks to take his poetic revolution to the level of graphic conventions in order to connect his poetry to speech. However, the clarity of his theory comes at a cost, for his concepts of nation language and nam too easily elide the linguistic, cultural, and identitarian complexities of the Caribbean. While he quite rightly sees questions of language and identity as inexorably related, he too readily relies on the rhetoric of strategic essentialism to describe the relation between nation language and nam. Moreover, while his ambition in creating Sycorax video-style—an ambition that seeks to fundamentally recast the relationship between writing and sound in poetry—is admirable, its achievement to date has been at best mixed. It sharpens his representation of nation language as different from Standard English, but it has not yet established the conventions necessary to connect reliably orthography with orality, sign with sound, text with speech.

While Brathwaite hears the voice of Eliot the cultural revolutionary, Walcott selectively attends to the voice of Eliot the cultural statesman, the established modernist who aspires for his poetry to refine the splintered voices of the age into a new ideal of common speech. Walcott transposes Eliot's aim to "purify" into a goal of "fusing" the "multitudinous dialects" of the Caribbean in order to inflect the poetry of Standard English with the sound of Caribbean speech. Whereas Brathwaite polarizes the difference between nation language and Standard English, Walcott aspires to make an "amalgam . . . of all the dialects" through the discipline of artistic form (Walcott, "Reflections Before and After Carnival" 42–43). Again, like Brathwaite's, the rhetoric of Walcott's ambition exceeds the results of his practice, for he still tends to write more *about* Creole as a theme or metaphor rather than *in* a recognizably Creole-inflected Standard English. Even more troubling, perhaps, is the fact that Walcott's poetics of speech has the potential to obscure the colonial hierarchies of power that established certain conventions of poetry and of speech as "standard." He considers it a risk worth taking because he believes that mastering these "standards" enables him to represent better his "darkening English," an effective means not only of asserting cultural independence but also of establishing a unifying, albeit contingent, poetic and cultural tradition in the Caribbean and the New World. Moreover, in the process of establishing this unifying tradition the older Walcott has become more and more willing to recognize the pain involved in resisting these colonial hierarchies of power.

In 1965 Harry Levin asks his famous question, "What was Modernism?" a question that seemed to mark the waning of modernism in Anglo-American academic circles. At about the same time, Brathwaite and Walcott seem to have been asking a quite different question: "How can Modernism be used in the Caribbean?" Their answers to this question are different but complementary, for they are drawn to different aspects of Eliot's modernism, but they share the objective of creating a distinctly Caribbean poetics of speech. They begin by selectively listening to Eliot, but they fully develop their ideas only by carefully listening to each other. Both men have their excesses—Brathwaite's appeals to strategic essentialism and Walcott's overly ambitious fusion of dialects—but they also have their triumphs—the rhythmic and visual originality of Brathwaite's verse and the masterful adaptation of "colonial" tropes, conventions, and language in Walcott's work. Together they illustrate that modernism continues to thrive, despite Levin's questioning of its demise, because writers as talented and as dissimilar as Walcott and Brathwaite recast its aesthetic principles to represent their own sense of the culture, language, and people of the New World. Modernism's central collocating method invites this disparate reception, and this disparate reception has enabled modernism to continue as a viable, discrepant, and cosmopolitan literary movement into this new century.

Together they illustrate not only the continued viability of modernist ideals in a New World context but also the rich possibilities for poetry to represent both the reality of linguistic fragmentation and the dream of a common language. Poetry is perhaps best suited to fulfill this task because its figurative complexity and linguistic sensitivity better register these contradictory realities of language. Indeed, postcolonial poetry is probably best equipped to make a contribution to the decolonizing objectives of postcolonial literature by fulfilling this role. Brathwaite and Walcott selectively listen to Eliot's poetics of speech because they both desire to renew this social function for poetry and to become themselves "public" poets. It is to their transposition of Eliot's advice on that subject that we turn next.

4 Public Poets

> Every poet would like, I fancy, to be able to think that he had some direct social utility.
>
> —T. S. Eliot, *The Use of Poetry*

> By luck, by blessing, I feel needed. I feel very needed. In the Caribbean, meeting people anywhere, on a beach somewhere, talking to poor people, to fishermen, a guy in a store, anybody, I feel as if I could speak for them. When that is missing, it's deadening.
>
> —Derek Walcott

> The poet's place in Bajan culture. . . . My place among us . . . Where I come from, how I come from. What I get, gain, lose, fit in, take out, give & give back.
>
> —Kamau Brathwaite, *Barabajan Poems*

IN THE SPRING of 1948 Eliot traveled to Aix-en-Provence, in the south of France, on behalf of the British Council to read, lecture, and perform the other ceremonial duties of a cultural ambassador, as well as to receive an award. It was a public role that he assumed more and more frequently following the success of *Four Quartets*.[1] While he would receive greater prizes that year—he had already been awarded the Order of Merit in January and would win the Nobel Prize in November—this particular occasion is important because of a phrase he used in this acceptance speech. He describes himself as a "persona umile e peregrina" (a person of humble birth and a pilgrim).[2] It is a scene and self-designation that neatly summarize Eliot's later career. In 1948 he is no longer the anxious young American worried about being accepted by the London literary world but a cultural emissary who traveled throughout the world for his adopted country of England. He truly is now more a Roman peregrine than a Greek metic. While both terms describe the status of aliens in an empire, the Greek metic was more likely to have earned the right to be there because of a special skill, whereas the Roman peregrine was more often considered to be a sojourner passing through the area.[3] Eliot has changed from colonial upstart to spiritual pilgrim, from constructing a cultural home from the fragments of many traditions to recognizing homelessness as an endemic spiritual condition of all people, from brash poetic revolutionary to representative public poet.

Indeed, Eliot's self-description resonates at multiple levels. It also evokes the image of the peregrine falcon, a bird known for its long migratory flights. This image deepens Eliot's representation of himself as a poet crossing national, cultural, and historical boundaries. Moreover, a quick etymological check reveals that Brunetto Latini's *Trésor* is a source from which the word *peregrine* enters into English *(Oxford English Dictionary).* Latini's name, of course, triggers another set of associations because he is Dante's teacher, and Dante is one of Eliot's "great masters" ("What Dante Means to Me" 127). Indeed, when Eliot imitates Dante in *Little Gidding,* he models his meeting with the familiar compound ghost on Dante's meeting with Latini in the *Inferno.*[4] He even has the ghost describe himself as "spirit unappeased and peregrine" (*Little Gidding, Complete Poems* 141). As these associations multiply, the larger significance of Eliot's allusions slowly becomes clear. Latini's final request to Dante is to "keep handy my *Thesaurus,* where I yet / Live on" (1.15.119–20). By revitalizing the word *peregrine* Eliot honors the request of his master's master and so quietly assumes the right to be considered their student and heir.

It is a literary memorial that illustrates Eliot's mature views of poetry's social function. Eliot contends that "the duty of poet, as poet, is only indirectly to his people; his direct duty is to his *language,* first to preserve, and second to extend and improve" ("Social Function" 20). By evoking the word *peregrine* Eliot first preserves its traditional associations with Latini and Dante and then extends its meaning to convey his contemporary sense of pilgrimage. In other words, Eliot stakes his claim to be a public poet on his capacity to represent and renew a community's tradition and language.

As Laurence Breiner argues, poetry plays "an unusually prominent role in West Indian society" primarily because it has a social "'function,' that it has a real reliable basis in the society" (*An Introduction* 13). Walcott and Brathwaite both see their work as making such a social contribution. Walcott also shifts his metaphors of self-description as he becomes more concerned about his public role. Beginning in the early 1980s he refers to himself as the "fortunate traveler" rather than as the isolated "castaway." Certainly this change in metaphors can be explained in part by his growing transience—since the late 1970s he has spent a part of each year teaching and speaking in the United States—but he also suggests that this shift represents a change in his relationship to the Caribbean. He still affirms his need for home: "I've never felt that I belong anywhere else but in St. Lucia. The geographical and spiritual fixity is there" (Walcott, "Art of Poetry" 115). He now recognizes more openly, however, his position of privilege vis-à-vis this community: "One is bound to feel the difference between these poor, dark, very small houses, the people in the streets, and yourself because you always have the chance of taking a plane out. Basically you are a fortunate traveller, a visitor, your luck is that you can always leave . . . yet the more I come back here the less I feel that I'm a prodigal or a castaway returning" (115). Indeed, this growing position of privilege has increased his sense of poetic responsibility. As a "wanderer" among the "ruins of civilizations" the younger Walcott saw himself as "bitter perhaps, but unencumbered" by any direct obligation to the community ("Muse" 3). As a "fortunate traveler" he feels compelled to return home to "see if what I write is not beyond the true experience of the person next to me on the bus" (Walcott, "Art of Poetry" 115). As a young "castaway" he testifies to his own existential loneliness, to being "afraid lest my own footprints multiply" ("The Castaway," *Collected Poems* 57). In *Omeros* his father urges him to speak for the larger community because its "multiplying feet / made your first rhyme" (75). More frequent travels abroad have sharpened his sense of obligation to home.

In his 1992 Nobel lecture Walcott directly addresses this issue of his public obligations as a Caribbean poet. He speaks of the "frightening duty" of representing both "a fresh language and a fresh people . . . I stand here in their name, if not their image—but also in the name of the dialect they exchange" *(Antilles)*. He chooses his words carefully to distinguish between two senses of representation—the artistic sense of depicting someone or something and the broadly political sense of serving as a substitute or proxy for another. Walcott recognizes that these two senses of representation are likely to be conflated, particularly at a Nobel award ceremony, so he feels compelled to stress the primacy of his artistic representation in this situation. He is a public representative of others, if at all, because of his artistic skill to represent their language and traditions and not because he is a representative, and perhaps a token, figure for their culture.[5]

Brathwaite serves as a useful counterexample in several ways. He too aspires after a more public role as a poet later in his career; however, in contrast to the conscious transformations in the careers of Eliot and Walcott, he has remained remarkably consistent in his ambition to speak primarily for and about the African diaspora in the Caribbean. He too shifts metaphors of self-description, but the difference between "rootless man of the world" and "X/Self" or between "Edward Kamau Brathwaite" and "Kamau Brathwaite" reflects a deepening rather than a changing of his basic poetic and ideological commitments.[6] Indeed, even the most noticeable change in Brathwaite's work, the development of his Sycorax video-style, is more of an extension of his earlier experiments to modify poetry's written conventions to represent nation language more accurately.

In aspiring to become public poets Eliot, Walcott, and Brathwaite represent not only a language and a community but also themselves. They sum up their careers to secure their reputations. As Lawrence Lipking suggests, this summing up involves a social function—"a mighty poet gathers his strength by embodying the essential thought of his age"—but it also involves a systematic rewriting of earlier work to complete its potential—"a great writer must be read as a tradition of one, his own continuum" (9, 66). It is this principle of repetition and advancement that provides structure to Eliot's *Four Quartets*.[7] It is also the process of revising and perfecting that makes Walcott's *Omeros* the culmination of his *Epitaph for the Young* and *Another Life*.[8] And it is this method of reformatting and exposition that gives coherence to Brathwaite's *Barabajan Poems*. In other words, they culminate their careers by revising their relationship, not only to traditions of other writers, but also to the tradition of their own writing. Eliot and Walcott recast earlier opinions to broaden the scope of their traditions; Brathwaite intensifies his commitment to an Afro-Caribbean folk tradition; and they all reorient the question of tradition to focus on poetry's relationship to language. In other words, each of them revisits the questions of tradition and language in order to envision the social function of his poetry and to establish himself as a public poet.

Indeed, this willingness to defend poetry's social utility is a distinguishing modernist characteristic of these poets. Much of contemporary Anglo-American postmodern poetry seems to be primarily concerned with the self-referential poetry of linguistic play, but Eliot, Walcott, and Brathwaite are concerned with connecting the linguistic play of their poetry to a broader social and cultural community. Their divergent but related defenses of poetry establish more broadly the contours of discrepant cosmopolitan modernism.

Several qualifications are in order about my use of the term *public poet*. I use *public* rather than *political* because the latter term too easily overstates the poet's influence on society. Poets today only rarely occupy positions of power through which they might initiate changes in the political or economic institutions that shape people's lives. Walcott may decry "the traitors / who in elected office, saw the land as views for hotels"

(*Omeros* 289), but he has no structural position in the political or economic institutions of Saint Lucia or the Caribbean from which to implement changes in the policies of development. Moreover, the "traitors" who do hold such positions are unlikely to be swayed, if they read poetry at all, by Walcott's critique. These economic and political reforms are crucial to creating a sense of cultural wholeness in the region, but no one expects poetry to offer specific programs. As Edouard Glissant contends, "Building a nation means today thinking first and foremost of systems of production, profitable commercial exchanges, betterment of the standard of living," but the artist contributes to this process by creating a "sense of collective personality" and by being a "voice to give expression to common ideals" (*Caribbean Discourse* 235–36).

Glissant's reference to "nation" raises my second qualification. While Benedict Anderson persuasively argues that the concept of the nation is "the most universally legitimate value in the political life of our time," and while it is a central concern of postcolonial theory,[9] I use the phrase *public poet* rather than *national poet* because each of these poets sees himself in relationship to a variety of collective identities. Each of them participates in, to adapt Anderson's key concept, a distinct series of "imagined communities" (6). The nation is, of course, the initial identification, but even this affiliation has its complexities. Eliot becomes a British citizen but thinks his work sounds "American" ("Tradition and the Practice of Poetry" 17). Walcott speaks of the "geographic and spiritual fixity" of Saint Lucia, but he has also written tellingly about the United States. Brathwaite contends that his work should be considered a part of both the Jamaican and the Barbadian national tradition (*Barabajan Poems* 22–23). At another level, each of them considers his work to serve a broader regional identification, Eliot relating himself to the "whole of the literature of Europe" ("Tradition and the Individual Talent" 14), Walcott speaking of himself as "primarily, absolutely a Caribbean writer" (Walcott, "Art of Poetry" 106), and Brathwaite claiming to be part of the "Caribbean as a whole" (*Barabajan Poems* 23). Finally, each of them conceives of himself as participating in an even broader, transcontinental and multilingual identity: Eliot imagines a broad "European" identity that encompass all of "Western" culture ("What Dante Means to Me" 134); for Walcott, it is a "New World" identity ("Culture" 50–57); and Brathwaite aligns himself with an "African Diaspora" community (*Barabajan Poems* 22).

It is important to recognize these different collective identities in order to avoid the simplifications that too often plague theorizing the postcolonial writer's larger social function, simplifications such as Fredric Jameson's claim that "all third-world texts are necessarily . . . *national allegories*" ("Third World" 69). As Aijaz Ahmad rightly contends, "If we replace the idea of the 'nation' with that larger, less restrictive idea of 'collectivity'" and if we consider the social function of the writer "not in nationalistic terms but simply as a relation between private and public, personal and communal," then it becomes possible to see that writers from the "so-called First and Third Worlds" share certain common aspirations and methods with respect to their social function (25). My use of the term *public* is in keeping with Ahmad's more comparative approach, but it also extends this approach to a more ideologically disparate group like Eliot, Walcott, and Brathwaite.

Finally, by *public* I do not necessarily mean "popular," for poetry demands an attention that often makes it less accessible to a mass audience. Each of these poets recognizes this tension in his own way. Eliot turns at the end of his career to compose West End poetic dramas as a way to bridge the gap.[10] Walcott knows that those who sing Bob Marley's songs will outnumber those who recite his poems, but he still affirms the power of poetry to offer its audience "The Light of the World" (*Arkansas Testament* 51). Brathwaite is the most consistent of the three in modeling his poetry on forms of popular culture, but he too laments the lack of attention given to poetry in the Caribbean (*Barabajan Poems* 23). These "public" poets recognize the limits of their political and popular appeal, but they still claim a public role in their capacity to represent the tradition and language of a people.

As Breiner rightly suggests, defending poetry's social function is difficult in the best of contexts and may seem hopelessly idealistic in the face of the difficulties of trying to live and publish as a poet in the West Indies, but this "does not diminish the value of a visionary program as an alternative to the debilitating assumption that most of society is inaccessible [to poetry] in principle" (*An Introduction* 23).

Critical Revisions

There is no mannerism more ubiquitous in Eliot's later essays than his casual dismissal of his earlier critical positions, both of his general pronouncements and of his evaluations of individual writers.[11] Critics have recognized and speculated on the significance of these revisions, but no one has examined how Eliot used these revisions to secure his own reputation as a public poet.[12] Consider, first, how he changes his conception of tradition. In 1936 Eliot gives a public lecture at University College, Dublin, a lecture that has only recently been published and in which Eliot gives a new response to a familiar question. He begins the lecture by asking, "What, in the practice of a particular art such as poetry, do we mean by tradition?" ("Tradition and the Practice of Poetry" 10).[13] In 1919 he answered this question primarily in terms of content. Tradition is knowledge of the relations among writers. It may seem like a "ridiculous amount of erudition (pedantry)," but whether poets "absorb knowledge" or "sweat for it," they must "procure the consciousness of the past" ("Tradition and the Individual Talent" 17). In 1936 Eliot answers this question more explicitly in terms of understanding how past poets have influenced their languages. "The great revolutions of poetry," he argues, "are revolutions in the sense of rhythm" ("Tradition and the Practice of Poetry" 11). In his earlier essay he abstractly claims that "the really new" work of art alters the "whole existing order" ("Tradition and the Individual Talent" 15); now he explains how this alteration occurs. "Literature may be renewed," he contends, only through the "cross-fertilisation" of rhythms from older or foreign literatures ("Tradition and the Practice of Poetry" 13). In other words, as he grows older he becomes more concerned with tradition in terms of poetic technique and versification, more concerned about a "fertilisation" of rhythms that "goes much deeper than the exact reception of ideas" (13). Eliot concludes that the English language is "without any historical parallel" because it has three distinct literatures—English, Irish, and American—the cross-fertilization of which has greatly "fortif[ied] the vitality of the language as a literary medium" (16).

It is striking how Eliot's argument about tradition and language anticipates more recent discussions of the use of English by colonial or postcolonial writers even as it exposes his own cultural and racial bias.[14] Eliot is keen to defend these three forms of English as equal, rejecting claims that either Irish English or American English is "*colonial* English" (15). It is a defense no doubt resulting in part from his having come to accept the "American" rhythms of his own work (17). He is also, however, eager to identify these traditions and languages as distinct: "The Irishman writing in English does not write English poetry. I should even say that the American writing in English does not write English poetry. It is not the trying to be American or Irish that does it, nor is it the choice of local subject matter, fundamentally; it is the different rhythm of the blood. I can't explain this to people who have no ear for poetry" (17). Unfortunately, Eliot's explanation of this different rhythm "of the blood" is muddled at best and perhaps racist at worse. Moreover, he was unwilling to recognize the possibility of other English rhythms. He dismisses summarily other Anglophone writers from the "British Dominions" for failing to "produce a distinct and impersonal idiom, a separate and peculiar rhythm" (16–17).

And he goes on to say that he cannot even imagine the development of other traditions in English, calling it a "question which lies in too remote a future to be discussed" (15).

Of course, Anglophone writers from around the world have proven him wrong during the last fifty years, but they have tended to prove him wrong on his own terms. These writers have created "separate and peculiar rhythm[s]" in English that are distinct from other Anglophone traditions. It is what Walcott means when he describes the effect of reading poetry in English in his own voice: "The temptation to become English was simply resisted by the fact that you wanted to make it breathe as naturally as you were speaking. Not only did it sound all right once you said it, but it enriched the language; it gave it extra melody" (Walcott, "Thinking Poetry" 177). And it is what Brathwaite means when he argues that nation language is not English "in terms of its rhythms and timbre, its own sound explosions . . . even though the words, as you hear them, would be English to a greater or lesser degree" ("History of the Voice" 266). Each of them strives, in Walcott's words, "to make just a small contribution to the sound of the world's hum" (Walcott, "Derek Walcott" 95).

Eliot also revises his opinion of individual poets—he revises his tradition—in order to bolster this argument that renewing the language is the mark of a public poet. Consider, for example, his treatment of Tennyson and Yeats.[15] In 1921 Eliot dismisses Tennyson as someone who merely "ruminated" ("Metaphysical Poets" 288) and Yeats as an "Irishman . . . outside of the tradition altogether" ("Andrew Marvell" 294). By 1936 Tennyson was a "great poet," not only because of his "technical accomplishment" but also because he "expresses the mood of his generation" ("In Memoriam" 337, 334). And in 1942 Eliot hails him as "The Voice of His Time" (2). Eliot's views of Yeats undergo a similar transformation.[16] By 1935 Eliot reverses himself completely and argues that Yeats "belonged" to English literature precisely because he was Irish. He contends that Yeats's Irish rhythms had a "fertilizing effect on *English*," an effect that Eliot describes as Yeats's "*literary* Nationalism," and declares him "the greatest poet of his time" ("A Commentary"). In 1940 Eliot completes the canonization. He eulogizes Yeats as a "great craftsman" and a "great poet" because "he was one of those few whose history is the history of their own time, who are a part of the consciousness of an age which cannot be understood without them" ("Yeats" 255, 262).

The conscious parallels between his description of these poets and his own career are obvious: the young innovative poet achieving a new technical mastery, the American poet fertilizing the language with a distinctive poetic rhythm, the urbane poet expressing the mood of a postwar generation, the prophetic poet decrying the secular drift of an age. At the beginning of his career he transformed traditions to enter and enlarge them. At the end he transforms his own critical opinions about tradition in general and about figures in that tradition in particular to claim a role as the representative voice of a generation. In the process, he shifts from being a poet who speaks in many voices to a poet who aspires to speak in his own voice for many people, from a poet who collocates diverse traditions to a poet who desires to consolidate his position as the public spokesperson for a particular tradition in a particular age.

Walcott's career follows an analogous trajectory as he modifies his earlier opinions and broadens his appeal as a public poet. Walcott even praises Eliot's contradictory approach as a model for his own changes in thinking. Like Eliot, he dismisses his early prose criticism as mere "reviewing" and not "really profound" (Walcott, "Conversation" [Smith] 194). He even questions his own ability to "think properly" because of his affinity for the "poetic process," a process that he contends works only through "inherent contradiction" (194). He sees this poetic process as antithetical to the creation of prose criticism except for the "great prose criticism" of writers like Coleridge and Eliot (194). He finds Eliot's criticism "wonderful" because for Eliot "the contradiction, . . . the opposite direction is much more fascinating than the one you're taking" (194–95). Walcott himself often takes the "opposite direction" in fascinating ways that suggest his desire to become a public poet.[17] Walcott concurs with Eliot that poetic achievement should be assessed in terms of poetic rhythm, but his concept of tradition is broader, reflecting a greater diversity of cultural experiences in the Caribbean.

No shift in Walcott's career is more dramatic than his changing attitude about African sources of culture for his New World tradition. In the early 1970s he castigates Afro-Caribbean "epic-poets" for glorifying the "tom-tom" and "ignoring the dynamo" ("Muse" 8); he scoffs at "pastoralists of the African revival" for trying to construct a culture out of "pathetic African carvings, poems and costume" ("Twilight" 10, 8); and in *Another Life* he damns them:

> I enclose in this circle of hell,
>
> . . . .
>
> Those who peel, from their own leprous flesh, their names,
> who chafe and nurture the scars of rusted chains,
> like primates favouring scabs, those who charge tickets

> for another free ride on the middle passage,
> those who explain to the peasant why he is African,
> (*Collected Poems* 269)

Yet some twenty years later *Omeros* advertises itself as an epic in which almost all of the central characters nurture wounds, in which most of the characters are from the "folk," in which two of the pivotal scenes involve imaginative returns to Africa, and in which the future, as represented by Helen's unborn child, will bear an African name. He retains some ironic distance from these characters with his self-conscious commentary—the wounds proliferate because "affliction is one theme / of this work" (28)—but in general he enlarges his New World classicism to incorporate more direct and sympathetic treatment of African-oriented cultural sources in the Caribbean.[18]

It is a shift, however, that needs to be understood in the context of Walcott's ideal of a cosmopolitan Caribbean tradition, language, and identity. As Rei Terada suggests, "In his later poems, Walcott calls more freely upon African-Caribbean language and folklore" as part of a growing "yearning after international community" (10). So, whereas Brathwaite remains committed to advancing an Afro-Caribbean nation language and folk identity as the primary purpose of his poetry, Walcott refers more sympathetically to Afro-Caribbean cultural sources as part of a general broadening of his New World tradition. Indeed, in his Nobel lecture he goes so far as to claim his right as a Caribbean writer to "the feast of Husein," "the Muslim epic," "the Chinese Dragon Dance," and "the rites of the Sephardic Jewish synagogue" *(Antilles)*. He also admits, with a new air of modesty, that he has not yet successfully incorporated these diverse cultural resources into his work *(Antilles)*.

This pattern of broadening and reaffirming his New World classicism also characterizes Walcott's more pronounced use of Creole in *Omeros*. As Terada contends, Walcott "increasingly enlarges and thematizes" his interest in using Creole in his poetry throughout his career (85). He has, of course, used it extensively throughout his drama, but he is careful to distinguish between representing the speech of dramatic characters, which he says is based "on real people talking," and representing his own voice in poetry: "For my poetry to be true, it had to be accurate, quietly accurate in terms of the sound of my own voice," and "I couldn't pretend that my voice was the voice of the St. Lucia peasant or fisherman" (Walcott, "An Interview" [Hirsch] 58). It is a distinction that he has honored in his later poetic experiments with dialect by creating personae—Shabine, Spoiler, the characters in *Omeros*—who speak English Creole and French patois. Indeed, he justifies this technique by appealing specifically to Brathwaite's example (Walcott, "An Interview" [Rowell] 130). However, important differences remain in their use of these personae. The mature Brathwaite recasts the meter, the length, and later the typeface of his poetic line to materialize these idiomatic rhythms, whereas Walcott continues to inflect classical prosodic techniques with creolized syntax and diction. The nation language of Brathwaite's Caliban breaks with Prospero's visual and phonetic conventions, whereas Walcott's Spoiler speaks nonstandard English in heroic couplets and Achille speaks French patois and English Creole in Homeric hexameters and Dantean terza rima. Brathwaite offers an important alternative vision of the poet's social function, to which we will return toward the end of the chapter. However, first let us explore how Eliot and Walcott represent their public ambitions in their poetic practice.

Receiving Tradition's Advice: Speaking with Dante about Speaking for an Age

Eliot's relationship to Dante has been well documented, but it is worth recalling the details to recognize fully how Eliot interprets Dante to defend the social function of his own poetry.[19] Eliot does not revise his opinion of Dante as he did his opinion of Tennyson, Yeats, and others; instead he speaks of Dante's influence as "*cumulative:* that is, the older you grow, the stronger the domination becomes" ("What Dante Means to Me" 130). However, when he comes to explaining this cumulative influence, he reiterates the same attributes that he celebrates in these other poets. He praises Dante, paradoxically, as the most "*universal* of poets" because he wrote in a "localiz[ed]" vernacular, Florentine Italian ("Dante" 238–39). He explains that Dante's speech was "very close to" the "common" language of the age, medieval Latin, but that it also invigorated that common language with its own unique rhythms (239). Later he attributes Dante's skill with language to his being the most "attentive student of the *art* of poetry" and the most "painstaking and *conscious* practitioner of the *craft*" ("What Dante Means to Me" 132). The result, according to Eliot, was that Dante created a language that was more "developed," "refined," and "precise" not only for other poets and philosophers but also for whoever "speaks that language," including "statesmen or railway porters" (133). Eliot also commends Dante for using this language to widen the range of human experience, "to find words for the inarticulate, to capture those feelings which people can hardly even feel, because they have no words for them" (134). Finally, he praises Dante's cosmopolitanism, contending that he was the "most *European*" of all poets because his "lessons of craft . . . and of exploration of sensibility" cut across cultural, linguistic, racial, and national traditions.[20] The parallels to Eliot's own aspirations are again apparent: he considers his "local" American dialect as both close to and invigorating for the common language of his age, Standard English; he works to perfect his craft so that he can develop this common language into a more effective medium for all Anglophone speakers; and he has cosmopolitan aspirations to become the representative speaker of modern Europe and America. The poet serves a social function by refining a common language to widen people's capacity to experience life, a benefit not only within a nation, culture, or race but also across nations, cultures, and races.

Walcott does not, of course, desire to become the most "European" of writers, but he still finds Dante's example important.[21] Indeed, while critics of Walcott's *Omeros* have understandably focused more on the significance of Homer, they have unduly neglected the influence of Dante. For example, Gregson Davis asks, "What does the narrator gain from invoking Homer while disowning the Homeric genre?" ("With No Homeric Shadow" 322). Similarly, Paul Breslin questions, "Why does the poet so obsessively devoted to forging parallels with the Homeric epics end up confessing, to the spirit of Homer himself, that he has never read them 'all the way through'. . . ?" (244).[22] In other words, why does Walcott so invest in his Homeric allusions and then undercut them with such irony? Davis suggests that Walcott is not "renouncing 'epic' so much as redefining it" ("With No Homeric Shadow" 328), whereas Breslin speculates that Walcott's self-critique of his Homeric allusions "emerged in the course of composition," and he "could not (or would not) integrate the portions he had already completed into his belated insight" (272). Both answers are plausible in relation to Walcott's treatment of Homer, but why does he not treat Dante with the same irony? Is it perhaps because he sees Dante as a more fitting model for the poet's public role?

Walcott speaks of Dante as a model because of his own desire to "fuse the noble and the common language, . . . in a tone that is true to my own voice, in which both accents are heard naturally" (Walcott, "An Interview" [Sjoberg] 83). And like Eliot, Walcott sees Dante as a writer who conveyed the ineffable, who testified to the "radiance that happens, a kind of sublimity that happens" in life (Walcott, "Derek Walcott" 104). However, while Eliot ascribes Dante's success to his ability to name, and so extend, the registry of people's emotional experiences, Walcott makes a more daring, even wildly speculative link between poetic transcendence and social utility. He admires Dante because the "horrors" he went through "are finally sublimated in love, a radiant light swirls backward into a center" (Walcott, "An Interview" [White] 155). He calls this poetics of transcendent love a "political answer in Dante," for it testifies to a power stronger than evil, to an endurance even in the face of suffering, to a survival despite oppression (160). Indeed, he explicitly associates Dante's poetics with the African diaspora's "strong love of the idea of worship" in the New World, claiming that this idea is the "greatest contribution the Afro-American has made to America" (155–56). This conflation reflects the reorientation of his idea of tradition. He defends poetry as a discourse of hope by bringing together Dante's poetry and storefront Baptist worship, classical Western and contemporary New World African cultural experiences.

Eliot and Walcott also explicitly recast scenes from Dante to defend poetry's social utility, Eliot in the "familiar compound ghost" canto in *Little Gidding* and Walcott in analogous scenes in books 1 and 7 of *Omeros*. In transposing Dante, each of them broadens his own understanding of tradition, expresses his own sense of magnanimity toward other writers, explores his own complicity with fame, and renews the English language with his own accent. Eliot is ultimately less successful in his transposition, for he tends to distort Dante's paradigm to defend the orthodoxy of his poetic aspiration. Walcott takes better advantage of the more mixed nature of Dante's model and productively renews it to suggest the social utility of his poetry in representing a Caribbean cultural identity.

The Multivocal Tradition of the Public Poet

Eliot and Walcott both rewrite Dante's reunion with his former poetic master, Brunetto Latini, because they find in this dramatic encounter a model for the public poet's relation to tradition, a model that recognizes the ideological differences among poets but affirms a common pursuit nonetheless. Dante places his former teacher in Hell but expresses surprise at meeting him there: "What, you here, Ser Brunetto? you!" (1.15.30). Even though Latini is damned, Dante still listens carefully to his advice and describes movingly his deep gratitude for his earlier instruction:

> for I keep with me still,
>
> Stamped on my mind, and now stabbing my heart,
> the dear, benign, paternal image of you,
> You living, you hourly teaching me the art
>
> By which men grow immortal;
> (1.15.81–85)

Dante thanks a specific individual, but Eliot and Walcott recognize less identifiable and more multifaceted figures as their poetic masters, not only because they have specific reservations about Dante's model but also because they see themselves as learning from a multivocal tradition rather that a single person.

Eliot's reservations are primarily theological. In a letter to John Hayward, his friend and literary adviser, Eliot offers two reasons for complicating the parallel between his encounter with the familiar compound ghost and Dante's meeting with Latini: "The first is that the visionary figure has now become somewhat more definite and will no doubt be identified by some readers with Yeats though I do not mean anything so precise as that. However, I do not wish to take the responsibility of putting Yeats or anybody else into Hell. . . . Second, although the reference to that Canto is intended to be explicit, I wished the effect of the whole to be Purgatorial which is more appropriate" (quoted in Gardner 64–65). Not as quick to condemn as Dante, Eliot quiets his reservations by proliferating his masters. With this proliferation, Eliot invites us to compare this "familiar compound ghost" to the shifting shapes of his earlier persona, Tiresias. In *The Waste Land* the young Eliot draws on comparative anthropology and the occult, as well as literary sources, to amalgamate "personages" like the one-eyed merchant, the Phoenician Sailor, and the figure of Tiresias. In *Little Gidding* the older Eliot creates this compound ghost predominantly from the voices of literary figures: the voices of writers whom Eliot always considered to be great, Dante and Shakespeare; the voices of those whom he reconsidered and elevated to greatness, Milton, Tennyson, and Yeats; and the voices of those whom he considered minor but important for their fertilizing effect on his own poetic language, Laforgue and Mallarmé.[23] Even though he complicates Dante's figure of tradition, it serves the same function: they both recognize masters in order to make them peers. In addition, Eliot does not ironize these voices to stretch the tradition as he does in *The Waste Land;* he conflates them to intensify the force of the advice given to the poet. Eliot's personification of tradition remains eclectic in its sources, but it now merges to speak with the conviction of one voice.

Walcott's recasting of this epic figure of tradition is more involved and less well known than Eliot's, so it deserves a more extended treatment.[24] Two specific examples—Walcott's reunion with his dead father at the end of book 1 of *Omeros* and his visit with Omeros/Seven Seas in book 7—best illustrate the older Walcott's understanding of his relationship to tradition. Toward the end of book 1, Walcott meets the ghost of his father,

Warwick, in his childhood home in Castries.[25] The house had been converted into a print shop, and Warwick emerges from a cheap duplication machine, a nicely sardonic comment on the material conditions of publishing "the tradition" in the Caribbean. Warwick carries a book of his own verse and asks Walcott:

> "In this pale blue notebook where you found my verses"—
> my father smiled—"I appeared to make your life's choice,
> and the calling that you practise both reverses
>
> and honors mine from the moment it blent with yours.
> Now that you are twice my age, which is the boy's,
> which the father's?"
> "Sir"—I swallowed—"they are one voice."
> (68)

In these stanzas Walcott represents his personal life as emblematic of his aspiration to become a public poet. He reaffirms the reality of loss in the Caribbean experience; he is an orphan literally because his father died when he was a young child and culturally because colonialism separated all people in the Caribbean from their cultural origins. However, Walcott responds to that loss with an invention: he imagines a father that embodies some of those lost cultural origins. This poetic practice both "reverses and honours" the past, the pun on *reverses* (both a rewriting and a redirecting) suggesting his resistance to the past and the word *honours* conveying his indebtedness to it. The goal of this practice is for the poet and the tradition to speak with "one voice" (68). Or as he says in an interview, he does not want to be "a poet but an anthology" because "every poet of any modesty hopes to make just a small contribution to the sound of the world's hum," which is not a "wish to be individual" (Walcott, "Derek Walcott" 95).

The table of contents of Walcott's anthology deserves closer attention. Warwick comes to instruct his son about the artist's vocation, so the scene evokes a variety of classical sources, not only Dante's meeting with Latini but also Odysseus's with Telemachus, and Anchises' with Aeneas. In each case the father returns to advise the son about his vocation. Walcott underscores his rewriting of this classical tradition of fathers and sons by composing *Omeros* in loose Homeric hexameters and Dantean terza rima. However, Walcott does not limit himself to classical sources; he also transposes his father's biography to make it resonate with Shakespeare's life and work. For example, he "reverses" the illegitimacy of his father's name by associating it with Shakespeare's home. Warwick explains that "my bastard father christened me after his shire: / Warwick. The Bard's county" (68). It is not the academic Shakespeare of an imposed colonial canon—the "foreign machinery known as Literature"—but an idealized Shakespeare of the amateur poet who reads and writes for the love of the craft—"It's that Will you inherit" (68). Walcott even has Warwick explain his own death in Shakespearian terms: "that disease / like Hamlet's old man's spread from an infected ear" (68). With this allusion to *Hamlet* Warwick expands exponentially his role as composite figure of tradition. The scene becomes a "reversing" not only of the classical sources but also of King Hamlet's admonitions to Hamlet to "Remember me." This convergence of the classical and the Shakespearean, then, triggers a series of modernist "colonial" parallels, not only Eliot's encounter with the familiar compound ghost in *Little Gidding* but also Stephen's theories of *Hamlet* in Joyce's *Ulysses*. This scene even echoes Walcott's contemporary and friend Seamus Heaney, who engages in similar rewriting in his meeting with Joyce's ghost in *Station Island*.[26] In other words, Walcott proliferates his correspondences to transform imitation into invention, to reorient the relations among writers so that tradition speaks for and about the Caribbean.

Walcott's proliferations renew Eliot's modernist strategy of representing tradition with multiple literary figures speaking as one voice, but Walcott modifies that strategy to reflect his discrepant Caribbean experience, a modification that becomes most readily apparent by briefly contrasting Walcott's and Joyce's biographical transpositions of *Hamlet*.[27] In the "Scylla and Charybdis" episode of Joyce's *Ulysses* Stephen identifies Shakespeare with King Hamlet, the father, rather than with Hamlet, the son, because he questions the validity of paternity as a trope for literary influence. He envisions the artist, not as a dutiful son carrying out the commands of the father, but as a self-authorizing figure who transcends the need for origins, the tracing of genealogies, or the imitation of literary predecessors. For most readers of Joyce, recounting Stephen's theory is all too familiar; for Walcott it is all too painfully true. The Caribbean experience of slavery and indentured servitude severed people's ties to origins, ruptured family genealogies, and fragmented traditions, events that place absence at the core of Caribbean culture. Stephen wonders glibly about the arbitrary significance of names, but Walcott recognizes experientially the alienation of having a father named for a county in England. Stephen dismisses paternity as a "legal fiction," but the legal fiction of "illegitimacy" cannot be so flippantly dismissed by those characterized as bastards, a characterization that has been applied not only to biological sons but also to colonial cultures. Stephen struggles with his biological, religious, and political fathers to become an artist. Bereft of real and literary fathers, Walcott dismisses this Oedipal model of literary tradition as less relevant to his New World context. Instead, he accepts the absence of paternal and cultural origins in the Caribbean as a privilege because it frees him to create his own origins, genealogy, and heritage. He does not struggle with an authoritative father whom he must depose but constructs an imagined father with whom he enjoys a reunion.[28]

Walcott's strategy is bold and innovative, but does it go far enough? If he is free to construct his cultural origins, why does he still allude almost exclusively to the Western literary tradition in imagining his father as a composite figure of tradition? How does this example recognize the Afro-Caribbean aspects of the region's cultural heritage? Walcott only partially addresses this question in this passage. When, as a younger poet, he selected Crusoe as his organizing persona, it was clear that he was creating a New World/Caribbean tradition by reorienting the Western tradition from within. When he chooses his father as his figure of tradition, he shifts the focus slightly to suggest the importance of his personal experience. Walcott still reorients Western literary figures in imagining his father as a composite figure of his New World/Caribbean tradition, but he now represents that controlling consciousness as an Afro-Caribbean from Saint Lucia. This shift does not, of course, fully respond to the criticism. There is no obvious reason why he could not have also alluded to literary or folk figures associated with Afro-Caribbean culture as part of creating this composite figure of tradition. He still makes a distinction, although more nuanced, between his relationship to Europe and his relationship to Africa, between his literary and personal traditions.

In the opening chapters of book 7 he addresses this issue more broadly in a scene that recasts his classical and modernist precursors more explicitly. Walcott's poet character wakes early one morning and sees some beach debris, a coconut and a driftwood log, churning in the surf. The changing light illuminates the debris so that the figures of Omeros and Seven Seas emerge alternatively, almost as photographic negatives of each other. Omeros is Walcott's Homeric character, and Seven Seas is an Afro-Caribbean folk character. In the direct light, Omeros appears as a "marble head . . . fringed with its surf curls and beard," but then, as the shadow of a cloud passes, Seven Seas' "visage reappeared / with ebony hardness" as a "foam-headed fisherman" (280–81). Omeros wears a "dripping chiton" and carries an "old leather goatskin"; Seven Seas has a "white, torn / undershirt" and a "plastic bag" (280–81). By conflating Omeros and Seven Seas,

Walcott creates another composite figure of tradition, but now his character brings together more explicitly the classical and the vernacular, the "Western" and the "African," the elite and the popular, the written and the oral cultural traditions of the Caribbean. Walcott also inserts details to echo Eliot's meeting with the "familiar compound ghost" and Stephen's walk along the Sandymount strand in the "Proteus" episode of *Ulysses*. This confluence of allusions in Omeros/Seven Seas better embodies Walcott's modernist strategy to represent the discrepant cosmopolitan traditions of the West Indies.

When Eliot and Joyce compare their modern characters to classical mythological figures, the past comments ironically on the present as these writers blend, in Richard Ellmann's words, the "two ends of the western tradition like a multitemporal, multiterritorial pun" (2). When Walcott mimics this strategy, he makes the ironic commenting reciprocal and widely broadens the ends of his New World tradition. He seeks to convey not only the classical nature of Caribbean culture but also the Caribbean quality of classical culture. As he contentiously puts it, "Part of what I'm saying in the book [*Omeros*] is that the Greeks were the niggers of the Mediterranean" (Walcott, "Thinking Poetry" 183). Indeed, he even claims that a classical approach is a more accurate way to represent what is "African" in the Caribbean because classical art is mimetic, whereas African art is not "representational" (183). For Walcott, the Caribbean and Greek cultures generate an exhilarating art because they combine disciplined form with ornate exuberance. By seeing classical Greek culture through the "freshness" of his Caribbean experience, he honors the "vigor and elation" of each culture (183).

Omeros, of course, only represents the familiar, "Western" half of Walcott's concept of tradition. Seven Seas, on the other hand, reflects the growing prominence of class and ethnicity in Walcott's New World classicism. Seven Seas is Walcott's new, poorer and darker version of the New World epic poet. Instead of the Crusoe figure driving to a beach house to compose poetry, Seven Seas lives in a simple seaside hut, makes coffee with a leaky kettle, and writes from a tin chair (*Omeros* 11–13). But in these ordinary circumstances Seven Seas has the extraordinary ability to recount the communal stories of the New World. He sings of the Middle Passage as an African griot (148–49); he recounts how the names of the trees mark the massacre of Caribs and Aruacs (163–64); and he recalls participating in the Ghost Dance as a Sioux shaman (164, 318). Even his name indicates the new ethnic awareness in Walcott's cosmopolitan ambition, for it suggests not only that people from the Caribbean are

"People of the Sea," as Benítez-Rojo suggests, but that their tradition should encompass the cultures of all of the people who traveled the "seven seas" to come to the New World (314). With Seven Seas, Walcott offers an alternative figure to represent Brathwaite's "folk" tradition, a figure who reflects the broadening cosmopolitanism of Walcott's New World tradition and who seeks to heal the injustice of colonialism. He represents the broadening cosmopolitanism of Walcott's tradition.

Again, however, the daring of Walcott's ambition opens him up to criticism for promising more than he delivers. Why, for example, does Seven Seas not tell the epic tales of East Indian, Jewish, or Chinese cultures? The older Walcott recognizes the disparity between his multicultural aspiration and his poetic achievement more openly. In the Nobel lecture he writes: "I was entitled to the feast of Husein, to the mirrors and crepe-paper temples of the Muslim epic, to the Chinese Dragon Dance, to the rites of that Sephardic Jewish synagogue that was on Something Street. I am only one-eighth the writer I might have been had I contained all the fragmented languages of Trinidad" *(Antilles)*. Walcott's acknowledging of this disparity does not, of course, eliminate it. An even more pressing concern is Walcott's sense of proportion among the different sources of culture in the Caribbean. Why represent the Caribbean tradition as half "Western" and half the rest of the world? Is the African heritage of the region unduly muted in the figure of Seven Seas? Indeed, Walcott's sometimes too easy transposition of cultures again risks unduly homogenizing Caribbean culture, as Paul Breslin seems to suggest when he argues, "As much as I admire Walcott for insisting, in a time of identity politics, on common ground in human experience, the metamorphosis of Sioux into Cherokee into African Americans who are also Afro-Caribbeans who in turn are like Homeric Greeks proceeds so rapidly, and with so little interest in the particular qualities of any of these peoples, that the universal becomes a blank category" (264).

By creating Omeros/Seven Seas, Walcott significantly broadens his concept of tradition, but he does not completely reverse his earlier position. He still represents literary sources as a dominating part of his Caribbean/New World tradition, but he is now more willing to recognize the oral and interethnic sources of culture in the region.[29] Even though the figure of Omeros/Seven Seas still falls short of Walcott's complete vision of the New World tradition, he is both more cosmopolitan and more discrepant than the poet's earlier Crusoe. It is a conscious revising and broadening of his concept of tradition, which suggests a growing openness to his critics even as he reaffirms his basic poetic commitments.

Magnanimity of the Public Poet

Eliot and Walcott transform Dante's single master into a composite figure of tradition and then extend his magnanimity toward this wider range of writers.[30] In Dante they find a person who acknowledges his poetic debts without compromising his ideological commitments. He thanks Brunetto for "teaching me the art / By which men grow immortal" (1.15.84–85) but still damns him for perverting that longing for immortality into a desire for earthly fame. Eliot is more reluctant to damn his predecessors, but he makes a similar distinction between poetry and ideology. Although a devout Anglo-Catholic, he freely praises the craft of poets like Milton, Tennyson, and Yeats while simultaneously rejecting their puritan, agnostic, and Celtic religious ideas.[31] For Walcott, this distinction is central to the integrity of his New World classicism. Walcott has spent a career showing that a poet can learn from precursors in a tradition without necessarily agreeing with their beliefs. Eliot and Walcott offer an unfashionable lesson to a critical world that sees poetry and ideology as coterminous, that expects iambic pentameter to advance an identity politics. These poets testify not only to the possibility of poetic exchange despite principled disagreement but also to the generosity of poets who acknowledge learning from those with whom they passionately disagree. For them, even the misguided mentor can appear, in Dante's words, "not like a loser, but the winning runner" (1.15.123–24).

This ideological tension exists not only between the poet and his predecessors but also between the poet and the ideological factions of his community. Again, Latini offers apt advice, for he warns Dante of the danger of poetic success, the danger of having his art co-opted by narrow political or ethnic affiliations: "Fortune has honors for thee—of such note, / Both sides will seek to snatch thee and devour" (1.15.70–72). The poet avoids this danger, Latini suggests, by perfecting his craft, for the well-crafted poem represents the complexity of experience in ways that avoid easy affiliations and that reorient common ideological divisions.

Postcolonial artists have felt this ideological pressure perhaps most keenly. Ever since Frantz Fanon encouraged the "native intellectual" to "shake the people" and create "a fighting literature, a revolutionary literature, a national literature" (222–23), postcolonial artists have often been expected to create an art that recognizably advances a national or regional political agenda. Walcott has resisted being co-opted by any simple ideological position throughout his career, resisting any either-or choice "between Africa and the English tongue I love" ("A Far Cry,"

Collected Poems 18). Indeed, he rejects as provincial and patronizing both the "eurocentric" and the "afrocentric" critics who assess his work exclusively from either of those perspectives (Walcott, "Art of Poetry" 121). And as Latini advises Dante, Walcott's father advises him to devote himself to his craft to maintain his independence:

> Measure the days you have left. Do just that labour
> which marries your heart to your right hand: simplify
> your life to one emblem, a sail leaving harbour
>
> and a sail coming in.
>
> (*Omeros* 72)

This movement of his hand back and forth across the page becomes the emblem of his commitment to the craft, both literally and figuratively, of writing poetry. It is a commitment that he must uphold because "all corruption will cry to be taken aboard" (73). Like Dante, Walcott suggests that this fidelity to craft operates as an antitoxin to the poisoning demand for ideological purity. Indeed, postcolonial poetry may well be better suited to representing these ideological complexities because it is a genre that employs metaphor and language in ways that more readily convey the ambivalences of the postcolonial condition.

For Eliot the lesson is more difficult. He composes *Little Gidding* in the midst of an ideological conflict, World War II, in which the sides seem pretty clear. He likely found Latini's advice for the poet to flee any ideological attachments unwise at best and perhaps even treasonous under his circumstances. Instead, Eliot transmutes Dante's evasion of ideological forces into his own obligation to mediate the spiritual significance of ideological conflict. Accordingly, he sees the poet as moving between two worlds, the spiritual and the temporal. He encounters his dead master in this liminal space: they meet at dawn, but it is also an "intersection time" with "no before and after"; they meet "between three districts" of London, but it is a "meeting nowhere"; and they speak to each other, but it is in a linguistic gap between "last year's words [which] belong to last year's language / and next year's words [which] await another voice" (*Little Gidding, Complete Poems* 141). Although his resolution of the problem may be less satisfying in a secular age, Eliot uses his craft, not to resist ideological conflict, but to subsume it through a theological perspective on temporal events. Dante employs a similar theological strategy in representing the role of fame for a public poet, the third issue to which Eliot and Walcott look to Dante for guidance.

Fame and the Public Poet

Should the poet aspire to achieve fame for himself or for his community? Does the desire for fame undermine the integrity of art? How can the public poet purify his ambition? In his comprehensive history of fame Leo Braudy identifies Dante as the first writer to mediate successfully the Christian understanding of fame as the transitory goal of fools and the Roman belief in fame as the permanent reward of true greatness. Braudy contends that Dante sacralizes the Roman urge to fame by defining it "as an inspiration by God to an exemplary true fame" (238). The poet should strive for fame, not to bring glory to himself, but to bring glory to God. Eliot is clearly much closer to Dante in his religious convictions, but it is Walcott who more successfully appropriates and transforms Dante's understanding of fame in fulfilling a poet's public function.

The contradictory nature of fame is evident in Dante's encounter with Latini. As Ricardo Quinones contends, Latini himself represents the Roman "love of glory" (23). He advises Dante to strive to achieve earthly fame through his art: "follow but thy star; / Thou canst not fail to win the glorious haven" (1.15.55–56). Dante charitably deflects Latini's advice with gratitude and self-deprecating humility, gratitude for learning from Latini the "art / By which men grow immortal" and humility about the fickleness of fame: "I can stand steady / So conscience chide not, facing unafraid / Whatever Fortune brings, for I am ready" (1.15.61–63). Virgil, however, quickly reprimands Dante for his apparent indifference to Latini's advice: "well-heeded is well-heard" (1.15.99). This reprimand implies that the public poet must redirect rather than reject the desire for fame. This redirection is suggested by the narrative structure of the scene itself. As a sodomite in Dante's Catholic world, Latini is damned not because of his desire but because his expression of that desire is viewed as the corruption of a heterosexual ideal. Similarly, he is damned not because he aspires after fame but because he corrupts that aspiration by limiting fame to a poet's earthly reputation. Dante teaches that the poet's fame can be exemplary only to the extent that it affirms an ideal that transcends his own experience and ambition.

Eliot is strict, almost ascetic, in renouncing his own fame. The familiar compound ghost neither predicts Eliot's future renown nor tempers Eliot's ascetic embrace of a strict humility. Instead, he sets a "crown" on Eliot's "lifetime's effort," a crown of regrets about a deteriorating physical body ("cold friction of expiring sense"), a degenerating civic society ("the conscious impotence of rage / At human folly"), and a repeating of personal moral failure ("the rending pain of re-enactment") (*Little Gidding, Complete Poems* 141–42). More strictly orthodox than his master, Eliot longs to achieve a state of Christian humility that eviscerates the public poet's need or desire for Roman fame:

And all shall be well and
All manner of thing shall be well
By the purification of the motive
In the ground of our beseeching.
(143)

Eliot's ascetic ideal distorts Dante's paradigm by seeing poetic fame exclusively in terms of personal ambition. Instead, Dante teaches that the public poet can use his fame to bring honor to the subject of poetry.

Walcott recasts this lesson to confront the unique challenges of fame for the New World/Caribbean poet. He agrees with Dante and Eliot that a longing for earthly fame can corrupt a poet, but he does not represent this problem exclusively in terms of personal moral character. Walcott also blames, at least in part, colonial and neocolonial institutions of power for their corrupting influence on the Caribbean poet. Walcott responds by recognizing both the necessity and the danger of poetic fame for the Caribbean poet. To understand this point, we must return to the scene of instruction between Warwick and Walcott.

After the initial discussion in their childhood home, Warwick invites his son to walk with him to the wharf and consider the dangerous allure of fame in the image of a tourist cruise ship.

At the corner of Bridge
Street, we saw the liner as white as a mirage,
its hull bright as paper, preening with privilege.

"Measure the days you have left. Do just that labour
which marries your heart to your right hand: simplify
your life to one emblem, a sail leaving harbour

and a sail coming in. All corruption will cry
to be taken aboard. Fame is that white liner
at the end of your street, a city to itself,

taller than the Fire Station, and much finer,
with its brass-ringed portholes, mounting shelf after shelf,
than anything Castries could ever hope to build."
(*Omeros* 72–73)

In keeping with Latini's advice to Dante, Warwick tells his son to give his first loyalty to his craft and free himself from the contaminating expectations of others. However, in making explicit that "fame is the white liner," Walcott transforms the issue of fame and the public poet to encompass the colonial experience. Fame remains a literary achievement—he compares the liner's white hull and its multilevel decks to books on a library shelf—but it is an achievement shaped by institutions with racial and economic identities. As he suggests, the perceived "whiteness" of the liner may in fact be only a "mirage," but he implies that race still serves as a powerful symbolic marker in the establishing of literary reputations. From his small harbor of creative activity in the Caribbean, this liner of literary fame still seems overwhelmingly white, privileged, and finer "than anything Castries could ever hope to build" (73).

Walcott then goes on to explain the pernicious effect of the liner's financial resources on Caribbean writers.

> [the liner's] humming engines spewed expensive garbage
> where boys balanced on logs, or riding old tires,
> shouted up past the hull to tourists on the rails
>
> to throw down coins, as cameras caught their black cries,
> then jackknife or swan-dive—their somersaulting tails
> like fishes flipped backwards—as the coins grew in size
>
> in the wobbling depth; then, when they surfaced, fights
> for possession, their heads butting like porpoises.
>
> (73)

Accordingly, the power of the white liner consists not only in establishing reputations but also in distributing money. Walcott recognizes the pressure on Caribbean writers to "perform" for metropolitan institutions in order to make a living, but he also shows that the results are often degrading and divisive. Their work is diminished to an intellectual souvenir, and they are reduced to fighting among themselves for scarce resources.[32]

To this point, the white liner represents all that is negative in aspiring after poetic fame. However, like Dante and unlike Eliot, Walcott recognizes that the public poet has a more ambivalent relation to fame. On the one hand, he knows that his ability to represent Saint Lucia and its people depends on the wealth, technology, and power of all that is symbolized by the liner—the publishers who distribute his books, the periodicals who review them, the readers who can afford to buy them, the foundations who grant him fellowships and award him prizes, and the universities that employ him. Yet, on the other hand, he knows that if he submits his ambition completely to the conditions of the metropolitan liner, he risks demeaning his own poetic practice to an exotic display for tourists. He will become just another "beach" boy skillfully diving for money amid the refuse of the metropolitan culture. He must find another image to suggest the relation between the liner and the Caribbean artist.

He finds it in the dignity of the hardworking women coal-carriers whose work literally fuels the liner's power, a cleverly ironic comment on the empire's need for the economic and, by implication, cultural resources of the colonies. These women were skilled, climbing with "baskets of coal / balanced on their torchoned heads, without touching them"; they were powerful, carrying hundredweight loads with a "spine straight as a pole, / and with a strength that never altered its rhythm"; and they were radiant, "ascending / the narrow wooden ramp built steeply to the hull / of a liner" with a "gait . . . made beautiful by balance" (74). Of course, they were also exploited because of their race and gender, receiving only a copper penny for every load, a point Walcott makes deftly by contrasting the heavy loads of black coal on the women's heads with the "white pith-helmets" shading the heads of the two tally clerks (74). Even though these women were exploited by the economic system of colonialism represented by the ship, Warwick still advises his son to follow them up the ladder to the top of the liner, for "only by its stages . . . will you achieve that height" where poetry can make a difference. In other words, Walcott acknowledges that his poetry remains inextricably linked to metropolitan institutions of power, but he wants to transform that power to retell the story of his home. No longer will Castries be viewed, by its inhabitants or others, as merely "unknown, raw, insignificant"; instead, his poetry can commemorate even the debased work of these women laborers as reflecting the beauty of their endurance.

Jonathan Martin criticizes Walcott for what he calls this "morally distasteful comparison between the work of poetry and the crushing labor of Caribbean slave women" (203–4). However, as Paul Breslin rightly argues, Walcott's analogy is more "one of reciprocity rather than unmitigated appropriation" (260). Walcott wants to recall not only the malevolence of the oppressors but also the skill, power, and radiance of the survivors. They have taught him, so he feels an obligation to represent them: his "own work owes them" because "no one knows them" (*Omeros* 75). It is an obligation that he believes he can best fulfill by perfecting his craft to expand the capacity of language to represent experience. Indeed, the formal aspects of poetry, rather than obscuring the communal ideal, as suggested by the realist assumption of so much of postcolonial literature and theory, become the means by which the communal obligation is met.

Language and the Public Poet

Eliot and Walcott reconfigure two distinctive elements of Dante's prosody—his terza rima stanza and his choice of the vernacular—to perfect their craft. Dante's stanzaic form is useful because its concatenated rhyme scheme conveys a sense of continuity and change. In Dante's Italian the prevalence of rhymes makes this movement both insistent and understated. Accordingly, it is an ideal poetic form for Eliot and Walcott, two poets who wish to establish in an insistent but understated way their continuity with, yet difference from, a poetic tradition. Eliot modifies the form by using masculine and feminine terminations rather than rhyme to link his tercets. While the feminine terminations obviously evoke Dante's hendecasyllabic line, Eliot explains this choice in terms of linguistic difference. He thought the scarcity of rhymes in English would make a rhymed imitation too "emphatic" to capture the effortlessness of Dante's Italian ("What Dante Means to Me" 128). Here again Eliot's self-asserting humility is evident: he meticulously avoids drawing too much attention to his verse by excising rhyme yet simultaneously adopts a form that will equate him with Dante.

Eliot is also less successful in his imitation of Dante's language, for he muffles the idiomatic rhythm of his own English in order to establish its universality. In his criticism he praises Dante's Italian vernacular for being closely related to the "universal" language of his age, medieval Latin. However, when he imitates Dante, he does not follow the obvious parallel; he does not write in a way that shows the relation between his own vernacular, an American English, and the international English of his day. Instead he selects English words and phrases with Latin derivations—"interminable," "intimate and unidentifiable," "laceration," "re-enactment," "valediction"—to establish a relationship between his English and a "universal" Latin. While Latin may have been the "literary Esperanto" of Dante's Europe in the fourteenth century, it is clearly not that of Eliot's Europe in the twentieth. The language of the passage is powerful, as many readers and critics have found, but it can also sound anachronistic at best and artificial at worst.[33] Seamus Heaney aptly describes it as a language that "gives the illusion of absolute authority [because of its] imperial lexicon" but also is "a hypnotic deployment of perfected latinate words" ("Envies" 9). Indeed, it is as if Eliot has heard only the second part of his ghost's advice: "our concern was speech, and speech impelled us / To purify the dialect of the tribe" (*Little Gidding, Complete Poems*

141). He may "purify" English by establishing its ties with a more "universal" Latin, but it is at the cost of writing in a language far removed from the rhythms of common speech. Indeed, he should have recognized that English needed less to be established as an international language and more to be renewed through the idiomatic rhythms of its variant national and regional forms. He needed to mimic Dante's Provencal Italian, not imitate his Latin.

Walcott faces the opposite challenge: not establishing English as an international language but identifying a viable vernacular language equivalent to Dante's Italian. He experiments with writing *Omeros* in French Creole—the common speech of Saint Lucia—and vestiges of those experiments still remain in the poem;[34] however, he abandons this approach because it "began to feel false" ("Reflections on *Omeros*" 245). He feels that writing in French Creole is too "forced" and "defensive" for him, too much of a desperate "act of aggression" to preserve a language, too much like trying to write in Gaelic or Welsh for nationalist writers from Ireland or Wales (245). He then considers using English Creole as the primary language of *Omeros* but decides that it too is "false to my interior tone" because "I do not think in dialect" (245). He concludes that he should write *Omeros* primarily in a Standard English but that this English should be inflected with his own "rhythm" or "accent" (245–46). He represents his choice as an affirmation of artistic integrity (his "interior tone") over ideological necessity (a nationalist recovery of a vernacular), but the choice is not that simple. Again, he seems reluctant to recognize that ideological forces also influence a writer's understanding of integrity, that he might feel "false" writing French or English Creole because colonial cultural and educational institutions had disparaged the use of those vernacular languages for generations. Poetry and ideology are neither coterminous nor autonomous. Walcott could do more to acknowledge the interdependence of these discourses in his own work.

Even so, he is more convincing than Eliot in his recasting of Dante's example. Eliot muffles the idiomatic rhythm of his American dialect by relying heavily on a Latinate diction and syntax to establish English as an international language. Walcott accepts English as a cosmopolitan medium and devotes his energy to infusing it with the melodic lilt of his own Caribbean accent. He occasionally conveys this interior tone through diction choices; for instance, he remembers sleeping under the "galvanize" and his father's "fob-watch" (*Omeros* 67, 76). More frequently, he underscores the importance of accent by specifically mentioning it: his father speaks "in an accent of polished weariness" (68); both Omeros and Seven Seas had the "look of men, . . . whose accents were born / from guttural shoal" (281); and the poet figure himself hears his "own voice correcting" the sound of the surf to pronounce Omeros's name properly (280). However, he is at his best in reworking Dante's terza rima to emphasize the unique rhythm of a Caribbean accent. "Accent is scansion," Walcott argues, and this principle animates his infusing of English with the rhythm of his own voice ("The Road Taken" 108).

Whereas Eliot minimizes rhyme in developing his English terza rima, Walcott makes rhyme more emphatic in order to adapt Dante's stanza to convey a distinct Caribbean rhythm. Consider, for example, the passage in which Warwick challenges him to speak for the women colliers:

> O Thou, my Zero, is an impossible prayer, *a*
> utter extinction is still a doubtful conceit. *b*
> Though we pray to nothing, nothing cannot be there. *a*
>
> Kneel to your load, then balance your staggering feet *b*
> and walk up that coal ladder as they do in time, *c*
> one bare foot after the next in ancestral rhyme. *c*
>
> Because Rhyme remains the parentheses of palms *d*
> shielding a candle's tongue, it is the language's *e*
> desire to enclose the loved world in its arms; *d*
>
> or heft a coal-basket; only by its stages *e*
> like those groaning women will you achieve that height *f*
> whose wooden planks in couplets lift your pages *e*
>
> higher than those hills of infernal anthracite. *f*
> There, like ants or angels, they see their native town, *g*
> unknown, raw, insignificant. They walk, you write; *f*
>
> keep to that narrow causeway without looking down, *g*
> climbing in their footsteps, that slow, ancestral beat *h*
> of those used to climbing roads; your own work owes them *i*
>
> because the couplet of those multiplying feet *h*
> made your first rhymes. Look, they climb, and no one knows them; *i*
> they take their copper pittances, and your duty *j*
>
> from the time you watched them from your grandmother's house *k*
> as a child wounded by their power and beauty *j*
> is the chance you now have, to give those feet a voice. *k*
>
> (*Omeros* 75–76)

With the telling couplet at the end of the second stanza, Walcott suggests an affinity between "time" and "rhyme," between the temporal and aural elements in this passage. He uses this affinity to solve a problem and to convey his unique rhythm. The problem is his hexameter line. He chooses it for its Homeric parallel, but as Paul Fussel suggests, any regular meter in an English line this long can become monotonous (125). Accordingly, he writes most of *Omeros* in a very loose iambic meter, so he does not tend to use meter to convey a distinct rhythm. Instead, he turns to end rhyme to transmit the exuberant pulse of Caribbean experience. In this passage he establishes the prevailing rhythm with Dante's rhyme scheme *(aba, bcb, cdc)*, but he subjects that scheme to endless variation, a syncopation found in this passage not only in the rhymed couplet of stanza 3 but also in the altered rhymes of stanzas 6 and 7. Walcott diverges from the pattern to draw attention to the representative nature of his poetic obligation to the woman coal-carriers—his "work owes them" for "no one knows them" (75)—an obligation that he fulfills by enunciating "that slow ancestral beat . . . of those multiplying feet" (75). In other words, he creolizes the Homeric line and the Dantean stanza to convey a unique Caribbean rhythm, an irregular beat that is most often heard in the popular music of jazz, calypso, or reggae; it is a way for his civic New World classicism to tap its foot to the beat of Mighty Sparrow or Bob Marley.[35] As Breslin suggests, in *Omeros* "both rhyme and meter have the homemade texture of creole traditions, stretching to accommodate many influences both high and low" (245).

Following what is now a familiar strategy, Walcott even makes the concept of rhyme a metaphor to suggest how the poet can use language to transfigure the degrading experiences of a colonial past:

> Because Rhyme remains the parentheses of palms
> shielding a candle's tongue, it is the language's
> desire to enclose the loved world in its arms;
>
> or heft a coal-basket;
>
> (75)

The metaphor is ingenious: just as the women lift, steady, and bear baskets of coal on their heads, so also the poet selects, balances, and carries forward words in a rhyme scheme; coal forms through the sedimentation of living material, and words emerge from the layering of cultures; coal feeds physical fires, and words stoke imaginative ones; and just as the women affirm their dignity through their work, so also the poet establishes his worth by perfecting his craft. However, Walcott does not only want to follow these women's example; he also wants to use his skill with language to transfigure their anonymous experience of suffering into a celebrated historical example of survival.

He conveys this ambition by alluding to Pentecost. According to the biblical account of Pentecost, the Holy Spirit appeared as a tongue of fire over the heads of the members of the early church and empowered them to speak their good news in different languages. Walcott suggests an analogous power for his poetic language: it anoints the coal-carriers' heads with its "candle's tongue" so that their story speaks to people across cultural, historical, political, and linguistic boundaries. And, just as the original Pentecost initiated the cosmopolitan community of the church, Walcott imagines a poetry that unites the dispossessed people of the New World into a new community of love after the devastation of colonialism. Walcott even suggests that language itself affirms this impulse. He imagines rhyme as the language's way of telling people that they ought to love one another—the affinity of sound modeling an ideal affinity between people. Accordingly, Walcott shows that the "political answer" of his poetry is the same as Dante's: poetry recognizes the evil in the world, but it responds best to this evil by representing an alternative ideal of love.

Walcott is not finished exploring the Dantean paradigm, for he not only follows these women to the top of the liner but also follows the composite figure of Omeros/Seven Seas up the goat trial to the sulphur pits of Soufrière. In book 1 "hell" is the "infernal anthracite hills" where the women colliers worked, but in book 7 hell is filled with anyone who exploits the region, not only the past colonial speculators, "Bennet & Ward," but also contemporary government officials, "who saw the land as views / for hotels," and "selfish" poets, who "saw only surfaces / in nature and men, and smile at their similes" (*Omeros* 74, 289, 293). Walcott includes himself in this group, saying that "pride in my craft" and "elevating myself" had landed him in this hell. This self-accusation is part of a larger shift in the final two books of *Omeros,* a shift that Walcott describes as "the point where my book pivots on itself and accuses itself of vanity" ("Reflections on *Omeros*" 233).[36] This accusation is made against the historian, Plunkett, and the poet narrator, Walcott, and it specifically challenges the "presumption [that the historian or artist is] able to elevate the ordinary, the common" (233). This challenge seems to qualify, even renounce, Warwick's earlier advice to Walcott that he perfect his craft to speak for and about the women colliers. In fact, this renunciation reinforces the priority that is implied in that earlier scene: the example of the women colliers elevates the artist rather than vice versa. It also does more. Walcott suggests that the "best poets" strive to convey the elation of the ordinary transparently, a representation in which the poet and his conventions are invisible (233). In *Omeros* he describes this transparency as the poet's desire to "enter that light beyond metaphor" (271). In an interview he points to the last few cantos of Dante's *Paradiso* as the best example of this light. It is a "light that is, . . . *beyond art.* To get beyond art is the ideal of the artist, for the anonymity is there" (Walcott, "Reflections on *Omeros*" 234).

It is aspiration fraught with paradox because language itself is inherently metaphoric. Indeed, Walcott cannot even describe it without relying on Dante's trope of light. Moreover, by describing this aspiration in terms of anonymity, he echoes another of Eliot's modernist precepts—that art should be impersonal—exactly the type of echo that he is trying to get beyond.[37] Walcott recognizes that this aspiration is quixotic, but he still represents it as his ideal of artistic humility for the public poet, an ideal of creating a work without echo, without ambition, but with gratitude for the given, for the ordinary, for the landscape and the people of the Caribbean. It is a far different Walcott from the one that Rohlehr predicts will emerge when in the late 1960s he criticizes Walcott's skepticism—his "failure to look for positives" when "he does directly observe the society"—and claims that he is "growing less and less capable of enjoying life" ("Withering" 218). Walcott does acknowledge that his claim sounds "embarrassing" and "so affected," but he still says that his "first intention" for writing *Omeros* was to "express my gratitude for the island—for the people of the island, the beauty of the island" ("Reflections on *Omeros*" 242). It is in this second Inferno scene that he tries to work through the paradoxes of this claim.

Omeros/Seven Seas leads the poet narrator into this second Inferno and saves him from slipping back into the hellish pit of selfish poets. However, just as Walcott is about to break free, a fist of ice grips him from the pit and challenges him to consider whether he has betrayed his subject to create his art:

> "You tried to render
> their lives as you could, but that is never enough;
> now in the sulphur's stench ask yourself this question,
>
> whether a love of poverty helped you
> to use other eyes, like those of that sightless stone?"
>
> (294)

The difficult interpretive question is, what is the nature of this artistic sight? Robert Hamner suggests that Walcott's "consideration of the poor has broadened his perspective," a suggestion that is accurate but too general (*Epic* 153). Rei Terada is more helpful when she argues that Walcott accuses himself of "depriving his subjects of life by *not* looking at them—which is to say, by looking at them with too visionary [eyes]" (209). However, the proper sight is more than just realism, more than what Terada describes as a faithful "gaze *upon* life" (209); indeed, at the beginning of this canto, he condemns poets

> with eyes
> who wrote with them only, saw only surfaces
> in nature and men,
>
> (293)

Instead, Walcott suggests that the great artists have both sight and insight, both the capacity to represent the ordinary things of life faithfully and the faith that those ordinary things will convey their own radiance.

He represents his own understanding of that mode by renouncing the echoes of his cultural origins.

> My own head sank in the black mud of Soufrière,
>
> while it looked back with all the faith it could summon.
> Both heads were turned like the god of the yawning year
> on whose ridge I stood looking back where I came from.
>
> The nightmare was gone. The bust became its own past,
> I could still hear its white lines in the far-off foam,
> I woke to hear blackbirds bickering at breakfast.
>
> (294)

The syntactical structure and pronominal references of this passage are difficult, but parsing the allusions to Janus helps to clarify Walcott's point. Terada interprets the reference to Janus ("the god of the yawning year") as a reminder that Walcott and Omeros "can be seen as two halves of a single head" (208–9). However, it is more consistent with the preceding sections to view this Janus figure as another iteration of Walcott's multifaceted tradition, as the two faces of the composite figure of tradition—Omeros and Seven Seas. This interpretation also makes more sense of the allusion. As the Romans would appeal to Janus, their god of beginnings and endings, to secure the outcome of their endeavors, Walcott petitions both Omeros and Seven Seas, his ideal of the fictive origins of a New

World tradition, to assure the present and future of his work. However, this mastering of cultural origins is not enough to achieve true poetic greatness because it still depends on metaphors and allusions. Instead, he suggests that he masters the past in order to renounce its importance and that this renunciation enables him to see and represent what is truly important in the present. He awakes from the nightmare of art and history, a nightmare in which the present is always compared with the past and the contemporary Caribbean is compared with the classical Greek, and revels instead in the wonder of the ordinary—"blackbirds bickering at breakfast" (294).

Walcott suggests that this nightmarish struggle with Omeros/Seven Seas has helped him to move "beyond art," even if only temporarily, by opening the next chapter with a simple declarative statement: "My light was clear" (294). This transparency cannot be sustained—the metaphoric fecundity of language and his own imagination tempt him on every page—but it remains his ideal for the public poet for the remainder of the book. It is the ordinary elation that he finds in the Caribbean sea, "a wide page without metaphors" (296); in the Caribbean sun, which gives him "that other sight" (298); and in the Caribbean people, who still believed "work was prayer" (301).

With his multicultural Pentecost and his purging of poetic ambition, Walcott modifies religious concepts that Eliot explores in a more orthodox way in *Little Gidding*. Eliot evokes and conflates the image of Pentecost and the need for penitence most directly in section 4 of *Little Gidding*. He connects this passage to his earlier Dantean canto by repeating a tightly interwoven rhyme scheme and the air-raid context. The earlier canto ends with the familiar compound ghost advising the poet to seek expiation for personal moral failure: "From wrong to wrong the exasperated spirit / Proceeds, unless restored by that refining fire" (142). The fourth section extends the ghost's advice into a collective lesson for a nation at war. Eliot transforms the nightly bombing runs over London into an image of an apocalyptic Pentecost that calls a country, if not a civilization, to repentance:

> The dove descending breaks the air
> With flame of incandescent terror
> Of which the tongues declare
> The one discharge from sin and error.
> The only hope, or else despair
> Lies in the choice of pyre or pyre—

To be redeemed from fire by fire.

Who then devised the torment? Love.
(143–44)

Pentecost, renunciation, and love are common themes for both poets, but there are differences in emphasis between Eliot's more orthodox and Walcott's more aesthetic understanding of these religious ideas. Walcott redeploys the imagery of Pentecost to suggest that his poetry is inspired by the heroic survival of ordinary people, whereas Eliot recasts this biblical trope as a prophetic call for ordinary people to repent. Walcott represents his confrontation with Omeros/Seven Seas as primarily an artistic challenge, a need to renounce his poetic strategies and ambition in order to "see" and depict the radiance of the ordinary. Eliot represents his confrontation with God as a common spiritual challenge, a decision that all people must face: whether to follow their own will, which leads to the fires of Hell, or to submit to God's will and the purging fires of Purgatory. Walcott imagines a poetics of love rooted in human affection and community; Eliot desires a poetics of redemption by Love as a personification of God.

These differences are, however, a matter of degree rather than of kind. Walcott and Eliot share a common modernist assumption about poetry's social function. They agree that poetry can communicate a message across national and cultural boundaries—it can speak in "different tongues"—both because it renews a particular language and because it conveys ideas that are not bound to a particular language. They also agree that poetry can offer ideals that advance a sense of cultural wholeness for a broader community: it can help people see beyond their individual experiences and affirm a common identity. And both affirm a poetic idealism that recognizes the alienation of human experience—the suffering of the colliers or the bombing of Britain—but responds to that alienation by offering alternative ideals to help humans understand that experience—the radiant courage of the colliers' survival or the call for contemporary repentance for a civilization. Readers may well accept or reject these particular idealist alternatives according to their own convictions; however, the idealist stance itself remains a powerful modernist rationale for poetry's social function. Indeed, this idealist stance may well be the most enduring feature of cosmopolitan modernism. As Edouard Glissant contends, "Artistic creation . . . remains vital" because "one needs a voice to give expression to common ideals" (*Caribbean Discourse* 235–36). Poets are particularly well equipped to fulfill that role because of their sensitivity to the language(s) that shape those ideals. By enriching the capacity of language to communicate, poets can expand the range of ideals that can be contemplated by a community, as well as express those ideals more precisely.

Walcott and Eliot aspire to fulfill this role by making their poetry more transparent, a refining of their craft, language, and personal motives to make their work a more perspicuous expression of their communities' ideals. In contrast, Brathwaite aspires to fulfill his public role by making the language of his poetry more opaque, by making visible the colonial conventions of poetry and language in order to replace them with conventions that represent an alternative cultural ideal. Brathwaite's example is important because it offers an alternative method (making language visible) for achieving the common modernist ambition (imagining a new cultural ideal).

Brathwaite's Visible Pentecost

In *Barabajan Poems* (1994) Brathwaite also evokes the trope of Pentecost, although he is reluctant to call it that, to suggest poetry's social function. It is a trope that illustrates the consistency of his commitment to representing both the Afro-Caribbean folk tradition and nation language. Indeed, *Barabajan Poems* itself uniquely enables readers to examine the persistence of Brathwaite's commitments, for he describes it not only as an autobiography but also as a "collected poems" and a critical self-commentary ("Newstead" 658). As Lawrence Lipking suggests, a volume of collected poetry such as this one should be considered the "modern equivalent of the epic," for it enables the reader to assess the achievement of the modern writer as a public poet (70). While Brathwaite has been criticized in the past for excessively recycling earlier poems in subsequent volumes, *Barabajan Poems* is different because of its use of Sycorax video-style and its expository approach.[38] He reiterates, revises, and expounds on earlier poems in his new visual style in an attempt to synthesize and extend the interrelated themes of his career. Poetry as a form of spiritual possession is one of those themes, and he develops it in *Barabajan Poems* by extensively reworking and commenting on "Angel/Engine" from *Mother Poem.*

He begins by explaining how he came to write "Angel/Engine." He returns to Barbados in 1972 to discover that the main part of his great-uncle Robert's house had been neglected to the point of ruin;[39] however, the carpentry shop, the "shattered Sunday shop" of "Ogun," had been saved and converted into a Zion meeting house (*Barabajan Poems* 166). Zionism or Zion Revivalism is a syncretistic Christian sect in the Caribbean arising from a Pan-African myalism and a Native Baptist tradition (Chevannes

6–7). Like Walcott's Soufrière, this carpenter shop resonates supernaturally in Brathwaite's own private mythology. He conceives of the shop as a mystical doorway, a "tonnelle," through which he can reverse the journey of the Middle Passage and reconnect Barbados to its cultural origins in Africa. In Soufrière, Walcott conflates Omeros/Seven Seas with Janus, the Roman god of beginnings and doorways, to secure a blessing for the genesis of his New World tradition. Brathwaite, on the other hand, still speaks of his uncle as "**Legba**—the limping/crippled Africa god of the crossroads of beginnings & opening doors" (172). Moreover, he still represents his uncle as a composite persona of the Afro-Caribbean cultural tradition, a persona that conflates religious (Legba, Shango, and Ogun), historical (Toussaint Louverture), folk (John Henry), and popular (Bob Marley, Duke Ellington, and John Coltrane) figures (*Barabajan Poems* 172–73). Walcott broadens his representation of the Caribbean tradition with Omeros/Seven Seas, but he still emphasizes the formative role of Western literary sources. In contrast, Brathwaite reconceives of his Uncle Bob'ob only to deepen his commitment to an Afro-Caribbean oral tradition that emerges primarily from African and popular sources of culture.

Brathwaite recounts arriving at his uncle's converted shop during a "Wednesday Night Prayer Meeting" and overhearing the singing, clapping, drumming, and dancing of the Zion ritual of "possession." Brathwaite employs this ritual of possession as a metaphor not just of the "cultural affirmation" of Afro-Caribbean life, as Rhonda Cobham suggests (302), but also of poetic inspiration. Brathwaite says of that evening: "I was privileged to xperience for the first time the ?phenomenon of possession & to ?discover that it increasingly ?coincides w/ the ?phenomenon of the writing of a poem" ("Newstead" 657). The question marks accentuate the difficulty of finding the right words to describe this experience. As he listens to the sounds arising from the service—the sounds of drums beating, tambourines clashing, hands clapping and rubbing, feet stamping, and voices singing—he slowly becomes aware of an "alteration of consciousness" occurring within this place, an alteration of a "Newstead peasant/'anglican'" religious service into a ritual of "possession" by a "transAfrican Shango" (657). Rohlehr describes this as a move from "Christian Pentecostalism" to "something older and closer to the primal, a movement truer to the first and original nature of the congregation" ("The Problem" 22). Citing Eliot's Sweeney, however, Brathwaite expresses his frustration in trying to describe this alteration in Standard English and with biblical allusions:

> ('I gotta use words/ I gotta use/ words when I talk/ to you') like *'And when the Day of Pentecost had fully come & they were gathered together in one place'* which I invoke because that at least you 'know' even if only by report but which you accept because it's *'in the Bible'* so? not so? no? (*Barabajan Poems* 170–71)

The allusion to Pentecost still aligns this Zion worship service too closely with Christianity, but Brathwaite cannot dispense with the allusion without risking the intelligibility and significance of the possession service for his audience. It is the same dilemma that he faces in developing his Sycorax video-style. He contends that to represent Afro-Caribbean culture and language accurately, he cannot rely on a colonial literary tradition or the conventions of Standard English; however, to represent Afro-Caribbean culture and language intelligibly, he must have some shared linguistic and cultural conventions. So, in developing his Sycorax video-style he sets himself the heroic task of establishing new linguistic and cultural conventions so that his audience might quite literally *see* how this religious service reveals "the presence—*persistence*— . . . in the Caribbean/New World generally—of **Legba**" (172).

Contrasting the moment of possession in "Angel/Engine" with Walcott's Pentecost image illustrates the difference between their alternative approaches. Whereas Walcott imagines "Rhyme" as a metaphor to suggest the language's love of the world, Brathwaite breaks words into their phonetic parts and shifts them to the right margin, a method both to disrupt standard conventions and to represent the recovery of the sound of African speech in nation language. At this prayer meeting in his uncle's shop Brathwaite hears "new languages tongues of the water we had not known before or rather had forgotten forgotten till this moment" (182). He describes them as "Bajan Igbo voices the voices of the clamourous returning tongues. . . . It's an xperience I say that can describe only as IGBO and that will have to stand for sign & symbol of what happened" (182). The sound of Shango's name becomes more pronounced in the poem, and the name of the Christian God becomes truncated and then disappears altogether. As Brathwaite describes this process, "the **g** (as in god) is contracted, then imploded to **gg**; & then the awesome 'task' of converting gutturals (**gg**'s) to sibilants—the snake voice of Damballa/ Shango in the oumfort" ("Newstead" 657). Brathwaite wants his poetry to serve a social function by bringing about this conversion, by recasting the visual representation of nation language to transform its capacity to signify the Afro-Caribbean experience, by deforming Standard English to replace it with nation language. However, he knows that he has not fully achieved this conversion. By the end of the poem the speaker still cannot fully name Shango as the God that possesses her (*Barabajan Poems* 201–2; see fig. 2).

Joseph Donahue contends that Brathwaite's speaker is unable to "say either 'God' or 'Shango'" because either "articulation or inscription will commit [her] to nothing less than a cosmology" (280). However, the speaker's inability seems less a question of ambivalence and more a question of capacity. It does not seem enough for Brathwaite, in other words, that he makes a figurative connection between a Zion prayer meeting and a Shango ritual of possession. He wants the poem to bring about an actual change in linguistic and cultural conventions and practice; he wants his poetry to enable the speaker and participants in the service to identify Shango. However, he also suggests that it may not be possible, that the "nature of the Caribbean experience . . . cuts some of our African experience off" (quoted in Rohlehr, "The Problem" 22). He laments not having more "time" to show how this "Xperience" leads to the "confidence & knowledge & skills of self & communal survival" and how to "cope with the persistent legacies of the plantation—loneliness . . . disappointment . . . dispossession . . . poverty & fear" (*Barabajan Poems* 184). However, it appears to be less a matter of time and more a matter of the difficulty of the task that he has set for himself, the task of radically changing the fundamental linguistic and cultural conventions of the community to the point that he would change the community's actual experience.

It is not right, however, to dismiss Brathwaite's poem simply because he has not met his own ambitious goals, just as it is not right to dismiss Walcott's poetry for failing to match the breadth of his interethnic rhetoric or for relying on figuration to speak of poetic transparency. Instead, we should respect the poetic innovations that emerge from their aspirations even if those innovations do not fully realize their ambitions. Indeed, even though the poetry of Walcott's *Omeros* is startlingly different in its tropes, conventions, and appearance from the poetry of Brathwaite's *Barabajan Poems,* the two books advance complementary arguments about the poet's social function. They both conceive of the poet's obligation to his community primarily in terms of an obligation to represent the community's tradition and language. Walcott's postcolonial Pentecost offers a poetic ideal of love by representing a reciprocal relationship between his poetry and the "poetry" of the language and lives of women coal-carriers from Saint Lucia. Brathwaite's Pentecost imagines a poetics of recovery

Shango

as she struggles to name almost names him the
train comin in/ comin in/ comin in wid de rain

i de go
huh

i de go
shhhhhhhhaaaaaaa

under de rattle & pain

i de go
huh

i de go
hah

an a black curl callin my name

praaaaze be to
praaaaze be to
praaaaze be

sh

praaaaze be to
praaaaze be to
praaaaze be to

shang

praaaaze be to

sh

praaaaze be to

gg

praaaaze be to
praaaaze be to
praaaaze be to

sssssssssssssssssssssssssssssssshhhhhhhhhhhhhhhhhhhhhhhhh

an de train comin in wid
de rain

['Angel/Engine', **Mother Poem**, pp98-103][52*]

Fig. 2. Sycorax video-style version of "Angel/Ængine" in Kamau Brathwaite's *Barabajan Poems, 1492–1992,* pp. 201–2 (Courtesy of Kamau Brathwaite and Savacou Publications)

for Barbadians by repossessing these women worshipers with the reality of their Igbo origins. Both repeat elements and tropes from Eliot's modernist defense of poetry, but both are convincing primarily because they express their own discrepant Caribbean experience of modernity. It is the difference between a poetry that is inspired by the swift or the train, and it is through examining this final set of tropes that this study of these discrepant cosmopolitan modernisms comes to a close.

Epilogue

THIS STUDY began with Eliot's travels to the Caribbean as a trope for the migration and naturalization of modernism by Brathwaite and Walcott, a trope that suggests how modernism has become what James Clifford calls a "traveling culture." Indeed, *modernism* functions in this study as *travel* functions in Clifford's theory: it is a "translation term" of "apparently general application used for comparison in a strategic and contingent way" (*Routes* 39). Such terms always carry the "taint of location by class, gender, race, and a certain literariness," but that tainted condition also is useful in reminding us of the limits of comparative concepts (39). As Clifford suggests, all translation terms of global comparison only "get us some distance *and* fall apart" (39). The theory of discrepant cosmopolitan modernism has sought to travel that distance and explain the complex interrelationships between these poets, all the while recognizing that it has the potential to "fall apart" at the termination point of any particular line of inquiry.

Eliot, Brathwaite, and Walcott also turn to the metaphor of travel to suggest their poetic aspirations, and it seems fitting to close this study of modernism's journey by comparing these poets' tropes of travel. These tropes reflect the different but related traditions that these writers construct for their poetry and their audiences. These tropes remind us of poetry's unique attention to language as the medium of human experience. They are important because they expand the possible justifications for poetry, justifications that are needed now more than ever as poetry finds its cultural sphere of influence increasingly curtailed by the pervasiveness and immediacy of television, film, music, and fiction. Finally, these tropes are important because they are different, and these differences deepen our understanding of modernism's discrepant cosmopolitanism.

In *Little Gidding* Eliot relies on bird figures—the peregrine and the dove, in particular—as his images of poetic inspiration. These birds convey Eliot's sense of poetic inspiration as a transcultural and spiritual experience. Just as the peregrine takes its long migratory flights without regard to political, cultural, or geographic borders, the poet too should travel imaginatively beyond political, cultural, geographical, and linguistic frontiers; the poet should be the "explorer beyond the frontiers of ordinary consciousness" ("What Dante Means to Me" 134). Eliot's imagery evokes the romantic sense of poetic inspiration as emerging from a transcendent source; and his "dove descending" recasts this experience of the transcendence in specifically Christian terms. He represents Christ's incarnation—the Word becoming flesh—as the paradigm of poetic inspiration: the inspired poet embodies eternal ideals in language to edify his or her community. As A. D. Moody argues, *Little Gidding* "offers itself as a religious ritual for the time—as *the* ritual by which a foundering civilisation might be recovered" (*Thomas Stearns Eliot* 262). Eliot enacts this ritual in a specific time and place, "a secluded chapel . . . now and England," but he implies its wider relevance for Europe, if not the world. While Brathwaite and Walcott neither affirm the ideology of Eliot's ritual nor define their communities similarly, they also employ tropes of traveling that represent poetic inspiration as a paradigmatic ritual to restore the wholeness of a community.

In his comments on "Angel/Engine" Brathwaite suggests that it is all right that the speaker does not "quite reach . . . 'Shango'" because "she is invested with the power of the train" (quoted in Rohlehr, "The Problem" 22). The "power of the train" is the power of this poetic ritual of possession to enable the speaker and her audience to take the metaphoric journey and reconnect Barbados in particular and the Caribbean in general with Africa. Brathwaite describes "Angel/Engine" as part of the folk and oral tradition of "trainsongs" of the African diaspora in the New World, a tradition that he finds, for example, in the work songs about John Henry, the spirituals about a train to glory, the jazz of John Coltrane, and the contemporary kaiso of Calypso Rose (*Barabajan Poems* 369–70). In "Angel/Engine" he hears the steam release of the engine in the hyperventilating breaths of the women; he detects the "characteristic forward moving rumble of trainwheels" in the stamping feet of the dancers; and he recognizes the train whistles in the wails and shrieks of the participants (*Barabajan Poems* 188–89, 369–70). This trope of the train aptly conveys Brathwaite's desire for a more immanent sense of inspiration. The inspired Afro-Caribbean poet is someone physically possessed by religious and cultural forces that originate in Africa but are currently expressed in Caribbean popular culture. Just as a train carries its passengers on a journey, Shango possesses the worshipers (and then the poet) to take them on a cultural journey. And just as the train's physical operations convey the hypnotic rhythm of the journey, Brathwaite represents the rhythms of nation language possessing these women in this religious and cultural ritual. The train travels on rails that establish a direct, contiguous, and physical link between a place of origin and a destination, and Brathwaite aspires to create an analogous poetic ritual that establishes the religious, linguistic, and cultural links between Africa and the Caribbean.

While Brathwaite's train metaphor suggests a more physical, more immanent understanding of poetic inspiration than Eliot's bird imagery, they use these tropes to claim surprisingly similar roles as public poets. Eliot aspires to become the most European of writers, and he seeks to fulfill that aspiration by becoming less "provincial" without ceasing to be "local" ("What Dante Means to Me" 134–35). Similarly, Brathwaite understands his poetry as contributing to the literature of the African diaspora in the New World, but it is a contribution that he achieves primarily by representing the specificity of his experience in Ghana, Barbados, and Jamaica (*Barabajan Poems* 22–23). In other words, Eliot and Brathwaite both conceive of their poetry in relation to a specific and a transatlantic cultural community, but they define that cosmopolitan community along different latitudinal lines. By definition, then, Eliot and Brathwaite create complementary modernist poetics that are, respectively, Eurocentric and Afrocentric in their orientation. Either writer's orientation limits the cosmopolitan scope of his modernism; considered together, both writers contribute to creating a cosmopolitan modernism that recognizes both orientations as important. Indeed, an evaluation of Eliot's or Brathwaite's cosmopolitan influence should depend, not on the propriety of their defending their poetry in relation to a particular cultural community—poets always write within a cultural context and to a particular audience—but on the potential of their poetry to become an object of transcultural exchange. Do they speak in a way that benefits not only those who identify with their cultural tradition but also those who consider themselves estranged from, if not completely outside, that tradition?

We are just beginning to be in a position to judge Eliot's achievement according to such a standard because enough time has passed for critics to begin to evaluate how several generations of poets have responded to his work. Charles Altieri and James Longenbach have led the way in telling the story of Eliot's positive influence on contemporary American poets, such as John Ashbery and Jorie Graham, but it is a narrative that needs to be expanded to include writers from a variety of other cultural backgrounds.[1] The purpose of this study has been in part to respond to that need and trace Eliot's influence on Brathwaite and Walcott, but the lessons of this study are repeated in a variety of other cultural contexts. For instance, Northern Ireland's Seamus Heaney says that "reading T. S. Eliot and reading about T. S. Eliot were equally formative experiences" in his career ("The Government" 91). The African American novelist Ralph Ellison claims that his "real transition to writing" came when "*The Waste Land* seized my mind" (202–3). The Nigerian poet John Pepper Clark-Bekederemo recalls introducing the "New Greats . . . Pound, Eliot, and Yeats" (quoted in Nwoga 203) to his friend and fellow Nigerian poet Christopher Okigbo, and both of them recast certain modernist poetic strategies in developing their own sense of a Nigerian/African Anglophone modernism. Or consider Agha Shahid Ali, a Kashmiri poet writing in English, who has written a critical study on Eliot's role as an editor and whose poetry reflects his deep and innovative engagement with Eliot's thought and poetry. Howard Young has edited a book of essays looking at Eliot's influence among Hispanic modernist writers,[2] and Sanford Schwartz contends that similar bibliographical and critical studies could be "assembled for Continental Europe, Africa, the Middle East, and various regions of Asia" in order for us to understand the "larger patterns" of Eliot's "international influence" ("T. S. Eliot" 253). As these examples make clear, Eliot's transcultural influence extends beyond the limits of his own Eurocentric focus.

It is still too early to assess fully Brathwaite's cosmopolitan influence, but he recognizes both the importance and the difficulty of achieving this goal: "My work starts from my yard while trying to speak to you in yours; but this predicates that you will be DOING THE SAME THING: speaking to me from yr yard & LISTENING w/ this understanding to me as I try to be listening w/ understanding to you" ("A Post-Cautionary Tale" 75). In other words, he recognizes that the capacity to generate transcultural, cross-generational exchange should be one of the measures of a poet's success, but he doubts the willingness of others to engage in this exchange. Breiner suggests that Brathwaite is achieving this type of influence in the Caribbean. He argues that *The Arrivants* "is the single most *consequential* event in the history of West Indian poetry to date" because of Brathwaite's skillful use of nation language and his oral performance of the poem in public readings and recordings. Breiner traces how these features created an audience ready to hear the work of contemporary West Indian poets such as David Dabydeen, Anthony McNeill, Linton Kwesi Johnson, and Michael Smith. Even though many of these writers do not overtly recognize Brathwaite's role, Breiner suggests that his poetry "moved the boundaries of expression to their present position, and thereby liberalized the climate of taste and critical judgment in which all West Indian poets work" (*An Introduction* 177, 180).[3]

However, Breiner also recognizes that the influence of Brathwaite's subsequent work in the Caribbean and beyond remains uncertain. The scope of Eliot's international influence depended, to a degree, on the cultural "marketing" force of Ezra Pound, Faber & Faber, and the New Critics. The young Walcott or Brathwaite perceived Eliot as a representative modern poet at least in part because he was one of the few modern poets readily available in the Caribbean, an availability largely determined by the decisions of publishers and educational institutions. In contrast, Brathwaite's relationship to these important cultural institutions seems more uncertain. Gordon Rohlehr has been the most forceful advocate for Brathwaite's poetry in the Caribbean and beyond during the last thirty years,[4] and a broadening critical interest is evidenced by books such as Silvio Torres-Saillant's *Caribbean Poetics* and Laurence Breiner's *Introduction to West Indian Poetry,* as well as the collections of essays edited by Stewart Brown *(The Art of Kamau Brathwaite)* and Timothy Reiss *(For the Geography of a Soul)*. Moreover, while Brathwaite has become estranged from some in the Caribbean academic community,[5] he has received more institutional support from the United States, his 1994 Neustadt Prize and his post as professor of comparative literature at New York University being the two most notable examples. These are promising signs that Brathwaite will receive the attention he deserves, but it still remains uncertain whether this interest will be sustained.

In particular, it may be difficult to sustain the interest in Brathwaite because finding publishers for his work has become more difficult as his visual experiments have grown bolder. While Oxford University Press published the individual volumes in his first two trilogies and *Other Exiles,* he has had to self-publish many of his more recent works, including *Sappho Sakyi's Meditations* (1989), *Shar* (1990), *Barabajan Poems* (1994), and *conVERSations with Nathaniel Mackey* (1999). He suspects that the metropolitan publishers have become more reluctant because his Sycorax video-style challenges the colonial conventions of publishing more directly and "because the ideas come from Caliban" ("An Interview" 30). Breiner is likely more accurate when he suggests that Brathwaite's later poetry may not "travel well" because its graphic conventions "make not just performance but even sense inaccessible" (*An Introduction* 193). Either way, Brathwaite is caught in a familiar postcolonial bind. The success of his effort to decolonize the visual conventions of poetry may well depend on the dissemination of his ideas by a neocolonial publishing industry that is largely responsible for perpetuating those conventions.

Again, the prospects are not completely bleak for the future publishing of Brathwaite's more experimental work. *The Zea Mexican Diary* (1994) and *DreamStories* (1994), both written in Sycorax video-style, were published by the University of Wisconsin Press and Longman, respectively. More significantly, New Directions Books has just recently published the first collected edition of Brathwaite's second trilogy, *Ancestors* (2001), a "reimagination" of *Mother Poem, Sun Poem,* and *X/Self* in Sycorax video-style. Brathwaite will need to continue to receive that publishing support if the influence of his New World modernist poetics is to spread.

Walcott does not face the challenge of publication, having established his relationship with the "ocean liner" of institutional support; however, that ocean liner is more a trope of necessity than of choice. He chooses the image of the swift, the "*Cypseloides Niger, l'hirondelle des Antilles*" (*Omeros* 88), to convey his idealist sense of poetic inspiration. "I followed a sea-swift to both sides of this text," his poet character claims toward the end of *Omeros* (319). It is an image that comes to him more by chance than by design: a friend is reported to have given him a pamphlet listing all of the birds of the Caribbean, and "there was so many it amazed me, and then I found myself thinking about scansion in the list, the rhythm, and so, there they are" (quoted in Bruckner 398). Even so, it is an apt image. James Bond, the ornithologist whom Maud relies on for information about birds in the West Indies, describes swifts as "members of a cosmopolitan family," the most "aerial of land birds," and "highly gregarious, usually associating in flocks and nesting in colonies" (129). Just as Eliot's peregrine represents his nomadic, spiritual pilgrimage as a public poet, Walcott's swift conveys an analogous understanding of his poetic relationship to the Caribbean experience.

Drawing on the swift's crisscross path and cruciform shape in flight, Walcott initially invokes the bird as a sign of transcendent blessing on the human capacity to create. So, for example, before Achille begins cutting down the tree for his canoe, he sees overhead "the swift / crossing the cloud-surf," and he responds by making "a swift sign of the cross" with his cutlass (*Omeros* 6). Indeed, the Christian God sends the sea-swift to Achille not only to lead him back to Africa but also to bless the trip, its wings representing "the sign of my crucifixion" (134). The swift is also sent to bless Walcott's poetic craft. Seven Seas tells him that "the sea-swift was sent to you: / to circle yourself and your island with this art" (291).

Walcott's character even imagines the act of writing, an act "like the sea-dipping swift," to be "holier" than the blessing of his friendship with Philoctete (295). By affirming the transcendence of poetic inspiration, Walcott contends for the sacredness of the public poet's task to reword experience.

John Figueroa challenges Walcott's image of the swift as being too transcendent and otherworldly. He suggests that it is not enough for "modern humans" who have experienced true exile and continuing injustice, people "driven from the islands, dragged from Africa, beaten across the snow-floured plains of North America, hastening from Poland and Nazi Germany," to be "consoled only from time to time by birds that are free to leave" and "consoled by something that is to happen *after this exile*" (209). However, Figueroa's criticism fails to give enough credit to the tangible and direct influence of the swift on the characters' lives, the capacity of poetry to change the past's influence on the present even if it cannot change the past events themselves.

For example, the swift plays a central role in both Achille's imagined return to Africa and Ma Kilman's healing of Philoctete's wound. For Achille the swift is a transatlantic muse who prompts him to question "his name and its origin" and who figuratively pulls his canoe "home" to Africa (*Omeros* 130–31). However, Walcott represents Achille's trip as an important intermediary step, but not the conclusive end, to his understanding of the relationship between African and Caribbean culture. On this trip Achille recognizes that he cannot recover Africa as his cultural home. He tries to invoke an African religious past, but the sacred circle of trees "ignored his incantation" (140). He tries to remedy the violence of slavery, but the vines of history "looped his tendon," and his art is damaged when he falls: "he fell hard . . . the bow beside him and the broken oar" (148). What is most important, Achille cannot recover his linguistic past, for he has not only forgotten Afolabe's language but also adopted a completely different conception of how language works. Afolabe affirms his belief in language's referential capacity—"a name means something" (137)—but Achille only understands language as mimicry: "the gift / of this sound whose meaning I still do not care to know" (138).

Walcott distances himself from Achille's trip, claiming that only "half of me was with him. One half with the midshipman / by a Dutch canal" (135); however, he represents this reversal of the Middle Passage in a way that reflects his more modulated views of the relationship between African and Caribbean culture. He still does not believe that he can invoke African gods, speak African languages, or change African history, but he is now more willing to recognize implicit cultural links—Achille sees the music and dancing at the tribe's feast as "the same, the same" as at a Carnival celebration (143)—and the importance of this basic claim of identity—when Achille sees the "sea-swift" writing "Afolabe" in the sky, he is finally ready to proclaim himself "the king going home" (159). As Hamner suggests, Achille gains his "birthright" through this experience of "racial memory," but "Africa is no longer his personal home" (*Epic* 77). It is an imaginative homecoming that begins with the dream of Achille, but it is only completed through the healing of Philoctete.

With Ma Kilman's healing of Philoctete, Walcott represents the source of Caribbean cultural healing in the transplanted roots of African experience. Instead of traveling east to take Achille to Africa, the swift in the Ma Kilman section travels west to the Caribbean, carrying "the strong seed in its stomach . . . the cure that proceeds every wound" (*Omeros* 238–39). The seed takes root in Saint Lucian soil and grows into a vine that is strengthened through suffering, "its power, / rooted in bitterness" (237). Indeed, Walcott suggests that what remains of African experience, a few fragments of its religious and cultural practice, is concentrated in the vine's "stinking flower" (242). In Africa, Achille could name the African gods, but he could not move them to act with his prayer. In Saint Lucia, Ma Kilman admits that these gods "had lost their names, / and, therefore, considerable presence," but she still feels that "their sounds were within her, / subdued in the river of her blood" (242). Achille is so culturally, linguistically, and spiritually dispossessed in Africa that he cannot heal the wounds of his ancestors' tribe. In contrast, Ma Kilman is possessed by Erzulie, Shango, and Ogun, and they lead her to the transplanted African flower that eventually cures Philoctete's wound. Even though this scene moves Walcott considerably closer to Brathwaite's position, he still represents this healing as a recovery from the shame of losing this African heritage rather than a recovery of the renewed presence of this heritage in the region. As Breslin suggests, the African gods are "resurrected" in *Omeros,* but as "metaphors rather than objects of belief" (258).

Indeed, compare Ma Kilman's possession with the possession of the women in Brathwaite's "Angel/Engine." When Brathwaite's women are possessed, they make sounds that establish the contemporary presence of African languages in the Caribbean experience. When Ma Kilman undergoes possession, she exorcizes the indignity of the loss of those languages. Brathwaite sees the possession service as material evidence that "**there is at last what there always was / Shango**" (*Barabajan Poems* 200–201). Walcott sees it as a way to cure the

tribal shame.
A shame for the loss of words, and a language tired

of accepting that loss, and then all accepted.
(*Omeros* 248)

This acceptance of loss is exemplified by the sacrifice of the swift. It survives its transatlantic flight to transplant the healing seed in Caribbean sand, but it dies "with one frail cry, since swifts are not given to song" (239). For Walcott the songs of African languages are no longer available to benefit his poetry, but their absence can still animate it. Moreover, while Brathwaite depicts the Wednesday-night prayer meeting as a recurring ritual that could develop into a growing communal awareness of Afro-Caribbean cultural connections, Walcott represents Ma Kilman's possession as a single event. Cultural healing begins with recognizing these Afro-Caribbean cultural roots, but it also depends on a cathartic acceptance of the loss of almost all of these African cultural, religious, and linguistic practices in the Caribbean. It is an acceptance that he describes as feeling "the shame, the self-hate / draining from all our bodies" (245) or as having the "memory still there although all the pain was gone" (277).

Critics differ on the extent of this healing. Thieme suggests that Philoctete is completely cured of his "ancestral wound . . . by reversing the trauma of the Middle Passage through an African-derived remedy" (186). Ramazani suggests that Philoctete and the narrator may not have achieved a "definitive healing" by accepting Ma Kilman's cure, but they are restored to the point that they can testify to the hope of the Caribbean future ("Wound" 414). In either case, after his cure Philoctete is more often referred to as Philo, a renaming that evokes his renewed capacity for brotherly love, and he also accepts the role of godfather to Helen's unborn child, a role that obligates him to ensure the child's future (*Omeros* 318). He is healed enough to serve the community.

Walcott's claim can be challenged both empirically and ideologically. It is not certain empirically that contemporary Caribbean cultural practices are as removed from African influences as Walcott seems to contend.[6] Moreover, even if Walcott's empirical assumptions are true, Brathwaite and others would challenge his ideological claims that this loss has generated a sense of "shame" and "self-hate" or that accepting this loss is the best way to expiate this shame. These challenges are formidable but not necessarily decisive, for Walcott defines his poetry in relation to a broader public than Brathwaite's Afro-Caribbean audience. While Walcott recognizes a distinct need for accepting loss without revenge in the Afro-Caribbean community, he also contends that this need is common to all human beings. As Ramazani shows, all of the major characters in *Omeros* suffer wounds that metaphorically speak of human loss—not just Philoctete's lacerated shin but also the death of Catherine Weldon's son, not just the narrator's failed marriage but also Plunkett's loss of Maud ("Wound" 414). By universalizing this need for healing, Walcott suggests that there is a common experience upon which he can rely to articulate his interethnic, cross-cultural, and cosmopolitan New World poetics. He illustrates, in other words, what Kwame Anthony Appiah identifies as the key contribution of postcolonial writers to contemporary poetics, their concern for the "ethical universal" of "humanism—the concern for human suffering" (*In My Father's House* 155).[7]

Indeed, Walcott responds most directly to this human concern through his description of Maud's quilt, a work of art that depicts Walcott's cosmopolitan ideal for the contemporary public poet. He describes Maud's quilt to show that the racial diversity of the Caribbean is the racial diversity of the world: "And those birds Maud Plunkett stitched into her green silk / with sibylline steadiness were what islands bred: / brown dove, black grackle, herons like ewers of milk" (*Omeros* 313). He also uses it to contend that English is enhanced as a common language when speakers from different cultural traditions choose to use it:

> The African swallow, the finch from India
> now spoke the white language of a tea-sipping tern,
> with the Chinese nightingales. . . ,
>
> . . . the Persian falcon, . . .
> . . . .
>
> . . . each origin
> enriching the islands to which their cries were sewn.
> (313–14)

And by depicting Maud's quilt as her shroud, he also suggests that his poetry brings about healing by commemorating the painful experience of loss, not only the postcolonial experience of losing one's cultural origins but also the human experience of losing a loved one.[8]

In short, Walcott defends poetry by accepting Plato's ancient critiques of it. He accepts that the poet is possessed, not by Plato's divine madness, Eliot's Holy Spirit, or Brathwaite's Shango, but by a sacred belief in the power of human creativity. He accepts that poetry is mimicry, not mimicry as a derivative copying of an ideal form but mimicry as exposing the absence of all origins, which in turn allows the poet to offer new ideals through which to imagine the contemporary human experience. And he accepts that poetry operates through its rhetorical skill with language, not to circumvent reason by arousing people's passion, but to promote cultural healing by serving as a "radiant affliction," a language that "carries its own cure" by opening and cauterizing the scars of the past so that people will live more fully in the present. Just as the swift weaves together "the Atlantic rift with a needle's line" to bring together the Old and New Worlds, Walcott composes a text that he hopes will heal "the rift in the soul" (319). And it is this vision of poetry as a means to imagine anew a cosmopolitan cultural whole that is so characteristically modernist in Walcott's poetics.

Moreover, while Walcott's vision of this cosmopolitanism is different from Brathwaite's, both poets affirm the integrative impulse of modernism, for each of them aspires to shore together different fragments from the Caribbean experience. The genius of modernism's method is that it encourages us to collocate rather than choose between these two positions. It encourages us to imagine a Caribbean modernist poetics, not as coextensive with either Walcott's New World classicism or Brathwaite's Afro-Caribbean folk tradition, but as a larger whole that holds these two positions together as complementary parts. Walcott and Brathwaite each develop a modernist poetics that has its own coherent integrity, but each of these poetics should contribute to a larger, more comprehensive understanding of Anglophone Caribbean poetry. Choosing one over the other or accepting them both but considering them incommensurable would impoverish our understanding of each of them because it is only by juxtaposing them that we discover how their overlapping strengths and weaknesses contribute to the larger whole.

Indeed, this integrative impulse of modernism should not be stopped at national, regional, ethnic, or linguistic boundaries. Eliot's European modernism is a part of both Walcott's New World classicism and Brathwaite's Afro-Caribbean folk tradition but not identical with either. Cosmopolitan modernism should be understood as more than just the allusive practice of European modernists: an understanding of the larger cultural whole should emerge from juxtaposing modernist writers transnationally, cross-linguistically, and interethnically, not just Eliot, Walcott, and Brathwaite but also Joyce, Yeats, Pound, Auden, Woolf, Ali, Rushdie, Rhys, Clark-Bekederemo, Goodison, and others. These modernisms are discrepant and cosmopolitan, rooted and traveling, local and international, and it is perhaps in trying to recognize completely these complementary elements that this theory of modernism's discrepant cosmopolitanism begins to "fall apart" (Clifford, *Routes* 39). The discrepancies can proliferate to the point that any shared cosmopolitanism seems forced, or the cosmopolitanism can simplify to the point that the discrepancies seem unduly homogenized. However, modernism remains a viable poetics at the beginning of the twenty-first century and in different cultural contexts primarily because it encourages writers and readers to hold these complementary elements of human experience together. Modernism traveled well during the twentieth century because it was changed by the journey. Mapping modernism's route through Eliot, Brathwaite, and Walcott should change our understanding of these writers and this literary movement. It should also remind us that we should

> not cease from exploration
> And the end of all our exploring
> Will be to arrive at where we started
> And know the place for the first time.
> (*Little Gidding, Complete Poems* 145)

Notes

Introduction

1. Brathwaite and Walcott are clearly more than just poets: Brathwaite is also a distinguished historian and social critic, and Walcott is the leading West Indian dramatist and an accomplished painter. However, this study focuses on their poetry as the best expressions of their modernist aesthetic.

2. Of course, whether Anglo-American modernism should be called the age of Eliot is a contentious issue. For example, Marjorie Perloff claims that "no one today . . . seems eager to call the first half of the twentieth century the Eliot Era" (*The Dance* 23). James Longenbach contests her conclusion by looking at the relationship between Eliot and poets such as Elizabeth Bishop, Randall Jarrell, John Ashbery, and Jorie Graham. Part of the task of the present work is to extend Longenbach's argument to writers outside of the standard Anglo-American tradition.

3. Dash does an excellent job of summarizing the historical development of the term *New World studies* and of probing some of its inherent ambiguities (*The Other America* 1–7).

4. For the theoretical emphasis, see Britton; and many of the essays in Edmondson. For the focus on fiction, see Renk; and again Edmondson.

5. Walcott and Brathwaite both suggest that they were introduced to Eliot during their preparatory training (Walcott, "An Interview" [Hirsch] 53; Brathwaite, *Barabajan Poems* 56).

6. June Bobb has published the only other book-length study of Brathwaite and Walcott, but she does not convincingly establish their complementary contributions to a larger Caribbean poetics. She claims that the "poetry of Brathwaite and Walcott must be positioned" at the "cusp of the Caribbean modernist movement," but she mostly sees modernism as a European aesthetic that must be overcome, claiming that "the annihilation of the self inculcated in the Caribbean people" was carried out "by both European and Caribbean colonials and their modernist counterparts" (8, 226).

7. Laurence Breiner's *Introduction to West Indian Poetry* is a notable exception to this claim. He accomplishes the goal that he sets for himself "to provide categories for thinking about [Anglophone Caribbean] poetry, and to investigate the poems *as poems,* rather than as documents of social/political developments" (ix).

8. As Laurence Breiner contends, "West Indians are positioned to perceive American literature in quite different ways: as a facet of an oppressive, colonizing culture; as a liberating alternative to British writing; or even as a fraternal enterprise, a (post-)colonial literature that has only recently made its way out from under metropolitan models. The shiftiness of the relations based on these perceptions seems to make poets less vulnerable to American poetry" (*An Introduction* 202). He then illustrates this point through a short description of Brathwaite's relationship to Eliot (202–4).

9. Indeed, Brathwaite has been instrumental in describing how creolization has defined Caribbean cultural formation. The specifics of Brathwaite's argument are important, and they are discussed more fully in the next chapter. For other helpful discussions of creolization, see Dash, "Psychology"; and Glissant, *Caribbean Discourse* 97–157, esp. 134–44.

10. See *Knowledge and Experience* 142; "Tradition and the Individual Talent" 14–16; and "'*Ulysses*,' Order, and Myth."

11. Jewel Spears Brooker favors the terms "dialectical imagination" and "logic of complementarity" (16–20); Charles Altieri speaks of Eliot's "constructivist aesthetic" (198); Jeffrey Perl describes Eliot's "ambivalence" as "comprehending opposites" and "relative poetics" (*Skepticism and Modern Enmity* 48, 66–85).

12. Clifford is also careful to qualify his assertion, claiming that he is "not saying there are no locales or home or that everyone is—or should be—traveling or cosmopolitan, or deterritorialised. This is not nomadology" (*Routes* 36). Instead, he is looking for "a comparative cultural studies approach" to analyze the "dwelling *and* traveling" of cultures.

13. Readings of Walcott's work are particularly at risk for this conflating of his cosmopolitanism and Euro-American universalism.

1. Postcolonial Modernism/Modernist Postcolonialism

1. For instance, Frank Davey argues that modernism is "an international movement, elitist, imperialist, 'totalizing,' willing to appropriate the local while being condescending toward its practice" (119). Simon During also defines the goal of postcolonialism in antimodernist rhetoric, the goal being "to achieve an identity uncontaminated by universalist or Eurocentric concepts or images" (125). Georg Gugelberger feels compelled to distinguish the "bilingual, even polyglot" language in "Third World Literature" from the "polyglot aspects of the Euro-American modernist tradition" (518). For a brief overview of this debate with extensive bibliographical materials, see Parry, "The Postcolonial"; and Hutcheon, "Colonialism and the Postcolonial Condition."

2. June Bobb makes the similar mistake of equating colonialism and modernism in her study of Brathwaite and Walcott. She argues that Brathwaite and Walcott create "a New World identity as a response to the annihilation of self inculcated in Caribbean people by both European and Caribbean colonials and their modernist counterparts" (226).

3. Arnold rejects any facile sense of an evolution from modernism to postmodernism in the Caribbean. He argues that the "two terms represent competing paradigms that organize concepts and data so differently as to offer quite divergent maps of the literary Caribbean" ("Caribbean Literary Theory" 103).

4. Other critics have disputed the relationship between Brathwaite and Eliot, but primarily with passing generalizations. For example, Bruce King claims that "Brathwaite's desire to establish a cultural tradition grounded in communal ritual and his concern with individual moments of escaping from the fragmented, chaotic present into an experience of oneness, in which the artist becomes the voice of culture and its beliefs, show that he has profoundly understood Eliot" (*New English Literatures* 137). In contrast, in his review of *The Arrivants* Hayden Carruth contends that Eliot's influence is "almost entirely limited to matters of organization and structure . . . and perhaps . . . rhyming. . . . In texture, in verbal technique, in almost everything, nothing could be further from Eliot's poetry than Brathwaite's" (318). Laurence Breiner offers a short but more nuanced discussion of Brathwaite's relationship to Eliot and rightly concludes that "Brathwaite, in effect, constructs for himself precisely the Eliot he chose to imitate" (*An Introduction* 204). Ten Kortenaar is closer to King and Breiner than to Carruth in his argument, but he has the advantage of a more well conceived and developed theoretical framework.

5. In his *Caribbean Poetics* Silvio Torres-Saillant contends for the isolation of the Caribbean literary tradition as a completely unique cultural phenomenon, and Harold Bloom is, of course, the most prominent advocate of the Oedipal model of literary influence.

6. Walcott does, in fact, look to Joyce as a useful precursor for his work. For studies of Joyce as a postcolonial writer, see Chang; Lawrence, *Transcultural Joyce;* and Attridge and Howes. For studies of Yeats, see Said's "Yeats and Decolonization" in *Cultural and Imperialism;* Lloyd; Kiberd; and Ramazani's "W. B. Yeats: A Postcolonial Poet?" in *Hybrid Muse.*

7. For discussions of Eliot's anti-Semitism, see Julius; Menand; Perl, *Skepticism;* and Ricks.

8. See Perl, *Skepticism* 25–40; and Brooker 208.

9. Consider, for example, Cynthia Ozick, who contends that looking "at the condition of most poetry in America today will disclose how far behind we have left Eliot" (153). Ronald Bush insightfully shows how Eliot's ideas have been oversimplified both by his New Critical admirers and his contemporary critics (191–204). Jeffrey Perl contends that the "New Critical reading of modernism was impossibly wrong" and that if modernism "is to have a future, it will need to be freed from the embrace of loved ones" ("Passing the Time" 33). For a summary of adverse responses to Eliot, see Perl, *Skepticism* 30–40.

10. For the best study of Eliot's anthropological imagination, see Crawford; and for his interest in Indic traditions, see Kearns.

11. For example, in 1968 Dennis Scott asks Walcott about Brathwaite's distinction, and he replies: "Well, I still don't like the division [between folk and humanist] because that is a personal statement and that is a statement that Eddy and I come from different roots or different backgrounds. That is completely not true" (Walcott, "Walcott on Walcott" 12). See also Walcott, "Conversation" [Smith] 189–90.

12. Brathwaite seems to have made similar challenges to Walcott at the Association for Commonwealth Literature and Language Studies (ACLALS) conference in Jamaica in January 1971 and at Yale in February 1988. In each case Walcott found a way to avoid direct conflict (King, *Derek Walcott: A Caribbean Life* 263, 476).

13. Several other recent critics have joined Collier in correcting this binary opposition between Walcott and Brathwaite. For example, John Thieme argues that this binary "contrast does a disservice to both writers, since it obscures the discursive subtleties of their poetry" (3), and correctly concludes that "while it would be mistaken to argue that significant differences between Walcott and Brathwaite do not exist, the lines dividing them are far more blurred than many critics suggest" (4). Similarly, Nana Wilson-Tagoe argues that Walcott and Brathwaite should be viewed not "so much as poets in opposition to each other but as artists relating with differing emphases on aspects of history in the region" (11).

14. See, e.g., the brief description of the concept in Ashcroft, Griffiths, and Tiffin in *The Empire Writes Back* (146–48). Surprisingly, Bobb devotes little attention to creolization in general and almost none to Brathwaite's understanding of the concept (168–69). Dash insightfully narrates the history of the concept of creolization in the Caribbean, including Brathwaite's place in that history, but he does not develop Brathwaite's ideas with any specificity ("Psychology"). Silvio Torres-Saillant offers the most helpful discussion to date on Brathwaite's theory of creolization (130–35). See also Huggan.

15. Brathwaite's *Contradictory Omens* is closely related to *The Development of Creole Society;* indeed, identical long passages appear in both works.

16. For hybridity and liminality, see Bhabha's *Location;* for rhizomes, see Glissant's *Caribbean Discourse* and *Poetics of Relation* and Benítez-Rojo; for chutnification, see Rushdie's *Midnight's Children;* and for *métissage,* see Retamar.

17. For Brathwaite's discussion of Maroon experience, see "African Presence in Caribbean Literature" 228–32, and "Caribbean Culture" 35–41.

18. While he refers to the concepts of Maroon and nam in earlier essays, they become more central to his thinking in his essays in the 1980s, essays such as "Caribbean Culture" and "World Order Models—A Caribbean Perspective."

19. Brathwaite defines *nam* similarly in other contexts: as the "indestructible and atomic core of man's culture" ("Gods of the Middle Passage" 18) or as "an essence, an indestructible culture-core, imparting to each group an identity which in normal times one is proud enough of, but which, at times of crisis, may be fiercely defended by its possessors" ("World Order Models" 56). See also "History, the Caribbean Writer, and *X/Self*" 32–33.

20. For instance, Bobb (174–75) and Torres-Saillant (151) mention the concept of *nam* only briefly and with no discussion of its relationship to Brathwaite's theory of creolization.

21. Dash argues that Brathwaite's classification system is "conceptually ill-equipped to deal with the radical openness of the creolist model" (*The Other America* 72). Ashcroft, Griffiths, and Tiffin also recognize this problem when they suggest that "the importance of the African connection" in Brathwaite's thought "has sometimes obscured his increasing concern with Creolization" (*The Empire Writes Back* 147).

22. See Terada 18–25. Dash does discuss both Brathwaite's creolization and Walcott's mimicry in his historical survey of Caribbean literary theory, but without comparative analysis ("Psychology" 48–53). Similarly, Bobb addresses Brathwaite's creolization and Walcott's theory of mimicry separately, but she also wrongly claims that Walcott resists mimicry in order to represent him as closer to Brathwaite (95, 168–69).

23. The key essays are "What the Twilight Says: An Overture" (1970), hereinafter referred to as "Twilight"; "The Muse of History" (1974), hereinafter "Muse"; "The Caribbean: Culture or Mimicry?" (1974), hereinafter "Culture"; and *The Antilles: Fragments of Epic Memory* (1992), hereinafter *Antilles.*

24. In "Jazz and the West Indian Novel" Brathwaite makes this point explicitly: "And if in this essay I stress the African aspects of this literature, it is not, I submit, because I am not aware of the other, but because in most of the critical work so far available on this subject, 'Africa' has been neglected in a way which makes it difficult, if not impossible, to view the West Indian contribution in a meaningful, West Indian way" (63).

25. In his Nobel lecture, for example, Walcott expands on this point: "I was entitled to the feast of Husein, to the mirrors and crepe-paper temples of the Muslim-epic, to the Chinese Dragon Dance, to the rites of that Sephardic Jewish synagogue that was once on Something Street. I am only one-eighth the writer I might have been had I contained all the fragmented languages of Trinidad" *(Antilles).* See also "Culture" 54; and "Muse" 17–18.

26. Gordon Rohlehr characterizes Walcott's antipathy to Brathwaite as being more pointed: "The instantaneous reception which Brathwaite's poetry received, especially since it appeared at the height of the Black Power movement, angered Walcott even more, since it seemed that the same wave of politics and history which had caused his work to be neglected . . . had catapulted an inferior writer to the forefront. Walcott's bitterness against 'History' and 'Politics' and 'Race' and 'Africa' increased, as did his need to negate Brathwaite's achievement, which he viewed as the mediocre embodiment of all these themes" (*Pathfinder* 111–12). For other views of the Black Power movement in the Caribbean, see Pantin; Nettleford; and Palmer.

27. For a broader discussion of the role of "Europe" and "Africa" in the development of West Indian poetry, see Breiner, *An Introduction,* chaps. 4 and 5.

28. See Benítez-Rojo; and Glissant, *Poetics of Relation.* For insightful comparison of these two theories of Caribbean poetry, see Sprouse; and de la Campa.

2. "Not Borrowers, But Bearers of a Tradition"

1. Critical comments on Eliot's views of tradition are voluminous, but for three useful discussions of the literary and philosophical underpinnings of Eliot's idea, see Lucy; Svarny; and Shusterman.

2. Pound's letter to Eliot's father offers a glimpse into the perceived importance of London for these young American poets. He writes: "But still you may bear in mind that London imposes her acceptance of a man's work on all the English speaking world and that she accepts no other standard than her own . . . and after some lapse of years that of Paris. At any rate if T. S. E. is set on a literary career, this is the place to begin it and any other start would be very bad economy" (Eliot, *Letters* 102). Many Caribbean writers express a similar anxiety about having their work measure up to London standards. See, e.g., Naipaul; and Lamming, *Pleasures of Exile.*

3. See esp. "Sir Galahad and the Islands" and "Roots," in which Brathwaite is one of the first critics to discuss the theme of exile in the novels of George Lamming, V. S. Naipaul, Samuel Selvon, and other novelists.

4. Eliot identifies Henry James as the model for an American to establish this European, transnational identity: "It is the final perfection, the consummation of an American to become, not an Englishman but a European—something which no born European, no person of any European nationality, can become" ("In Memory" 44).

5. After graduating from the University of the West Indies, in Jamaica, in 1953, Walcott spent a few years teaching in Grenada, Saint Lucia, and Jamaica. In 1958 he went to New York for a year on a Rockefeller fellowship to study theater. He spent most of the next two decades in the Caribbean, particularly Trinidad, working as a reporter, teacher, poet, and playwright. Since the late 1970s he has split his time between the United States and various Caribbean islands. For a comprehensive study of Walcott's life, see King, *Derek Walcott: A Caribbean Life.*

6. Of course, the obvious exception to this generalization is the Amerindians. As a younger poet-critic, Walcott assumes that the Amerindian culture has been destroyed. He writes that "there were those who did not survive, not by weakness but by a process of imperialistic defoliation which blasted defiance; and this process, genocide, is what destroyed the original, destroyed the Aztec, and American Indian, and the Carib-bean Indian" ("Culture" 56). He later modulates this view in *Omeros,* but he still emphasizes the destruction of this culture as a defining feature of Caribbean life.

7. See, e.g., "Notes for a Revised History of English Poetry," in Brooks. For different analyses of the relationship between Eliot and Brooks in forming the New Critical canon, see Guillory; Graff 204–6; and Perl, "Passing the Time."

8. In "The Three Provincialities" (1922) he contends that "not one but three English literatures exist: that written by Irishmen, that written by Americans and that composed by the English themselves" and that "the traditions of the language, not the traditions of the nation or the race, are what first concern the writer" (38, 39).

9. In a similar vein, Fred D'Aguiar argues that Walcott develops as a writer in response to two traditions, "divided along African and European lines, with a communal orientation in the former and a more individual base for the latter" (157). He commends Walcott for grappling with these twin traditions even though he does quite articulate as well as Wilson Harris what D'Aguiar calls the "plural vision" of a "kaleidoscopic whole" in Caribbean culture (167).

10. The issue of a poet's tradition is addressed in this chapter, and that of a poet's relation to society is addressed in chapter 4.

11. Michael Levenson carefully traces the relationship between Eliot's concept of tradition and his interest in comparative anthropology (*A Genealogy* 165–212).

12. Eliot publishes "Tradition and the Individual Talent" in two parts in the *Egoist,* the first in September 1919 and the second in December 1919. He publishes his review of *The Path of the Rainbow* in the *Athenaeum* in October 1919.

13. See Levenson, *A Genealogy* 193–212; Crawford 120–32; and Spurr.

14. While the interviewer attributes the phrase "unbroken arc" to Eliot, it is likely a loose paraphrase of Eliot's claim that "the historical sense compels a man to write not merely with his own generation in his bones, but with a feeling that the whole of the literature of Europe from Homer and within it the whole of the literature of his own country has a simultaneous existence and composes a simultaneous order" ("Tradition and the Individual Talent" 14).

15. Michael Levenson aptly describes Eliot's tradition as "a kind of trailer park of literary greatness" ("End of Tradition" 163).

16. Walcott has, however, experimented a bit with East Indian sources; see, for example, "Laventille" and "The Saddhu of Couva" in *Collected Poems* 85–88 and 372–74.

17. The role of Creole in this debate is obviously important, and it is addressed in detail in the next chapter.

18. Brathwaite's claim has turned out to be prescient, for Eliot scholars are only now beginning to reevaluate his relationship to forms of popular culture. For example, David Chinitz claims that Eliot did not seek to preserve a distinction between high and low art, as is so often thought, but rather to offer a more permeable view of the divide between levels of culture. See also Schuchard 87–118; and Knowles.

19. Indeed, Griffith seems to misunderstand modernism's relation to tradition, claiming that Brathwaite has to "acknowledge the positives of West Indian tradition, grounded in 'folk' sensibility, before exhausting the potential of Modernism's rejection of tradition" (76).

20. Brathwaite typically identifies four "sociocultural orientations" to describe this fragmentation, but he does not always name the same four. In "Timehri" (1973) they are "European, African, indigeno-nationalist, and folk" (30). In "Contradictory Omens" (1974) he identifies them as "European, Euro-creole, African-creole (or folk), and creo-creole or West Indian" but also recognizes "East Indians, Chinese and others" as a subsequent complication of this fragmentation (25).

21. Walcott and Brathwaite both recognize that these poems are central to defining their initial views of tradition. See Walcott, "Walcott on Walcott" 15–16; Walcott, "Art of Poetry" 107–8; and Brathwaite, *Barabajan Poems* 150–63.

22. For two representative views of this debate over the role of Tiresias, see Levinson, *A Genealogy* 186–93; and Bedient, ix, 129–38.

23. Wilson Harris also looks to Tiresias as a figure of the writer. He writes that "Tiresias is the embodiment of death as well as life, masculine as well as feminine, because it is through him that the writer lays bare a fiction corresponding to a community whose wholeness in reality cannot exist except by confessing its own insubstantial limits" ("Writer" 49).

24. For a brief survey of this strategy, see Ashcroft, Griffiths, and Tiffin, *The Empire Writes Back* 189–94.

25. Indeed, theorists have long used the characters of *The Tempest* as representative of the cultural pressures of colonialism (see Mannoni; Dorsinville; and Retamar). For critical studies that examine this strategy, see Brydon; Zabus; Nixon; and Lie and D'haen.

26. Walcott's example illustrates, in a much more straightforward way, Homi Bhabha's point about cultural agency in a postcolonial context: "My contention, elaborated in my writings on postcolonial discourse in terms of mimicry, hybridity, sly civility, is that this liminal moment of identification—eluding resemblance—produces a subversive strategy of subaltern agency that negotiates its own authority through a process of iterative 'unpicking' and incommensurable, insurgent relinking" (Bhabha, *Location* 185). Like Bhabha, Walcott sees an oppositional agency in his iterating and

relinking these different figures of Crusoe. He would not, however, see these relinkings as incommensurable but rather as a process of forming a broader tradition that would unite these particular iterations into a new whole. This distinction illustrates the difference between Walcott's more modernist and Bhabha's more postmodernist poetics.

27. Indeed, Brathwaite says as much in *Barabajan Poems* when he explains the "deep religious & mythological significance" of his uncle's being a carpenter: "A carpenter is a person in touch, through his wood, with Nature, with Super Nature. Christ was a carpenter, for instance" (155).

28. To underscore this point, Brathwaite positions "Ogun" as the central poem in the section entitled "Possession."

29. Brathwaite employs *roots* as a metaphor throughout his prose and poetry (see, e.g., the essays "Roots" and "The African Presence in Caribbean Literature" in the collection entitled *Roots,* and the poems "The Cabin" *[Rights of Passage],* "The Forest" *[Masks],* and "Nametracks" *[Mother Poem]).* For a critique of Brathwaite's use of *roots* as a central metaphor for Caribbean tradition and identity, see Arnold, "Caliban" 240–43. Arnold suggests that the metaphor *rhizomes,* first articulated in the Caribbean by Antonio Benítez-Rojo and Edouard Glissant, is more useful for representing identity in the Caribbean cultural context.

30. Brathwaite provides footnotes for *Mother Poem, Sun Poem,* and *X/Self* when they are published individually; however, there is only the occasional prose commentary when he publishes the complete trilogy as *Ancestors.*

31. For this neglect of poetry in conceiving of the strategies of postcolonial literature, see Ramazani, "Wound" 413–14. For examples of this neglect, see otherwise useful discussions in Ashcroft, Griffiths, and Tiffin, *The Empire Writes Back* 189–94; Gugelberger; Lawrence, *Decolonizing Tradition;* and Adam and Tiffin.

32. Jahan Ramazani makes a similar argument with respect to postcolonial poetry's use of metaphor when he argues that "the movement of metaphor across ethnic, regional, and gender boundaries is well suited to the hybrid and intercultural character of postcolonial literature. . . . Forced and voluntary migration, crossings of one people with another, linguistic creolization, and racial miscegenation—these are the sorts of displacements, wanderings, and interminglings that poetic metaphor can powerfully encode in the fabric of a postcolonial text" ("Wound" 414).

33. Brathwaite, in fact, has expended great effort trying to recover a definitive list of poets from and poems about Barbados (see *Barabajan Poems,* app. 3).

34. For Eliot as an American poet, see Gordon, *Eliot's New Life;* Sigg; Chinitz; Childs; and Oser. For Eliot in the English context, see Marshall; Ellis; and Davie. And pedagogically, he must appear frequently on syllabi for courses in either American or British literature, for he is one of the few writers to appear in both *The Norton Anthology of American Literature* and *The Norton Anthology of English Literature.*

35. "Tradition and the Individual Talent" is collected in both Eliot's own *Selected Essays* and Kenner's volume of Eliot's selected prose. It has also been republished extensively in popular teaching texts such as *The Norton Anthology of English Literature* and *The Norton Anthology of American Literature.*

3. Listening to Eliot: Poetic Revolution and Common Speech

1. Breiner does an excellent job of summarizing a variety of Caribbean poets' responses to this question (*An Introduction* 164–94).

2. For a helpful introduction to these issues of language in the Caribbean, see Roberts.

3. Indeed, later in his career Eliot willingly admits that he had written his "earlier criticism" to defend "the sort of poetry that I and my friends wrote," but he carefully distinguishes that work from his later "more detached and . . . judicial essays" ("To Criticize the Critic" 16). On Eliot's critical self-revisions, see Levenson, "End of Tradition."

4. For a summary of these debates, see Ashcroft, Griffiths, and Tiffin, *The Empire Writes Back,* chaps. 2 and 3.

5. Ngũgĩ articulates, not the first, but the most forceful defense of the proposition that African literature should be written in African languages. Ngũgĩ credits Obi Wali as the first one to declare that "the whole uncritical acceptance of English and French as the inevitable medium for educated African writing is misdirected, and has no chance of advancing African literature and culture" (quoted in Ngũgĩ, *Decolonizing the Mind* 24).

6. Ngũgĩ and Brathwaite met in London in 1966, worked together during Brathwaite's stay in Nairobi on a City of Nairobi Fellowship in 1972, and have worked together recently in the Department of Comparative Literature at New York University. The relationship appears to be close: Brathwaite received the name Kamau as part of a welcoming party held by Ngũgĩ at his home village in Kenya, and Brathwaite composed a poem to celebrate the birth of Ngũgĩ's daughter. For more details on the relationship between Brathwaite and Ngũgĩ, see Brathwaite's *Barabajan Poems* 236; and Ngũgĩ's "Kamau Brathwaite."

7. For an insightful discussion of the African influence on Anglophone speech in the Caribbean, see Allsopp xxxi–xxxiv.

8. The categories diglossic and polyglossic indicate a general distinction; there are clearly examples of polyglossia in the African context, pidgin and Swahili being the most prominent examples of liminal forms of speech in Africa.

9. For example, Eliot contends that "because we have never learned to criticize Keats, Shelley, and Wordsworth (poets of assured though modest merit), Keats, Shelley, and Wordsworth punish us from their grave with the annual scourge of the Georgian Anthology" ("Observations" 69). A few years later he argues that the "only cure for Romanticism is to analyze it" ("Romantic Patrician" 266).

10. He defines this continuum in terms of "imperial" languages (English, French, Dutch, or Spanish), "creole" languages (an adaptation of an imperial language to the Caribbean environment and to other imported languages), "nation language" (an imperial language spoken by the slaves and laborers brought to the Caribbean), and "ancestral" languages (the survival of Amerindian, Hindi, Chinese, and various African languages) ("History of the Voice" 259–60).

11. See North, chap. 3; Chinitz; and Schuchard, chaps. 4–5. Brathwaite is not the only creative writer of the African diaspora to make this connection. Ralph Ellison also claims that "*The Waste Land* seized my mind" because "its rhythms were often

closer to those of jazz than were those of Negro poets" (203). For Ellison's relationship to Eliot, see Helmling.

12. For example, Hayden Carruth contends for the singularity of Brathwaite's experiments, claiming that "in texture, in verbal technique, in almost everything, nothing could be further from Eliot's poetry than Brathwaite's" (310), whereas King argues that Brathwaite's adapting of Eliot's techniques "show[s] that he profoundly understood Eliot" (*New English Literatures* 137). However, neither of them provides much textual analysis to support his conclusions. Even the most astute critic of Brathwaite's work, Gordon Rohlehr, describes this important intertextual relationship in only the most general of terms, arguing that Eliot's "contrasting sequences and stylistic variety served as a model for Brathwaite's experiments with various tones of voice, and his alternation between prosaic flatness and song, . . . [and] in the way Brathwaite operates through personae rather than a number of self-contained lyrics" (*Pathfinder* 66–67).

13. Chinitz has convincingly argued that critics have misleadingly seen Eliot as only a defender of high culture; he contends that Eliot appreciated, although somewhat condescendingly, music-hall, jazz, and other forms of "low" culture because these forms could trigger audience participation (see Chinitz; and Schuchard, 87–118).

14. *Rights of Passage,* first published in 1967, was later republished as the first volume, along with *Masks* (1968) and *Islands* (1969), in *The Arrivants: A New World Trilogy* in 1973.

15. See Allsopp for a fuller understanding of the common usage of *miraculous bush.*

16. As in this passage, Brathwaite often comments on the central speakers of *The Arrivants* through cryptic allusions to Shakespeare's Caliban, Othello, and Edgar.

17. Moody dates the initial draft of *Sweeney Agonistes* to April 1923 (*Thomas Stearns Eliot* 114).

18. For more about Eliot's interest in anthropology, see Crawford; and Spurr. For a concise discussion of Eliot's views on ritual creating community, see Chinitz.

19. Brathwaite seems drawn to this line because it expresses the difficulty of poetic communication and because its rhythm and diction implicitly recognize the prevalence of English dialects. For examples, see "Jazz" 74; and *Barabajan Poems* 170.

20. Indeed, North argues that Eliot's repetitive use of language in *Sweeney Agonistes* conforms to Henry Louis Gates Jr.'s definition of the African American idiom as "paradigmatic (y-axis) substitutions determined by phonetic rather than semantic similarity" (89).

21. Indeed, he seems to have his experiments in *Sweeney Agonistes* in mind when he makes this assertion. He recalls his experiment with an unfinished "verse play" just before he makes this assertion about finding the origin of poetry in the beat of a drum (*Use of Poetry* 147–48).

22. For Brathwaite's experiments with jazz forms in other poems, see Rohlehr, *Pathfinder;* James, "Brathwaite and Jazz"; and Weinstein.

23. Brathwaite claims that the best Caribbean "jazz" novelists employ a similar technique whereby their "words, then, are the notes of this New Orleans music" ("Jazz" 65).

24. Rohlehr describes the Ska as a "dance which Jamaica's deprived classes created in the late fifties, from a mixture of traditional mento songs, pukkumina hymns,

work-songs, and American Rhythm and Blues, jive, be-bop, and rock and roll" (*Pathfinder* 96).

25. As Rohlehr suggests, Brathwaite draws upon the imagery of Revelation 18, the passage that describes Babylon and is so central to Rastafarian beliefs, in writing this second section (Rohlehr, *Pathfinder* 96–97). On the Rastafarian understanding of Babylon, see Jacobs 99–105; and Chevannes 208–30.

26. For example, Jorie Graham describes how she was called to poetry when she passed a classroom and overheard the reading of lines from Eliot's "Love Song of J. Alfred Prufrock" (Schiff 64). Seamus Heaney praises Eliot for teaching him the "right way to listen" to poetry ("Learning from Eliot" 29).

27. Eliot cites this line in "Note sur Mallarmé et Poe" (1926); in the third Turnball lecture (1933), reprinted in Eliot, *Varieties of Metaphysical Poetry* 281–95; and in "American Literature and Language" (1953).

28. Consider, for example, Bernard Sharratt, who contends that Eliot's conservatism is ripe for new appropriations by people with "regressively conservative tendencies" (234).

29. Brathwaite himself acknowledges his predecessors in dialect poetry, such as Louise Bennett, in "History of the Voice," 274–304. For a useful summary of this history of dialect poetry in the West Indies and Brathwaite's place in it, see Breiner, *An Introduction* 164–94.

30. Even here, however, the overlapping nature of twentieth-century poetry is evident, for Eliot helps to introduce Saint-John Perse to the Anglophone world by translating his *Anabasis* in 1930.

31. Indeed, only five years after publishing this essay Walcott himself contends for the metaphoric power of Saint Lucian patois when he says that "once I knew that the richness of Creole was a whole uncharted territory for a writer, I became excited. I also knew that it couldn't be separated from the landscape, because the things I saw around me were being named by people in a new language, even if that language was being called Creole, or vulgar, or patois, or a dialect, or whatever. The metaphors that one heard from peasants describing a tree, a flower, an insect, anything, were not like the Latin names for things" (Walcott, "An Interview" [Hirsch] 58).

32. While Walcott usually focuses on the relationship between his Creole and Standard English, he recognizes his linguistic heritage as being more complex. For example, in an interview with J. P. White he says: "The reality is I grew up in two languages, Creole and English. And, of course, tonal English with a Creolized inflection. So there were actually three languages or even four. There was French, which was not spoken too much on the island, French Creole, English and then French Accent" (Walcott, "An Interview" [White] 152).

33. In his review of *Rights of Passage* Walcott resists Brathwaite's claim to the legacy of Césaire, concluding that "there is nothing in 'Rights of Passage' that equals the fan-poem 'Cahier d'un Retour Au Pays Natal'" ("Tribal Flutes" 41).

34. For an example of this distinction, consider Walcott's praise of Robert Frost for achieving an American "vernacular elation in tone, not with the cheap device of dialect spelling or rustic speech, but with a clear ear and fresh eye" ("The Road Taken" 98).

35. See, e.g., the discussions of "Names" in Ramsaran; Terada 98–101; and Breslin 114–16. Bobb mentions the dedication but limits her comparative analysis to Walcott's and Brathwaite's allusions to "pebbles" as a metaphor for the power of the Caribbean language (146–47). Thieme does suggest that Walcott dedicates "Names" to Brathwaite "presumably as a response to his project of *Afro*-Caribbean renaming" but does not follow up that assertion (97).

36. Walcott makes the same point in "Culture" when he writes that "we cannot focus on a single ancestor, that moment of ape to man if you wish, . . . when the black felt that he had crossed the meridian, when the East Indian had, or the Portuguese, or the Chinese, or the Old World Jew. There was no line in the sea which said, this is new, this is the frontier, the boundary of endeavor, and henceforth everything can only be mimicry. But there was such a moment for every individual American, and that moment was both surrender and claim, both possession and dispossession. The issue is the claim" (54).

37. This trope of breath shaping language as wind shapes a tree is one of Walcott's favorites. See, e.g., part 6 of "*The Schooner* Flight," in which Shabine says it does not matter whether a tree is called a "casuarina," "cypress" or "cedar," because the wind "bent them . . . all the same" (*Collected Poems* 353).

38. Even good critics of Brathwaite's work, such as Breiner, Torres-Saillant, or Rohlehr, who discuss extensively his use of nation language, tend only to mention and simply define Brathwaite's concept of nam. Elaine Savory does examine the concept of nam in the context of Brathwaite's critical essays and early poetry, but she does not explain in enough detail the nature of the relationship between nam and nation language. Instead, she makes correct but more general claims, such as, "Words then, for Brathwaite, are absolutely vital carriers of living experience, cultural ancestry and spiritual survival" ("Returning" 213).

39. For some of the variations in Brathwaite's definition of *nam,* see *Mother Poem* 121n61; *Sun Poem* 104; "World Order Models" 56; "History, the Caribbean Writer, and *X/Self*" 33–34; and *Barabajan Poems* 235–65.

40. While Césaire is not, of course, the only exponent of negritude, he has the most influence on Brathwaite's development of the concept of nam. For other seminal statements concerning negritude, see Senghor; and esp. Sartre.

41. See Arnold, *Modernism and Negritude* 37–38.

42. Césaire also clarifies his understanding of negritude by distinguishing himself from Senghor: "It seemed to me that Senghor made a kind of metaphysics out of negritude; there we parted company. He tended rather to construct negritude into an essentialism as though there were a black essence, a black soul, . . . but I never accepted this point of view" (quoted in Arnold, *Modernism and Negritude* 44).

43. Antonio Benítez-Rojo and Edouard Glissant both appropriate Gilles Deleuze and Félix Guattari's concept of the rhizome as a better metaphor for imagining identity and language in the Caribbean. Glissant writes that the "root is unique; a stock taking all upon itself and killing all around it. In opposition to this they propose the rhizome, an enmeshed root system, a network spreading either in the ground or in the air, with no predatory rootstock taking over permanently. The notion of rhizome maintains, therefore, the idea of rootedness but challenges that of a totalitarian root. Rhizomatic

thought is the principle behind what I call the Poetics of Relation" (*Poetics of Relation* 11; see also Benítez-Rojo, *Repeating Island* 291n24). For an analysis of how Benítez-Rojo and Glissant employ the concept of rhizome, see Sprouse. Walcott's assimilating poetics of speech is more in keeping with this rhizome model, for it recognizes the diversity of sources for speech and identity in the Caribbean. The rhizome trope has its own shortcomings, however, for it assumes an equality among sources of identity in the Caribbean, an assumption that disregards the historical denigration of certain identities under colonialism.

44. Gayatri Spivak defines *strategic essentialism* as the "*strategic* use of a positivist essentialism in a scrupulously visible political interest" ("In a Word" 126). She later qualifies this definition by suggesting that her "critique of essentialism" is an "acknowledgment of the dangerousness of what one must use" (129). Brathwaite's use of nam is a form of this type of strategic essentialism.

45. In this earlier essay Walcott is ambivalent in his praise of Césaire. He describes Césaire's *Return* as a work of "magnificent optimism" ("Necessity" 21) but considers the concept of negritude to be too "French" (22) and not reflective of "our complete identity, since that is mixed and shared by other races, whose writers are East Indian, white, mixed" (23). King argues that Walcott later "thought Césaire a loud but tremendous poet" (*Derek Walcott: A Caribbean Life* 236).

46. See, e.g., Brathwaite's "Caribbean Culture" 42–45; "History, the Caribbean Writer, and *X/Self*" 38–45; and *Barabajan Poems* 235–65.

47. Brathwaite says that "O'Grady says" is the same as the U.S. game "Simon says" (*Barabajan Poems* 245).

48. George Lamming's *Pleasures of Exile* and Césaire's *Une tempête* are arguably the most important appropriations of this motif in Caribbean literature. For postcolonial theory's appropriation of this motif, see Mannoni; Fanon; and Retamar. For critical summaries of how this motif has been used, see Nixon; and Lie and D'haen.

49. In "Caliban" Brathwaite revises the Caliban myth by shifting the focus from colonialism to neocolonialism, from Caliban's being the slave of Prospero to his being beguiled by Trinculo and Stephano, from the Caribbean's political struggle with European powers to its cultural and economic struggle with North America.

50. Brathwaite defines *nomminit* as a "nation-language sound/word" for "cultural domination," literally the "gobbling up of the (other's) name" (*Mother Poem* 121n64).

51. In contrast, Allsopp offers a more comprehensive, subtler approach. He recognizes the interplay of myriad imperial and ancestral languages in the development of Caribbean English (xxxi–xxxiv, xli–xliii). He also defines Caribbean Standard English as "the literate English of educated nationals of Caribbean territories and their spoken English such as is considered natural in formal social contexts" (lvi), but he recognizes that the broader concept of Caribbean English involves four different levels of formality: "formal" (educated and internationally accepted English), "informal" (accepted as familiar, well-structured, casual speech), "anti-formal" (conscious rejection of formal speech), and "erroneous" (lvi–lvii). Brathwaite's nation language encompasses both Allsopp's informal and antiformal categories, so it obscures the intention of the speaker in his or her use of the language.

52. For summaries of those differences, see Roberts 85–104; and Allsopp xli–xlii.

53. See Allsopp, s.v. "nation language," for examples of Brathwaite's ambiguous use of this term. Allsopp clarifies this distinction much better by identifying national Standard Englishes, e.g., Barbadian or Jamaican, and Caribbean Standard English, a conglomeration of those national Standard Englishes (lv–lvi).

54. "Letter Sycorax" was first published as "X/Self's Xth Letters from Thirteen Provinces" in *X/Self* (1987). Brathwaite subsequently revises the poem to employ more of his Sycorax video-style and publishes it as "Letter Sycorax" in *MiddlePassages* (1992).

55. Brathwaite also mentions the damage to his personal archive by Hurricane Gilbert (1988) and being robbed at gunpoint in his home in Jamaica (1990) as contributing to the creation of this new style ("Newstead" 658).

56. Rhonda Cobham explains in useful detail how Brathwaite's personal computers, not only Sycorax but also Stark, relate to the development of his Sycorax video-style and "have become symbolic presences in their own right in the poet's private iconography" (304).

57. For insightful critical commentary on this movement in Anglo-American poetry, see Perloff, *Radical Artifice;* and McGann.

58. The first version of this poem is entitled "X/Self's Xth Letters from the Thirteen Provinces," and it appears in one version in *X/Self* and in a revised version in *Ancestors.* Brathwaite first employs more of the Sycorax video-style in the "Letter Sycorax" version in *MiddlePassages.* Brathwaite does not, however, engage in wide-ranging typographical experiments until *Barabajan Poems,* a volume he published himself, which gave him more control over the publication process. For a discussion of the rewards and difficulties of publishing Brathwaite's Sycorax video-style, see Rigby; and Savory, "Returning."

59. In *The Zea Mexican Diary* Brathwaite speaks of his wife as the muse of his poetry: "But she was my wife/the perfect poet's wife—I mean the perfect wife of/for the poet. She made it possible. Created from the very start & kept it go/ing to the last moments of her very life. The perfect temperature & space for the poems to be/come" (152).

60. Of course, quoting passages from "Letter Sycorax" or any of the other of Brathwaite's poems written in Sycorax video-style immediately raises the challenge of his new poetics of speech because of the difficulty of reproducing the exact size, boldness, or font of the typeface given conventional publishing constraints. Several of the more significant examples of his Sycorax video-style have been reproduced or approximated, but others, regrettably, have been "standardized" to conform to "accepted" conventions.

61. Indeed, Brathwaite describes his Sycorax video-style as "the nearest I can get to what the athlete or the dancer or the actor says" (*Barabajan Poems* 378).

62. In his interview with Nathaniel Mackey, Brathwaite implies that he has never asserted a binary approach to the problem of cultural independence, that he has "never [been] concerned with Caliban's so-called curse" (Brathwaite, "An Interview" 45). It is, however, difficult to reconcile this statement with the overtly binary structure of "Nametracks." Rather, Brathwaite seems to modify his approach in "Letter Sycorax" because such an adversarial poetics reinforces cultural and linguistic hierarchies.

63. For a description of the role of *mkissi* (also known as *n'kisi*) in BaKongo culture, see MacGaffey 135–68.

64. As Stewart Brown points out, Brathwaite revises the ending of the poem when he publishes "Letter Sycorax" by eliminating an allusion to "The Dust"—"why is dat? // what it / mean?" ("Writin" 128). Brown suggests that the original ending offers an "intriguing echo, the poet perhaps inviting his readers to see the connection between the quest for a language and the 'solution' the computer offers. . . ?" (128). Perhaps Brathwaite agrees, for he has restored that ending in the version printed in *Ancestors* (2001).

65. Rohlehr rightly argues that this arbitrariness is fitting in the context of Brathwaite's *DreamStories* because it corresponds "to the arbitrariness of the different dream-world of these stories" ("Dream Journeys" ix); however, he does not address how this arbitrariness affects Brathwaite's capacity to convey the sound of nation language in his poetry.

66. Brathwaite himself has expressed uncertainty about reading Sycorax video-style to an audience because it must be both seen and heard (*ConVERSations* 210). One could imagine a videotape or computer version of a Sycorax video-style text in which the sound and text are more closely matched. However, it remains an open question whether such versions of the poems would be able to establish the conventions necessary to enable readers or listeners to replicate the experience or, in the terms of the musical metaphor, to read the notes.

67. For example, in "Roseau Valley" he laments that his "gift . . . cannot pay back this island / enough" because it "gave no communion / of tongues" (*Arkansas Testament* 19), and in "A Latin Primer" he recalls finding his poetic "voice" when he recognized for the first time the metaphoric richness of the multiple forms of speech in the Caribbean (*Arkansas Testament* 23–24).

4. Public Poets

1. See Gordon, *Eliot's New Life* 191–94.

2. The quotation is from Dante's *Paradiso,* canto 6, line 135, and was first brought to wider attention by A. D. Moody (*Thomas Stearns Eliot* 251, 369n59). A typescript of the speech is in the Hayward Collection at King's College, Cambridge. While Moody dates this speech to December 1947, Peter Ackroyd says that this trip to Aix-en-Provence was postponed to April 1948 (287).

3. See entries for *metic* and *peregrine* in *The Oxford Classical Dictionary* and *The Oxford English Dictionary.*

4. Eliot revised the passage in *Little Gidding* to blur the specific allusion to Latini so that readers would not identify Latini with Yeats. Even so, the passage still contains many details of Dante's encounter with his former teacher (see Gardner 63–66; and Moody, *Thomas Stearns Eliot* 248–59). Of course, Eliot also alludes to Dante's meeting with Latini in the London Bridge scene in *The Waste Land.*

5. By admitting his position of privilege, Walcott seeks to avoid the danger that Gayatri Spivak describes as the "first-world intellectuals masquerading as the absent nonrepresenter who lets the oppressed speak for themselves," a warning that she extends to "postcolonial intellectuals," who must "learn that their privilege is their loss" ("Can the Subaltern Speak?" 87, 82).

6. In *Barabajan Poems* Brathwaite describes the ceremony in which he received the name Kamau from members of Ngũgĩ wa Thiong'o's family in the early 1970s. In the mid-1980s he decides to "own" and "use" the name as an "important statement of cultural position/commitment/orientation" (237).

7. Indeed, the older Eliot measures the success of a poet not in terms his or her ability to alter the "*whole* existing order" of tradition but in terms of the coherence of the poet's career: "The difference between major and minor poets . . . is whether a knowledge of the whole, or at least of a very large part, of a poet's work, makes one enjoy more, because it makes one understand better, any one of his poems. That implies a significant unity in his whole work" ("What Is Minor Poetry" 49–50).

8. Walcott himself describes *Epitaph for the Young* as the "urtext" for *Another Life* (Walcott, "Conversation" 23), and Rei Terada rightly notes that *Epitaph* prefigures *Omeros* in its rewriting of *The Divine Comedy* and *Little Gidding* (231n35).

9. In his *Imagined Communities* Anderson offers the best historical argument about reciprocal relationship between culture and nationalism, but it is a topic that has also occupied postcolonial theorists from Frantz Fanon to Homi Bhabha. For examples of the more influential discussions of this concept, see Fanon, chaps. 3 and 4; Gellner; Chatterjee; Hobsbawm; and the essays in Bhabha, *Nation and Narration.*

10. Eliot argues that "the poet naturally prefers to write for as large and miscellaneous audience as possible, and that it is the half-educated and ill-educated, rather than the uneducated, who stand in the way: I myself should like an audience which could neither read nor write. The most useful poetry, socially, would be one which could cut across all the present stratifications of public taste—stratifications which are perhaps a sign of social disintegration. The ideal medium for poetry . . . is the theatre" (*Use of Poetry* 152–53).

11. For instance, as an older critic Eliot declines to "defend" the continued viability of phrases like the "dissociation of sensibility" and "objective correlative" but merely claims that they were "useful" when coined ("To Criticize the Critic" 19). For changes in his views of individual writers, consider, for example, his essays "Wordsworth and Coleridge," "In Memoriam," and "Yeats." For a general review of these changes, see Schwartz, "Literary Dictatorship"; and Levenson, "End of Tradition."

12. For example, Delmore Schwartz discusses these critical revisions and concludes that "Eliot, in revising this initial revaluation of English poetry, has permitted experience to teach him" ("Literary Dictatorship" 329). Michael Levenson argues that these changes reflect Eliot's growing understanding of the historicity of his own thought ("End of Tradition" 158).

13. First published in the *Southern Review,* the lecture was republished as part of a collection of essays entitled *T. S. Eliot: Essays from the Southern Review,* edited by James Olney. Eliot's title for the essay has been lost, but A. Walton Litz has aptly renamed it "Tradition and the Practice of Poetry."

14. For example, Chinua Achebe argues that "the African writer should aim to use English in a way that brings out his message best without altering the language to the extent that its value as a medium of international exchange will be lost. He should aim at fashioning out an English which is at once universal and able to carry his peculiar experience" (100). Salman Rushdie makes a similar point when he argues that the

"British Indian writer" cannot "simply use the language in the way the British did"; instead "it needs remaking for our own purposes" ("Imaginary Homelands" 17). Gabriel Okara contends that "living languages grow like living things, and English is far from a dead language. There are American, West Indian, Australian, Canadian and New Zealand versions of English. All of them add life and vigour to the language while reflecting their own respective cultures" (quoted in Ngũgĩ, *Decolonizing the Mind* 9).

15. One could make a similar analysis of Eliot's views of Milton, Dryden, Goethe, Wordsworth, and Coleridge (see Levenson, "End of Tradition"; and Schwartz, "Literary Dictatorship").

16. Eliot's changing opinion of Yeats is different because Yeats was publishing new poetry in the intervening years. However, the interesting point is that Eliot's rationale is the same for each poet.

17. Of course, the young Walcott is no stranger to contradictions. In his early essays he often inverts what others see as a deficiency into an advantage (i.e., a loss of history, a hybrid or mulatto identity, or an excessive mimicry). However, it is the larger contradictions in the course of his career that best illustrate the scope of his ambition to become a public poet.

18. While the contrast is most striking between Walcott's earlier critical statements and *Omeros,* the change is not, of course, that abrupt. Several of his earlier poems make reference to Africa, including the often anthologized "A Far Cry from Africa," which speaks of his struggle between "Africa and the English tongue I love," and "Laventille," which describes the cultural trauma of the Middle Passage (*Collected Poems* 17–18, 85–88). In addition, a central part of the action of his *Dream on Monkey Mountain* involves an imaginative return to Africa. However, the younger Walcott tends to satirize these African-oriented allusions. In *Omeros* he presents these allusions more sympathetically.

19. For two of the best studies on Eliot and Dante, see Moody, *Thomas Stearns Eliot;* and Manganiello.

20. In his earlier essay on Dante, Eliot ties Dante's use of language to this European identity: "Some of the character of this universal language [medieval Latin] seems to me to inhere in Dante's Florentine speech; and the localization seems if anything to emphasize the universality, because it cuts across the modern division of nationality" ("Dante" 239).

21. In a recent interview Walcott rejects the idea that his work sounds like Eliot but welcomes a general comparison to Dante: "If somebody told me it sounded like Dante, I'd say, well, thanks. But even then, that's not true, because it's not the same language" (Walcott, "Thinking Poetry" 219). For a detailed discussion of Walcott's use of Dante in *Omeros,* see Fumagalli.

22. For other examples, see Terada 183–212; Burnett 281–312; and Figueroa 203–6.

23. For a more specific discussion of the role of Dante and Yeats in this passage, see Gardner 63–69, 171–96. For the other allusions, see Smith, *T. S. Eliot's Poetry* 290.

24. For example, in the special issue of the *South Atlantic Quarterly* devoted to Walcott, four of the seven articles discuss *Omeros,* but only one mentions these key scenes, and then only in a cursory fashion (Burian 371–74). Or consider Robert Hamner,

who rightly describes Walcott's meeting with his father in book 1 as a "useful vehicle for establishing literary roots uncannily deep in the English tradition" but then only discusses the scene in relationship to Shakespeare's *Hamlet* and *King Lear* and Virgil's *Aeneid* (*Epic* 53–58).

25. For the actual biographical details about Walcott's father, see King, *Derek Walcott: A Caribbean Life* 4–20.

26. Joyce's advice to Heaney parallels, in part, Warwick's to Walcott in focusing on the craft of poetry ("cultivate a work-lust"), in claiming the language ("the English language / belongs to us"), in avoiding a simplistic art of protest ("that subject people stuff is a cod's game"), and in evading the prescribed requirements of others for his poetry ("keep at a tangent. / When they make the circle wide, it's time to swim / out on your own") (Heaney, "Station Island" 192–93). However, Walcott seems more concerned with the communal obligations of the poet. In "Station Island" Joyce concludes by advising Heaney "to swim / out on your own and fill the element / with signatures on your own frequency" (193), whereas in *Omeros* Warwick tells Walcott to remember the women coal-carriers by giving "those feet a voice" (84).

27. Joyce has been a part of Walcott's anthology since the beginning of his career. He recalls choosing that "blasphemous, arrogant Stephen Daedalus" as his "current hero" when he was eighteen ("Leaving School" 31), and he declares himself as "I Stephen" in the first epic that he publishes, at nineteen, *Epitaph for the Young* (1949). He negotiates his relationship to Joyce better in *Another Life* (1973), an autobiographical epic in which the speaker of the poem searches for fathers, experiences epiphanies, equates sexual awakening with encountering the muse, resists political nationalism, and flees the provincialism of his island home. In other words, it is a Portrait of the Caribbean Artist as a Young Man. While he tends to downplay the relationship between his *Omeros* and Joyce's *Ulysses,* it represents his most successful reworking of Joyce's themes and ideas (Walcott, "Thinking Poetry" 184). Indeed, he pays high tribute to Joyce in his epic, calling him "our age's Omeros, undimmed Master" and joining voices with him: "I blessed myself in his voice" (200). Little critical attention has been paid to this relationship, but see Pollard, "Traveling with Joyce"; Alleyne; Baugh, "The Poem"; and Hamner, *Epic* 112–17.

28. Indeed, *Omeros* is filled with these imagined reunions between fathers and sons, not just Walcott and his father, but Achille and Afolabe, the midshipman and Plunkett, and Helen's baby and his father.

29. As Olaniyan argues, Walcott's choice to start from the "Western tradition . . . is not necessarily a negative thing, but only with a self-conscious acknowledgment that it is only one tradition in many open to the Caribbean artist: the choice is not natural, self-evident, or automatic but thoroughly ideological" (*Scars* 114–15). Walcott could address the ideological significance of his choices more directly.

30. Moody rightly argues that Dante extends a greater magnanimity to Latini because he does not try "to convert him into an expression of his own point of view" (*Thomas Stearns Eliot* 253). He sees Eliot as indulging the opposite impulse because he "is not concerned with the *otherness* of his masters" (253–54). Indeed, Eliot and Walcott both seem more concerned with the advice of the masters than with the gratitude of the poet. Even so, Moody seems unduly critical. Part of Eliot's, and presumably Walcott's,

point is to recognize the composite nature of tradition. The blending of voices, of necessity, means a muting of the "otherness" of particular masters.

31. This split between poetry and ideology reoccurs throughout Eliot's later criticism. He contends that others can study Milton with "profit to their poetry and to the English language," but he continues to find Milton's personality, politics, and theology "antipathetic" ("Milton II" 161; "To Criticize the Critic" 23). Of Tennyson's "In Memoriam," Eliot argues that while its "technical accomplishment" is an "amazing *tour de force*," its attitude of "vague hopefulness" is "mistaken" ("Voice of His Time" 212). He describes Yeats' poetry as a "great and permanent example . . . of moral, as well as intellectual, excellence" while at the same time claiming to be "unsympathetic" to aspects of his "thought and feeling" ("Yeats" 257, 262).

32. The effect of financial support on artistic integrity has worried Walcott for a long time. In 1957 he argues that the lack of financial support for the arts in the Caribbean either kills artists' capacity to work at home or forces them into exile ("Society and the Artist" 15–17). In 1965 he makes a similar argument lyrically when he writes: "Once I thought love of country was enough, / now, even if I chose, there's no room at the trough. / I watch the best minds root like dogs / for scraps of favour" ("Codicil," *Collected Poems* 97).

33. See, e.g., Moody, *Thomas Stearns Eliot,* which recognizes not only the "limitations and defects" but also the "great power and authority" of this passage. He contends that this passage "is an extraordinary kind of inferior writing that can be regarded . . . as a supreme achievement of poetic genius" (250).

34. See, e.g., chapter 3 of *Omeros,* where Walcott engages in these experiments in a more extended fashion and where he suggests the limitation of this approach. Most of the "folk" characters—Hector, Achille, Ma Kilman, Philoctete—speak in French Creole, a reminder to the reader of the common speech of Saint Lucia, but Walcott also feels compelled to translate this dialogue into English Creole.

35. Walcott explicitly makes this suggestion in "The Light of the World," in *The Arkansas Testament,* in comparing his work with that of Bob Marley.

36. The shift begins in book 6, where he first accuses himself of nostalgia: "Didn't I want the poor / to stay in the same light so that I could transfix / them in amber, the afterglow of the empire / preferring a shed of palm-thatch with tilted sticks / to that blue bus-stop? . . . Hadn't I made their poverty my paradise?" (*Omeros* 227–28).

37. Eliot develops his theory of impersonality in the second half of "Tradition and the Individual Talent," and critics have recognized its influence on subsequent poets even if they dispute Eliot's own faithfulness to the concept. For example, Charles Altieri identifies it as one of three major factors in Eliot's impact on writers in the Anglo-American tradition (199–201).

38. For example, Dash criticizes Brathwaite's recycling of poems in his review of *The Visibility Trigger* and *Jah Music.* He contends that this recycling gives the appearance of "a seemingly inexhaustible stream of publications" but is really a despondent clutching "to the word in order not to surrender to silence" (87–88). See also Rohlehr's response to Dash, "Brathwaite."

39. It is a neglect that Brathwaite laments and takes as an indication of the lack of concern in Barbados to preserve its cultural heritage: "We allow(ed) the pox & pot &

rat & warm & damp & rat & rot & sworms of our **neglect neglect neglect** to ravage & destroy these things becau(se) we didn't earn or care about Mile&Quarter &/or Bob'ob & his 'maroon' world becau(se) we didn't know or care about our history & the people who have help(ed) to make it what it cd still far better be" (*Barabajan Poems* 161). In this complaint Brathwaite echoes his own accusation against the University of the West Indies administrators for failing to act to preserve his archives in Jamaica following Hurricane Gilbert in 1988 (see *Barabajan Poems,* app. 5).

Epilogue

1. See Altieri; and Longenbach 85–101, 158–76.

2. See Young, *T. S. Eliot and Hispanic Modernity.*

3. David Dabydeen dismissively describes Brathwaite's nation language as "polite" and "conventional" (quoted in Breiner, *An Introduction* 179). Brathwaite himself laments the "lack of continuity" and the "ignorance of that continuity" in the Caribbean because it prevents "dub" poets from recognizing a relationship between their oral poetry and his own (Brathwaite, "An Interview" 28).

4. Brathwaite himself recognizes Rohlehr as the "Xception" because he has "been a most formidable champion of the poetry in the face of som(e) pretty hostile & culturally prejudiced—esp *local*—response to my work" (*Barabajan Poems* 24). See Rohlehr's study on *The Arrivants (Pathfinder)* and his essays on *The Sun Poem, X/Self,* and *DreamStories* in *The Shape of That Hurt.*

5. Brathwaite's estrangement from some in the Caribbean academic community has emerged from what Brathwaite perceives as a general indifference on the part of some at the University of the West Indies to the death of his wife and the destruction of his personal archives. For Brathwaite's discussion of this estrangement, see *Zea Mexican Diary* 169–86; *Shar;* and *Barabajan Poems* 362–66.

6. For the influence of African languages on Caribbean Anglophone speech, see, e.g., Allsopp xvii–lvii. For the role of African religious rituals in contemporary Caribbean literature and experience, see Brathwaite, "African Presence in Caribbean Literature."

7. Appiah specifically rejects "master narratives of modernism" in defining his "postmodern" humanism, but he once again oversimplifies the modernist concept of identity. For example, Eliot's Tiresias surely qualifies as a "provisional, historically contingent, antiessentialist" character who understands that suffering "can still be demanding" on the formation of a poetics (*In My Father's House* 155).

8. Walcott has used this image before. In "The Season of Phantasmal Peace" (1981) he imagines that "all the nations of birds lifted together / the huge net of the shadows of this earth / in multitudinous dialects and twittering tongues" (*Collected Poems* 464). They lifted this net of shadows so that men could see the "phantasmal light" of "Love, made seasonless" (464–65). He concludes by reaffirming the enticing ephemerality of this love: "This season lasted one moment, . . . but, for such as our earth is now, it lasted long" (465).

Bibliography

Abrams, M. H., ed. *The Norton Anthology of English Literature*. 6th ed. Vol. 2. New York: Norton, 1993.

Achebe, Chinua. "The African Writer and the English Language." In *Morning Yet on Creation Day: Essays,* 91–103. Garden City, NY: Anchor, 1975.

Ackroyd, Peter. *T. S. Eliot: A Life*. New York: Simon & Schuster, 1984.

Adam, Ian, and Helen Tiffin, eds. *Past the Last Post: Theorizing Post-colonialism and Post-modernism*. Calgary: Univ. of Calgary Press, 1990.

Ahmad, Aijaz. *In Theory: Classes, Nations, Literatures*. New York: Verso, 1992.

Ali, Agha Shahid. *T. S. Eliot as Editor.* Ann Arbor, MI: UMI Research Press, 1986.

Alighieri, Dante. *The Divine Comedy: Inferno*. Trans. Dorothy L. Sayers. 1949. Reprint, New York: Penguin, 1980.

Alleyne, Keith. Review of *Epitaph for the Young,* by Derek Walcott. In Hamner, *Critical Perspectives on Derek Walcott,* 98–105.

Allsopp, Richard, ed. *Dictionary of Caribbean English Usage*. Oxford: Oxford Univ. Press, 1996.

Altieri, Charles. "Eliot's Impact on Twentieth-Century Anglo-American Poetry." In Moody, *Cambridge Companion to T. S. Eliot,* 189–209.

Anderson, Benedict. *Imagined Communities: Reflections on the Origin and Spread of Nationalism*. Rev. ed. New York: Verso, 1991.

Appadurai, Arjun. *Modernity at Large: Cultural Dimensions of Globalization*. Minneapolis: Univ. of Minnesota Press, 1996.

Appiah, Kwame Anthony. "Cosmopolitan Patriots." *Critical Inquiry* 23, no. 3 (1997): 617–39.

———. *In My Father's House: Africa in the Philosophy of Culture*. Oxford: Oxford Univ. Press, 1992.

———. "Is the Post- in Postmodernism the Post- in Postcolonial?" *Critical Inquiry* 17, no. 2 (1991): 336–57.

Arnold, A. James. "Caliban, Culture, and Nation-Building in the Caribbean." In Lie and D'haen, *Constellation Caliban,* 231–44.

———. "Caribbean Literary Theory: Modernist and Postmodern." *New West Indian Guide* 69, nos. 1–2 (1995): 103–9.

———. Introduction to *Lyric and Dramatic Poetry, 1946–82*. Charlottesville: Univ. Press of Virginia, 1990.

———. *Modernism and Negritude: The Poetry and Poetics of Aimé Césaire*. Cambridge: Harvard Univ. Press, 1981.

———, ed. *A History of Literature in the Caribbean*. Vol. 3. Philadelphia: John Benjamins Press, 1997.

Ashcroft, Bill, Gareth Griffiths, and Helen Tiffin. *The Empire Writes Back: Theory and Practice in Post-colonial Literatures*. New York: Routledge, 1989.

———. *The Post-colonial Studies Reader.* New York: Routledge, 1995.

Attridge, Derek, and Marjorie Howes, eds. *Semicolonial Joyce*. Cambridge: Cambridge Univ. Press, 2000.

Auden, W. H. "American Poetry." In *The Dyer's Hand, and Other Essays,* 354–68. London: Faber & Faber, 1975.

Baker, Houston A., Jr. *Modernism and the Harlem Renaissance*. Chicago: Univ. of Chicago Press, 1987.

Baugh, Edward. "The Arkansas Testament." In Brown, *Art of Derek Walcott,* 123–38.

———. "The Poem as an Autobiographical Novel: Derek Walcott's 'Another Life' in Relation to Wordsworth's 'Prelude' and Joyce's 'Portrait.'" In *Awakened Conscience: Studies in Commonwealth Literature,* ed. C. D. Narasimhaiah, 226–35. New Delhi: Sterling Press, 1978.

———. "Poetry as Ritual: Reading Kamau Brathwaite." *Journal of West Indian Literature* 8, no. 1 (1998): 1–9.

———. "Review of *Rights of Passage*." *Bim* 1, no. 47 (1968): 66–68.

Baym, Nina, ed. *The Norton Anthology of American Literature*. 5th ed. Vol. 2. New York: Norton, 1998.

Bedient, Calvin. *"He do the police in different voices": The Waste Land and Its Protagonist*. Chicago: Univ. of Chicago Press, 1986.

Benítez-Rojo, Antonio. *The Repeating Island: The Caribbean and the Postmodern Perspective*. Durham, NC: Duke Univ. Press, 1992.

Bhabha, Homi. *The Location of Culture*. London: Routledge, 1994.

———. "Unsatisfied: Notes on Vernacular Cosmopolitanism." In *Text and Nation: Cross-Disciplinary Essays on Cultural and National Identities,* 191–207. Columbia, SC: Camden House, 1996.

———, ed. *Nation and Narration*. New York: Routledge, 1990.

Bloom, Harold. *The Breaking of the Vessels*. Chicago: Univ. of Chicago Press, 1982.

———. "The Central Man: Emerson, Whitman, Wallace Stevens." *Massachusetts Review* 7 (Winter 1966): 23–42.

———. "The Internalization of Quest-Romance." In *Romanticism and Consciousness,* ed. Harold Bloom, 3–23. New York: Norton, 1970.

———. Introduction to *T. S. Eliot: Modern Critical Views*. New York: Chelsea House, 1985.

———. "Reflections on T. S. Eliot." *Raritan* 8, no. 2 (1988): 70–87.

Bobb, June. *Beating a Restless Drum: The Poetics of Kamau Brathwaite and Derek Walcott*. Trenton, NJ: African World Press, 1998.

Bond, James. *Birds of the West Indies*. Boston: Houghton Mifflin, 1971.

Bradbury, Malcolm, and James McFarlane, eds. *Modernism: A Guide to European Literature, 1890–1930.* New York: Penguin, 1976.

Brathwaite, Edward Kamau. "The African Presence in Caribbean Literature." In Brathwaite, *Roots,* 190–259.

———. "An Alternative View of Caribbean History." In *The Colonial Encounter,* 43–65. University of Mysore, Center for Commonwealth Literature and Research, Karnataka, India, 1984.

———. *Ancestors.* New York: New Directions, 2001.

———. *The Arrivants: A New World Trilogy.* Oxford: Oxford Univ. Press, 1973.

———. *Barabajan Poems, 1492–1992.* New York: Savacou North, 1994.

———. "Caribbean Culture: Two Paradigms." In *Missile and Capsule,* ed. Jürgen Martini, 9–54. Bremen, Germany: Univ. of Bremen Press, 1983.

———. *Contradictory Omens: Cultural Diversity and Integration in the Caribbean.* Mona, Jamaica: Savacou, 1974.

———. *ConVERSations with Nathaniel Mackey.* New York: We Press and Xcp: Cross-Cultural Poetics, 1999.

———. *The Development of Creole Society in Jamaica, 1770–1820.* Oxford: Clarendon, 1971.

———. *DreamStories.* London: Longman, 1994.

———. "Edward Brathwaite." In *Contemporary Poets of the English Language,* ed. R. Murphy, 128–30. London: St. James Press, 1970.

———. *Folk Culture of the Slaves in Jamaica.* London: New Beacon, 1980.

———. "Gods of the Middle Passage: A Tennament." *Caribbean Review* 11, no. 4 (1982): 18–19, 42–44.

———. "History, the Caribbean Writer, and *X/Self.*" In *Crisis and Creativity in the New Literatures in English,* ed. Geoffry V. Davis and Hena Maes-Jelinek, 23–45. Atlanta: Rodopi, 1990.

———. "History of the Voice." In Brathwaite, *Roots,* 259–304.

———. "An Interview with Kamau Brathwaite." By Nathaniel Mackey. In Brown, *Art of Kamau Brathwaite,* 13–32.

———. "Jazz and the West Indian Novel." In Brathwaite, *Roots,* 55–110.

———. *MiddlePassages.* New York: New Directions, 1992.

———. *Mother Poem.* Oxford: Oxford Univ. Press, 1977.

———. "Newstead to Neustadt—Kamau Brathwaite." *World Literature Today* 68, no. 4 (1994): 653–60.

———. *Other Exiles.* Oxford: Oxford Univ. Press, 1975.

———. "A Post-Cautionary Tale of the Helen of Our Wars." *Wasafiri* 22 (Autumn 1995): 69–78.

———. "Roger Mais." In Lindfors and Sander, *Twentieth-Century Caribbean and Black African Writers,* 78–81.

———. "Roots." In Brathwaite, *Roots,* 28–54.

———. *Roots.* Ann Arbor: Univ. of Michigan Press, 1993.

———. *Sappho Sakyi Meditations.* Mona, Jamaica: Savacou, 1989.

———. *Shar.* Mona, Jamaica: Savacou, 1992.

———. "Sir Galahad and the Islands." In Brathwaite, *Roots,* 7–27.

———. *Sun Poem.* Oxford: Oxford Univ. Press, 1982.

———. "Timehri." In Coombs, *Is Massa Day Dead?* 29–44.

———. *Wars of Respect: Nanny, Sam Sharpe, and the Struggle for People's Liberation.* Kingston, Jamaica: Agency for Public Information, 1977.

———. "World Order Models—A Caribbean Perspective." *Caribbean Quarterly* 31, no. 1 (1985): 53–63.

———. *X/Self.* Oxford: Oxford Univ. Press, 1987.

———. *The Zea Mexican Diary.* Madison: Univ. of Wisconsin Press, 1994.

Braudy, Leo. *The Frenzy of Renown: Fame and Its History.* Oxford: Oxford Univ. Press, 1986.

Breiner, Laurence A. "Edward Kamau Brathwaite." In Lindfors and Sander, *Twentieth-Century Caribbean and Black African Writers,* 8–28.

———. *An Introduction to West Indian Poetry.* Cambridge: Cambridge Univ. Press, 1998.

———. "Tradition, Society, and the Figure of the Poet." *Caribbean Quarterly* 26, nos. 1–2 (1980): 1–12.

Brennan, Timothy. *At Home in the World: Cosmopolitanism Now.* Cambridge: Harvard Univ. Press, 1997.

Breslin, Paul. *Nobody's Nation: Reading Derek Walcott.* Chicago: Univ. of Chicago Press, 2001.

Britton, Celia. *Edouard Glissant and Postcolonial Theory.* Charlottesville: Univ. Press of Virginia, 1999.

Brooker, Jewel Spears. *Mastery and Escape: T. S. Eliot and the Dialect of Modernism.* Amherst: Univ. of Massachusetts Press, 1994.

Brooks, Cleanth. *Modern Poetry and The Tradition.* Oxford: Oxford Univ. Press, 1939.

Brown, Stewart. "'Between me and thee is a great gulf fixed': The Crusoe Presence in Walcott's Early Poetry." In *Robinson Crusoe: Myths and Metamorphoses,* ed. Lieve Spass and Brian Stimpson, 210–23. New York: St. Martin's, 1996.

———. "'Writin in Light': Orality-thru-typography, Kamau Brathwaite's Sycorax Video Style." In *The Pressures of the Text: Orality, Texts, and the Telling of Tales,* ed. Stewart Brown, 125–36. Birmingham, UK: Centre of West African Studies Press, 1995.

———, ed. *The Art of Derek Walcott.* Bridgeend, Wales: Poetry Wales Press, 1991.

———. *The Art of Kamau Brathwaite.* Bridgeend, Wales: Poetry Wales Press, 1991.

Bruckner, D. J. R. "A Poem in Homage to an Unwanted Man." In Hamner, *Critical Perspectives on Derek Walcott,* 396–99.

Brydon, Diana. "Rewriting *The Tempest.*" *World Literature Written in English* 24, no. 2 (1984): 75–88.

Burian, Peter. "'All That Greek Manure under the Green Bananas': Derek Walcott's Odyssey." In Davis, "Poetics of Derek Walcott," 359–77.

Burnett, Paula. *Derek Walcott: Politics and Poetics.* Gainesville: Univ. Press of Florida, 2000.

Bush, Ronald. "T. S. Eliot and Modernism at the Present Time: A Provocation." In *T. S. Eliot: The Modernist in History,* 191–204. Cambridge: Cambridge Univ. Press, 1991.

Carey, Peter. *Jack Maggs*. New York: Knopf, 1997.

Carruth, Hayden. "Poetry Chronicle." Review of *The Arrivants,* by Edward Brathwaite. *Hudson Review* 27, no. 2 (1974): 308–20.

Césaire, Aimé. *Notebook of a Return to the Native Land.* Trans. Clayton Eshleman and Annette Smith. In *Aimé Césaire: The Collected Poetry.* Berkeley: Univ. of California Press, 1983. Originally published as *Cahier d'un retour au pays natal* (Paris: Présence Africaine, 1947).

———. *Une tempête: d'apres 'La Tempête' de Shakespeare—Adaptation pour un théatre nègre.* Paris: Editions du Seuil, 1974.

Chamberlin, J. Edward. *Come Back to Me My Language: Poetry and the West Indies.* Urbana: Univ. of Illinois Press, 1993.

Chang, Vincent J. *Joyce, Race, and Empire.* Cambridge: Cambridge Univ. Press, 1995.

Chatterjee, Partha. *Nationalist Thought and the Colonial World: A Derivative Discourse.* London: Zed, 1986.

Chevannes, Barry. *Rastafari: Roots and Ideology.* Syracuse: Syracuse Univ. Press, 1994.

Childs, Donald. "T. S. Eliot's American Dissent/Descent." In *Cohesion and Dissent in America,* ed. Carol Colatrella, 77–94. Albany, NY: SUNY Press, 1994.

Chinitz, David. "T. S. Eliot and the Cultural Divide." *PMLA* 110, no. 2 (1995): 236–47.

Clifford, James. *The Predicament of Culture: Twentieth-Century Ethnography, Literature, and Art.* Cambridge: Harvard Univ. Press, 1988.

———. *Routes: Travel and Translation in the Late Twentieth Century.* Cambridge: Harvard Univ. Press, 1997.

Cobham, Rhonda. "K/Kam/Kam/Kama/Kamau: Brathwaite's Project of Self-Naming in *Barabajan Poems.*" In Reiss, *For the Geography of a Soul,* 297–315.

Coetzee, J. M. *Foe.* New York: Penguin, 1987.

Coleridge, Samuel Taylor. *Biographia Literaria.* Vol. 7 of *The Collected Works of Samuel Taylor Coleridge.* Ed. James Engell and W. Jackson Bate. Pt. 2. Princeton: Princeton Univ. Press, 1983.

Collier, Gordon. "Artistic Autonomy and Cultural Allegiance: Aspects of the Walcott-Brathwaite Debate Re-examined." *The Literary Half-Yearly* 21, no. 2 (1980): 93–105.

Coombs, Orde, ed. *Is Massa Day Dead? Black Moods in the Caribbean.* Garden City, NY: Anchor, 1974.

Crawford, Robert. *The Savage and the City in the Work of T. S. Eliot.* Oxford: Oxford Univ. Press, 1987.

D'Aguiar, Fred. "Ambiguity without a Crisis? Twin Traditions, The Individual and Community in Derek Walcott's Essays." In Brown, *Art of Derek Walcott,* 157–70.

Dash, J. Michael. *Edouard Glissant.* Cambridge: Cambridge Univ. Press, 1995.

———. "Edward Brathwaite." In *West Indian Literature,* ed. Bruce King, 210–27. Hamden, CT: Archon, 1979.

———. *The Other America: Caribbean Literature in a New World Context.* Charlottesville: Univ. Press of Virginia, 1998.

———. "Psychology, Creolization, and Hybridization." In *New National and Post-Colonial Literatures: An Introduction,* ed. Bruce King, 45–58. Oxford: Clarendon, 1996.

———. Review of *The Visibility Trigger* and *Jah Music,* by Kamau Brathwaite. *Journal of West Indian Literature* 1, no. 2 (1987): 87–90.

Davey, Frank. *Reading Canadian Reading.* Winnipeg, MB: Turnstone, 1988.

Davie, Donald. "Anglican Eliot." In *Eliot in His Time: Essays on the Occasion of the Fiftieth Anniversary of The Waste Land,* ed. A. Walton Litz, 181–96. Princeton: Princeton Univ. Press, 1973.

Davis, Gregson, ed. "The Poetics of Derek Walcott: Intertextual Perspectives." Special issue of *South Atlantic Quarterly* 96, no. 2 (1997): 227–377.

———. "'With No Homeric Shadow': The Disavowal of Epic in Derek Walcott's *Omeros.*" In Davis, "Poetics of Derek Walcott," 320–33.

de la Campa, Román. "Resistance and Globalization in Caribbean Discourse: Antonio Benítez-Rojo and Edouard Glissant." In Arnold, *History of Literature in the Caribbean,* 87–118.

D'haen, Theo. "(Post) Modernity and Caribbean Discourse." In Arnold, *History of Literature in the Caribbean,* 303–24.

Donahue, Joseph. "Kamau Brathwaite's Videolect: Spirit and Letter." In *Ngũgĩ wa Thiong'o: Texts and Contexts.* Ed. Charles Cantalupo. Trenton, NJ: African World Press, 1995: 271–82.

Dorsinville, Max. *Caliban without Prospero.* Erin, ON: Press Porecpic, 1974.

During, Simon. "Postmodernism or Post-colonialism Today." In Ashcroft, Griffiths, and Tiffin, *Post-colonial Studies Reader,* 125–29.

Eagleton, Terry. *Criticism and Ideology: A Study in Marxist Literary Theory.* London: Verso, 1978.

Edmondson, Belinda, ed. *Caribbean Romances: The Politics of Regional Representation.* Charlottesville: Univ. Press of Virginia, 1999.

Eliot, T. S. "American Literature and the American Language." In Eliot, *To Criticize the Critic,* 43–60.

———. "Andrew Marvell." In Eliot, *Selected Essays,* 292–304.

———. *Christianity and Culture.* New York: Harcourt Brace Jovanovich, 1960.

———. "A Commentary." *Criterion* 14, no. 57 (1935): 610–13.

———. *The Complete Poems and Plays, 1909–1950.* New York: Harcourt Brace Jovanovich, 1971.

———. "Dante." In Eliot, *Selected Essays,* 237–80.

———. "From Poe to Valéry." In Eliot, *To Criticize the Critic,* 27–42.

———. "In Memoriam." In Eliot, *Selected Essays,* 328–40.

———. "In Memory." *Little Review* 5, no. 4 (1918): 44–47.

———. Introduction to *Savonarola: A Dramatic Poem by Charlotte Eliot.* London: R. Cobden-Sanderson, 1926.

———. *Knowledge and Experience in the Philosophy of F. H. Bradley.* London: Faber & Faber, 1964.

———. "The Last Twenty-five Years of English Poetry." Draft lecture. 1940. Quoted in Christopher Ricks, ed., *Inventions of the March Hare* (New York: Harcourt Brace, 1996), 388.

———. *The Letters of T. S. Eliot. Volume 1, 1898–1922.* Ed. Valerie Eliot. New York: Harcourt Brace Jovanovich, 1988.

———. "Marie Lloyd." In Eliot, *Selected Essays,* 456–59.
———. "The Metaphysical Poets." In Eliot, *Selected Essays,* 281–91.
———. "Milton II." In Eliot, *On Poetry and Poets,* 146–61.
———. "The Music of Poetry." In Eliot, *On Poetry and Poets,* 26–38.
———. *Notes towards the Definition of Culture.* London: Faber & Faber, 1962.
———. "Note sur Mallarmé et Poe." *La Nouvelle Revue Française* 14, no. 158 (1926): 524–26.
———. "Observations." *Egoist* 5, no. 5 (1918): 69–70.
———. *On Poetry and Poets.* 1957. Reprint. London: Faber & Faber, 1979.
———. "Reflections on Contemporary Literature." *Egoist* 6, no. 3 (1919): 39–40.
———. "A Romantic Patrician." *Athenaeum,* 2 May 1919, 265–67.
———. *Selected Essays.* 1932. Reprint. London: Faber & Faber, 1972.
———. *Selected Prose of T. S. Eliot.* Ed. Hugh Kenner. New York: Harcourt Brace Jovanovich, 1975.
———. "The Social Function of Poetry." In Eliot, *On Poetry and Poets,* 15–25.
———. "Swinburne." *Athenaeum,* 16 January 1920, 72–73. Reprinted as "Swinburne as Poet," in Eliot, *Selected Essays,* 323–27.
———. "Tarr." *Egoist* 5, no. 8 (1918): 105–6.
———. "The Three Provincialities." *Essays in Criticism* 1, no. 1 (1951): 38–41. First published in *The Tyro: A Review of the Arts of Painting, Sculpture, and Design* 2 (1922): 11–13.
———. "To Criticize the Critic." In Eliot, *To Criticize the Critic,* 11–26.
———. *To Criticize the Critic.* London: Faber & Faber, 1965.
———. "Tradition and the Individual Talent." In Eliot, *Selected Essays,* 13–22.
———. "Tradition and the Practice of Poetry." In Olney, *T. S. Eliot,* 7–25. First published in *Southern Review* 21, no. 4 (1985): 873–88.
———. "'*Ulysses,*' Order, and Myth." In Eliot, *Selected Prose,* 175–78.
———. *The Use of Poetry and the Use of Criticism.* 1933. Reprint. Cambridge: Harvard Univ. Press, 1994.
———. *The Varieties of Metaphysical Poetry.* Ed. Ronald Schuchard. New York: Harcourt Brace, 1993.
———. "The Voice of His Time: T. S. Eliot on Tennyson's 'In Memoriam.'" *Listener* 27 (12 February 1942): 211–12.
———. "War-Paint and Feathers." *Athenaeum* 17 October 1919, 1036.
———. *The Waste Land: A Facsimile and Transcript of the Original Drafts Including the Annotations of Ezra Pound.* Ed. Valerie Eliot. London: Faber & Faber, 1971.
———. "What Dante Means to Me." In Eliot, *To Criticize the Critic,* 125–35.
———. "What Is Minor Poetry?" In Eliot, *On Poetry and Poets,* 39–52.
———. "Wordsworth and Coleridge." In Eliot, *Use of Poetry,* 58–77.
———. "Yeats." In Eliot, *On Poetry and Poets,* 252–62.
———, trans. *Anabasis.* By Saint-John Perse. London: Faber and Faber, 1930.
Ellis, Steve. *The English Eliot: Design, Language, and Landscape in "Four Quartets."* London: Routledge, 1991.
Ellison, Ralph. "Hidden Name and Complex Fate." In *The Collected Essays of Ralph Ellison,* ed. John F. Callahan, 189–209. New York: Modern Library, 1995.

Ellmann, Richard. *Ulysses on the Liffey.* London: Faber & Faber, 1972.

Fanon, Frantz. *The Wretched of the Earth.* Trans. Constance Farrington. New York: Grove, 1963.

Figueroa, John. "Omeros." In Brown, *Art of Derek Walcott,* 193–213.

Flanagan, Hallie. *Dynamo.* New York: Duell, Sloan & Pearce, 1943.

Fumagalli, Maria Cristiana. "Derek Walcott's *Omeros* and Dante's *Commedia:* Epics of the Self and Journeys into Language." *Cambridge Quarterly* 29, no. 1 (2000): 17–36.

Fussell, Paul. *Poetic Meter and Poetic Form.* Rev. ed. New York: McGraw-Hill, 1979.

Gardner, Helen. *The Composition of the "Four Quartets."* Oxford: Oxford Univ. Press, 1978.

Gates, Henry Louis, Jr. *Figures in Black: Words, Signs, and "Racial" Self.* New York: Oxford Univ. Press, 1987.

———. *Loose Canons.* Oxford: Oxford Univ. Press, 1992.

Gellner, Ernest. *Nations and Nationalisms.* Ithaca, NY: Cornell Univ. Press, 1983.

Gikandi, Simon. *Writing in Limbo: Modernism and Caribbean Literature.* Ithaca, NY: Cornell Univ. Press, 1992.

Gilroy, Paul. *The Black Atlantic: Modernity and Double Consciousness.* Cambridge: Harvard Univ. Press, 1993.

Glissant, Edouard. *Caribbean Discourse: Selected Essays.* Trans. J. Michael Dash. Charlottesville: Univ. Press of Virginia, 1989.

———. *Poetics of Relation.* Trans. Betsy Wing. Ann Arbor: Univ. of Michigan Press, 1997.

Gordon, Lyndall. *Eliot's Early Years.* Oxford: Oxford Univ. Press, 1977.

———. *Eliot's New Life.* Oxford: Oxford Univ. Press, 1988.

Graff, Gerald. *Professing Literature: An Institutional History.* Chicago: Univ. of Chicago Press, 1987.

Griffith, Glyne. "Kamau Brathwaite as Cultural Critic." In Brown, *Art of Kamau Brathwaite,* 75–85.

Gugelberger, Georg. "Decolonizing the Canon: Considerations of Third World Literature." *New Literary History* 22, no. 3 (1991): 505–24.

Guillory, John. "The Ideology of Canon-Formation: T. S. Eliot and Cleanth Brooks." *Critical Inquiry* 10, no. 1 (1983): 173–98.

Hamner, Robert. *Epic of the Dispossessed: Derek Walcott's Omeros.* Columbia: Univ. of Missouri Press, 1997.

———, ed. *Critical Perspectives on Derek Walcott.* Washington, DC: Three Continents Press, 1993.

Harris, Wilson. "History, Fable, and Myth in the Caribbean and Guianas." In Harris, *Selected Essays,* 152–66.

———. "The Making of Tradition." In *Explorations: A Selection of Talks and Articles,* ed. Hena Maes Jelinek, 88–96. Geding Sovej, Denmark: Dangaroo, 1981.

———. "Quetzalcoatl and the Smoking Mirror: Reflections on Originality and Tradition." In Harris, *Selected Essays,* 184–95.

———. *Selected Essays of Wilson Harris: The Unfinished Genesis of the Imagination.* Ed. A. J. M. Bundy. London: Routledge, 1999.

———. "Tradition and the West Indian Novel." In Harris, *Tradition, the Writer, and Society,* 28–47.

———. *Tradition, the Writer, and Society.* London: New Beacon, 1967.

———. "The Writer and Society." In Harris, *Tradition, the Writer, and Society,* 48–64.

Heaney, Seamus. "Envies and Identifications: Dante and the Modern Poet." *Irish University Review: A Journal of Irish Studies* 15, no. 1 (1985): 5–19.

———. "The Government of the Tongue." In *The Government of the Tongue: Selected Prose, 1978–1987,* 91–108. New York: Farrar, Strauss, & Giroux, 1988.

———. "Learning from Eliot." *Agenda* 27, no. 1 (1989): 20–33.

———. "Station Island." In *New and Selected Poems, 1966–1987,* 163–93. London: Faber & Faber, 1990.

Heidegger, Martin. "Letter on Humanism." Trans. Frank A. Capuzzi and J. Glenn Gray. In Martin Heidegger, *Basic Writings,* ed. David Farrell Krell, 189–242. New York: Harper & Row, 1977.

Helmling, Steven. "T. S. Eliot and Ralph Ellison: Insiders, Outsiders, and Cultural Authority." *Southern Review* 25, no. 2 (1989): 841–58.

Hobsbawm, Eric J. *The Age of Empire, 1875–1914.* New York: Pantheon Books, 1987.

Hollinger, David. *Postethnic America.* New York: Basic Books, 1995.

Hornblower, Simon, and Antony Spawforth, eds. *The Oxford Classical Dictionary.* 3rd ed. Oxford: Oxford Univ. Press, 1996.

"How Far Are Derek Walcott and Edward Brathwaite Similar? Is it Impossible for the Caribbean to Choose between the Two, If So, Which Way Should They Choose and Why?" *Busara* 6, no. 1 (1974): 90–100.

Huggan, Graham. "Opting out of the (Critical) Common Market: Creolization and the Post-Colonial Text." *Kunapipi* 11, no. 1 (1989): 27–40.

Hutcheon, Linda. "Circling the Downspout of Empire: Post-colonialism and Postmodernism." *Ariel: A Review of International English Literature* 20, no. 4 (1989): 149–75.

———. "Colonialism and the Postcolonial Condition: Complexity Abounding." *PMLA* 110, no. 1 (1995): 7–16.

Ismond, Patricia. "Walcott Versus Brathwaite." In Hamner, *Critical Perspectives on Derek Walcott,* 220–38.

Jacobs, Virginia Lee. *Roots of Rastafari.* San Diego: Avant Books, 1985.

James, Cynthia. "Caliban in Y2K?—Hypertext and New Pathways." In Reiss, *For the Geography of a Soul,* 351–61.

James, Louis. "Brathwaite and Jazz." In Brown, *Art of Kamau Brathwaite,* 62–74.

———. "Review of *Rights of Passage.*" *Caribbean Quarterly* 13, no. 1 (1967): 38–41.

Jameson, Fredric. *Postmodernism, or the Cultural Logic of Late Capitalism.* Durham, NC: Duke Univ. Press, 1991.

———. "Third World Literature in the Era of Multinational Capitalism." *Social Text* 15 (1986): 65–88.

Jay, Gregory S. "Postmodernism in *The Waste Land:* Women, Mass Culture, and Others." In *Rereading the New: A Backward Glance at Modernism,* ed. Kevin Dettmar, 221–46. Ann Arbor: Univ. of Michigan Press, 1992.

Joyce, James. *Ulysses.* 1922. Reprint. London: Penguin, 1986.

Julius, Anthony. *T. S. Eliot, Anti-Semitism, and Literary Form.* Cambridge: Cambridge Univ. Press, 1995.

Kearns, Cleo M. *T. S. Eliot and Indic Traditions: A Study in Poetry and Belief.* Cambridge: Cambridge Univ. Press, 1987.

Kenner, Hugh. Introduction to Eliot, *Selected Prose.*

Kiberd, Declan. *Inventing Ireland.* Cambridge: Harvard Univ. Press, 1996.

King, Bruce. *Derek Walcott: A Caribbean Life.* Oxford: Oxford Univ. Press, 2000.

———. *Derek Walcott and West Indian Drama: "Not Only a Playwright but a Company": The Trinidad Theatre Workshop, 1959–1993.* Oxford: Oxford Univ. Press, 1995.

———. *The New English Literatures: Cultural Nationalisms in a Changing World.* New York: St. Martin's, 1980.

Knowles, Sebastian. "'Then You Wink the Other Eye': T. S. Eliot and the Music Hall." *ANQ* 11, no. 4 (1998): 20–31.

Lamming, George. *Natives of My Person.* London: Allison & Busby, 1971.

———. *The Pleasures of Exile.* London: Michael Joseph, 1960.

Lawrence, Karen, ed. *Decolonizing Tradition: New Views of Twentieth-Century "British" Literary Canons.* Urbana: Univ. of Illinois Press, 1992.

———. *Transcultural Joyce.* Cambridge: Cambridge Univ. Press, 1998.

Levenson, Michael. "The End of Tradition and the Beginning of History." In *Words in Time: New Essays on "Four Quartets,"* ed. Edward Lobb, 158–78. Ann Arbor: Univ. of Michigan Press, 1993.

———. *A Genealogy of Modernism: A Study of English Literary Doctrine, 1908–1922.* Cambridge: Cambridge Univ. Press, 1983.

Levin, Harry. "What Was Modernism?" In *Refractions: Essays in Comparative Literature,* 271–95. New York: Oxford Univ. Press, 1966.

Lie, Nadia, and Theo D'haen, eds. *Constellations Caliban: Figurations of a Character.* Atlanta: Rodopi, 1997.

Lindfors, Bernth, and Reinhard Sander, eds. *Twentieth-Century Caribbean and Black African Writers: Second Series.* Vol. 125 of *The Dictionary of Literary Biography,* 78–81. Detroit: Gale Research, 1993.

Lipking, Lawrence. *The Life of the Poet: Beginning and Ending Poetic Careers.* Chicago: Univ. of Chicago Press, 1981.

Lloyd, David. *Anomalous States: Irish Writing and the Post-Colonial Moment.* Durham, NC: Duke Univ. Press, 1993.

Longenbach, James. *Modern Poetry after Modernism.* Oxford: Oxford Univ. Press, 1997.

Lucy, Sean. *T. S. Eliot and the Idea of Tradition.* London: Cohen & West, 1960.

MacGaffey, Wyatt. *Religion and Society in Central Africa: The BaKongo of Lower Zaire.* Chicago: Univ. of Chicago Press, 1986.

Manganiello, Dominic. *T. S. Eliot and Dante.* London: Macmillan, 1989.

Mannoni, Oscar. *Prospero and Caliban: The Psychology of Colonization.* New York: Praeger, 1964.

Marshall, Alan. "England and Nowhere." In Moody, *Cambridge Companion to T. S. Eliot,* 94–107.

Martin, Jonathan. "Nightmare History: Derek Walcott's *Omeros*." *Kenyon Review* 14, no. 3 (1992): 197–204.

Materer, Timothy. "T. S. Eliot's Critical Program." In Moody, *Cambridge Companion to T. S. Eliot,* 48–59.

McClintock, Ann. "The Angel of Progress: Pitfalls of the Term 'Post-colonialism.'" In Williams and Chrisman, *Colonial Discourse,* 291–304.

McGann, Jerome. *Black Riders: The Visible Language of Modernism.* Princeton: Princeton Univ. Press, 1993.

Menand, Louis. "Eliot and the Jews." Review of *T. S. Eliot, Anti-Semitism, and Literary Form,* by Anthony Julius. *New York Review of Books* 53 (1996): 34–41.

Mishra, Vijay, and Bob Hodge. "What Is Post(-)Colonialism?" In Williams and Chrisman, *Colonial Discourse,* 276–90.

Moody, A. D. *Thomas Stearns Eliot: Poet.* 2nd ed. Cambridge: Cambridge Univ. Press, 1994.

———, ed. *The Cambridge Companion to T. S. Eliot.* Cambridge: Cambridge Univ. Press, 1994.

Morris, Mervyn. "The Broken Ground: Edward Brathwaite's Trilogy of Poems." *New World Quarterly* 5, no. 3 (1970) 14–26.

———. "Is English We Speaking." In *"Is English We Speaking" and Other Essays,* 1–16. Kingston, Jamaica: Ian Randle, 1999.

———. "Overlapping Journeys: *The Arrivants.*" In Brown, *Art of Kamau Brathwaite,* 117–31.

———. "Walcott and the Audience for Poetry." In Hamner, *Critical Perspectives on Derek Walcott,* 174–92.

Moyers, Bill. *Derek Walcott.* Videocassette. Dir. Bill Moyers. Princeton, NJ: Films for the Humanities and Sciences, 1994.

Naipaul, V. S. *Mimic Men.* New York: Penguin, 1967.

Nettleford, Rex M. *Identity, Race, and Protest in Jamaica.* New York: William Morrow, 1972.

Ngũgĩ wa Thiong'o. *Decolonizing the Mind: The Politics of Language in African Literature.* Portsmouth, NH: Heinemann, 1986.

———. "Kamau Brathwaite: The Voice of African Presence." *World Literature Today* 68, no. 4 (1994): 677–79.

Nixon, Rob. "Caribbean and African Appropriations of *The Tempest.*" *Critical Inquiry* 13, no. 3 (1987): 557–78.

North, Michael. *The Dialect of Modernism: Race, Language, and Twentieth-Century Literature.* New York: Oxford Univ. Press, 1994.

Nwoga, Donatus Ibe. "Christopher Okigbo." In Lindfors and Sander, *Twentieth-Century Caribbean and Black African Writers,* 200–224.

Olaniyan, Tejumola. "Derek Walcott: Liminal Spaces/Substantive Histories." In Edmonson, *Caribbean Romances,* 199–214.

———. *Scars of Conquest; Masks of Resistance: The Invention of Cultural Identities in African, African-American, and Caribbean Drama.* New York: Oxford Univ. Press, 1995.

Olney, James, ed. *T. S. Eliot: Essays from the Southern Review.* Oxford: Clarendon, 1988.

Oser, Lee. *T. S. Eliot and American Poetry.* Columbia: Univ. of Missouri Press, 1998.

Ozick, Cynthia. "A Critic at Large: T. S. Eliot at 101." *New Yorker,* 20 November 1989, 119–54.

Palmer, Colin. "Identity, Race, and Black Power in Independent Jamaica." In *The Modern Caribbean,* ed. Franklin W. Knight and Colin A. Palmer, 111–28. Chapel Hill: Univ. of North Carolina Press, 1989.

Pantin, Raoul. *Black Power Day: The 1970 February Revolution.* Santa Cruz, Trinidad: Hatuey Productions, 1990.

Parry, Benita. "The Postcolonial: Conceptual Category or Chimera?" *Yearbook of English Studies* 27 (1997): 3–21.

———. "Problems in Current Theories of Colonial Discourse." *Oxford Literary Review* 9, no. 1 (1987): 27–58.

Perl, Jeffrey. "Passing the Time: Modernism versus New Criticism." In Witemeyer, *Future of Modernism,* 33–48.

———. *Skepticism and Modern Enmity.* Baltimore: John Hopkins Univ. Press, 1989.

Perloff, Marjorie. *The Dance of the Intellect: Studies in the Poetry of the Pound Tradition.* New York: Cambridge Univ. Press, 1985.

———. *Radical Artifice: Writing in the Age of Media.* Chicago: Univ. of Chicago Press, 1991.

Pollard, Charles. "Traveling with Joyce: Derek Walcott's Discrepant Cosmopolitan Modernism." *Twentieth Century Literature* 47, no. 2 (2001): 197–216.

Pollard, Velma. "The Dust—Tribute to the Folk." *Caribbean Quarterly* 26, nos. 1–2 (1980): 41–48.

———. "Language in the Poetry of Edward Brathwaite." *World Literature Written in English* 8, no. 1 (1980): 62–74.

Quinones, Ricardo. *Dante Alighieri.* New York: Twayne, 1998.

Rabinow, Paul. "Representations Are Social Facts: Modernity and Post-Modernity in Anthropology." In *Writing Culture: The Poetics and Politics of Ethnography,* ed. James Clifford and George Marcus, 234–61. Berkeley and Los Angeles: Univ. of California Press, 1986.

Ramaiah, L. S. *Indian Responses to T. S. Eliot: A Bibliographical Guide to Writings in English.* Calcutta: Writers Workshop, 1988.

Ramazani, Jahan. *The Hybrid Muse: Postcolonial Poetry in English.* Chicago: Univ. of Chicago Press, 2001.

———. "Is Yeats a Postcolonial Poet?" *Raritan* 17, no. 3 (1998): 64–89.

———. "The Wound of History: Walcott's *Omeros* and the Postcolonial Poetics of Affliction." *PMLA* 112, no. 3 (1997): 405–17.

Ramchand, Kenneth. *An Introduction to the Study of West Indian Literature.* Kingston, Jamaica: Thomas Nelson, 1976.

Ramsaran, J. A. "Derek Walcott: New World Mediterranean Poet." *World Literature Written in English* 21, no. 1 (1982): 133–47.

Ray, Sangeetha. "Shifting Subjects Shifting Ground: The Names and Spaces of the Post-Colonial." *Hypatia: A Journal of Feminist Philosophy* 7, no. 2 (1992): 188–201.

Redfield, Robert. *Peasant Society and Culture.* Chicago: Univ. of Chicago Press, 1956.

Reiss, Timothy J., ed. *For the Geography of a Soul: Emerging Perspectives on Kamau Brathwaite.* Trenton, NJ: African World Press, 2001.

Renk, Kathleen. *Caribbean Shadows and Victorian Ghosts.* Charlottesville: Univ. of Virginia Press, 1999.

Retamar, Roberto Fernández. *"Caliban" and Other Essays.* Minneapolis: Univ. of Minnesota Press, 1989.

Rhys, Jean. *Wide Sargasso Sea.* New York: Norton, 1966.

Ricks, Christopher. *T. S. Eliot and Prejudice.* London: Faber, 1988.

Rigby, Graeme. "Publishing Brathwaite: Adventures in the Video Style." *World Literature in Review* 68, no. 4 (1994): 708–14.

Robbins, Bruce. *Secular Vocations: Intellectuals, Professionalism, Culture.* New York: Verso, 1993.

Roberts, Peter A. *West Indians and Their Language.* Cambridge: Cambridge Univ. Press, 1988.

Rohlehr, Gordon. "'Black Sycorax, My Mother': Brathwaite's Reconstruction of *The Tempest.*" In Reiss, *For the Geography of the Soul,* 277–95.

———. "Brathwaite with a Dash of Brown: Crit, the Writer, and the Written Life." In Rohlehr, *The Shape of That Hurt, and Other Essays,* 209–46.

———. "Dream Journeys." Introduction to *DreamStories,* by Kamau Brathwaite, iii–xvi. London: Longman, 1994.

———. *Pathfinder: Black Awakening in The Arrivants of Edward Kamau Brathwaite.* Port of Spain: Gordon Rohlehr, 1981.

———. "The Problem of the Problem of Form: The Idea of an Aesthetic Continuum and Aesthetic Code-switching in West Indian Literature." In Rohlehr, *The Shape of That Hurt, and Other Essays,* 1–65.

———. "The Rehumanization of History: Regeneration of Spirit: Apocalypse and Revolution in Brathwaite's *The Arrivants* and *X/Self.*" In Brown, *Art of Kamau Brathwaite,* 163–207.

———. *The Shape of That Hurt, and Other Essays.* Port of Spain, Trinidad: Longman, 1992.

———. "Withering into Truth: A Review of Derek Walcott's *The Gulf, and Other Poems.*" In Hamner, *Critical Perspectives on Derek Walcott,* 212–19.

Rushdie, Salman. "Imaginary Homelands." In *Imaginary Homelands: Essays and Criticism, 1981–1991,* 9–21. London: Granta Books, 1991.

———. *Midnight's Children.* New York: Penguin, 1980.

Said, Edward. *Cultural and Imperialism.* New York: Knopf, 1993.

Sartre, Jean-Paul. "Black Orpheus." Trans. John MacCombie. In *The Black American Writer,* ed. C. W. E. Bigsby, 2:5–40. Deland, FL: Everett, 1969.

Savory, Elaine. "Returning to Sycorax/Prospero's Response: Kamau Brathwaite's Word Journey." In Brown, *Art of Kamau Brathwaite,* 208–30.

———. "The Word Becomes *nam:* Self and Community in the Poetry of Kamau Brathwaite and Its Relationship to Caribbean Culture and Postmodern Theory." In *Writing the Nation: Self and Country in the Post-Colonial Imagination,* ed. John C. Hawley, 23–44. Amsterdam: Rodopi, 1996.

———. "Wordsongs and Wordwounds / Homecoming: Kamau Brathwaite's *Barabajan Poems.*" *World Literature Today* 68, no. 4 (1994): 750–57.

Schiff, Steven. "Big Poetry." *New Yorker,* 14 July 1997, 60–67.

Schmidt, A. V. C. "Eliot and the Dialect of the Tribe." *Essays in Criticism* 33, no. 1 (1983): 36–48.

Schuchard, Ronald. *Eliot's Dark Angel: Intersections of Life and Art.* Oxford: Oxford Univ. Press, 1999.

Schwartz, Delmore. "The Literary Dictatorship of T. S. Eliot." In Schwartz, *Selected Essays,* 312–31.

———. *Selected Essays of Delmore Schwartz.* Ed. Donald A. Dike and David H. Zucker. Chicago: Univ. of Chicago Press, 1970.

———. "T. S. Eliot as the International Hero." In Schwartz, *Selected Essays,* 120–28.

———. "T. S. Eliot's Voice and His Voices." In Schwartz, *Selected Essays,* 129–42.

Schwartz, Sanford. "The Postmodernity of Modernism." In Witemeyer, *Future of Modernism,* 9–31.

———. "T. S. Eliot." In *Prospects for the Study of American Literature: A Guide for Scholars and Students,* ed. Richard Kopley, 241–65. New York: New York Univ. Press, 1997.

Senghor, Léopold. *Anthologie de la nouvelle poésie nègre et malgache de langue française.* 2nd ed. Paris: Presses Universitaires de France, 1969.

Sharpe, Jenny. *Allegories of Empire: The Figure of Woman in the Colonial Text.* Minneapolis: Univ. of Minnesota Press, 1993.

Sharratt, Bernard. "Eliot: Modernism, Postmodernism, and After." In Moody, *Cambridge Companion to T. S. Eliot,* 223–35.

Shusterman, Richard. *T. S. Eliot and the Philosophy of Criticism.* London: Duckworth, 1988.

Sigg, Eric. *The American T. S. Eliot: A Study of the Early Writings.* Cambridge: Cambridge Univ. Press, 1989.

Slemon, Stephen. "Modernism's Last Post." *Ariel: A Review of International English Literature* 20, no. 4 (1989): 3–17.

Smith, Grover. *T. S. Eliot's Poetry and Plays: A Study in Sources & Meaning.* 2nd ed. Chicago: Univ. of Chicago Press, 1974.

Spivak, Gayatri. "Can the Subaltern Speak?" In Williams and Chrisman, *Colonial Discourse,* 66–111.

———. "In a Word: Interview." By Ellen Rooney. *Differences* 1, no. 2 (1989): 124–56.

Sprouse, Keith Alan. "Introduction to Caribbean Poetics." In Arnold, *History of Literature in the Caribbean,* 79–86.

Spurr, David. "Myths of Anthropology: Eliot, Joyce, Lévy-Bruhl." *PMLA* 109, no. 2 (1994): 266–80.

Svarny, Erik. *"The Men of 1914": T. S. Eliot and Early Modernism.* Philadelphia: Open Univ. Press, 1988.

Ten Kortenaar, Neil. "Where the Atlantic Meets the Caribbean: Kamau Brathwaite's *The Arrivants* and T. S. Eliot's *The Waste Land.*" *Research in African Literature* 27, no. 4 (1996): 15–27.

Terada, Rei. *Derek Walcott's Poetry: American Mimicry.* Boston: Northeastern Univ. Press, 1992.

Thieme, John. *Derek Walcott.* Manchester: Manchester Univ. Press, 1999.

Torres-Saillant, Silvio. *Caribbean Poetics: Toward an Aesthetic of West Indian Literature.* Cambridge: Cambridge Univ. Press, 1997.

Walcott, Derek. *Another Life.* New York: Farrar, Straus & Giroux, 1973.

———. *The Antilles: Fragments of Epic Memory.* New York: Farrar, Straus & Giroux, 1993.

———. *The Arkansas Testament.* New York: Farrar, Straus & Giroux, 1987.

———. "The Art of Poetry XXXVII: Derek Walcott." By Edward Hirsch. In Walcott, *Conversations with Derek Walcott,* 95–121.

———. "The Caribbean: Culture or Mimicry?" In Hamner, *Critical Perspectives on Derek Walcott,* 51–57.

———. *The Collected Poems, 1948–1984.* New York: Farrar, Straus, & Giroux, 1984.

———. *Conversations with Derek Walcott.* Ed. William Baer. Jackson: Univ. of Mississippi Press, 1996.

———. "Conversation with Derek Walcott." By Robert D. Hamner. In Walcott, *Conversations with Derek Walcott,* 21–33.

———. "A Conversation with Derek Walcott." By Richard Smith. In *Our Other Voices: Nine Poets Speaking,* ed. John Wheatcroft, 178–95. Lewisburg, PA: Bucknell Univ. Press, 1991.

———. "Derek Walcott." In *Points of Departure: International Writers on Writing and Politics,* by David Montenegro, 80–109. Ann Arbor: Univ. of Michigan Press, 1991.

———. *Dream on Monkey Mountain, and Other Plays.* New York: Farrar, Straus & Giroux, 1970.

———. *Epitaph for the Young: A Poem in Twelve Cantos.* Bridgetown, Barbados: Advocate, 1949.

———. "The Figure of Crusoe." In Hamner, *Critical Perspectives on Derek Walcott,* 33–40.

———. "An Interview with Derek Walcott." By Edward Hirsch. In Walcott, *Conversations with Derek Walcott,* 50–63.

———. "An Interview with Derek Walcott." By Charles H. Rowell. In Walcott, *Conversations with Derek Walcott,* 122–34.

———. "An Interview with Derek Walcott." By Leif Sjoberg. In Walcott, *Conversations with Derek Walcott,* 79–85.

———. "An Interview with Derek Walcott." By J. P. White. In Walcott, *Conversations with Derek Walcott,* 151–74.

———. "Leaving School." In Hamner, *Critical Perspectives on Derek Walcott,* 24–32.

———. "The Muse of History: An Essay." In Coombs, *Is Massa Day Dead?* 1–28.

———. "Necessity of Negritude." In Hamner, *Critical Perspectives on Derek Walcott,* 20–23.

———. *Omeros.* New York: Farrar, Straus & Giroux, 1989.

———. "Reflections Before and After Carnival: An Interview with Derek Walcott." By Sharon Ciccarelli. In Walcott, *Conversations with Derek Walcott,* 34–49.

———. "Reflections on *Omeros.*" In Davis, "Poetics of Derek Walcott," 229–46.

———. "The Road Taken." In *Homage to Robert Frost,* 93–117. New York: Farrar, Straus & Giroux, 1996.

———. *Sea Grapes*. New York: Farrar, Straus & Giroux, 1976.

———. "Society and the Artist." In Hamner, *Critical Perspectives on Derek Walcott,* 15–17.

———. "Thinking Poetry: An Interview with Derek Walcott." By Robert Brown and Cheryl Johnson. In Walcott, *Conversations with Derek Walcott,* 175–88.

———. "Tribal Flutes." In Hamner, *Critical Perspectives on Derek Walcott,* 41–44.

———. "T. S. Eliot—Master of an Age." *Trinidad Guardian,* 10 January 1965, 3.

———. "Walcott on Walcott." By Dennis Scott. In Walcott, *Conversations with Derek Walcott,* 10–16.

———. "What the Twilight Says: An Overture." In Walcott, *Dream on Monkey Mountain, and Other Plays,* 3–40.

Weinstein, Norman. "Jazz in the Caribbean Air." *World Literature Today* 68, no. 4 (1994): 715–18.

Williams, Patrick, and Laura Chrisman, eds. *Colonial Discourse and Post-colonial Theory: A Reader.* New York: Columbia Univ. Press, 1994.

Wilson-Tagoe, Nana. *Historical Thought and Literary Representation in the West Indies*. Gainesville: Univ. Press of Florida, 1998.

Witemeyer, Hugh, ed. *The Future of Modernism.* Ann Arbor: Univ. of Michigan Press, 1997.

Wordsworth, William. "Preface to the Lyrical Ballads." In *The Prose Works of William Wordsworth,* ed. W. J. B. Owen and Jane Worthington Smyser, 1:118–60. Oxford: Clarendon, 1974.

Young, Howard, ed. *T. S. Eliot and Hispanic Modernity (1924–1993)*. Denver: Society of Spanish and Spanish-American Studies, 1994.

Zabus, Chantal. "A Calibanic Tempest in Anglophone and Francophone New World Writing." *Canadian Literature* 104 (Spring 1985): 35–50.

Index

New World Studies

New World Studies publishes interdisciplinary research that seeks to redefine the cultural map of the Americas and to propose particularly stimulating points of departure for an emerging field. Encompassing the Caribbean as well as continental North, Central, and South America, books in this series examine cultural processes within the hemisphere, taking into account the economic, demographic, and historical phenomena that shape them. Given the increasing diversity and richness of the linguistic and cultural traditions in the Americas, the need for research that privileges neither the English-speaking United States nor Spanish-speaking Latin America has never been greater. The series is designed to bring the best of this new research into an identifiable forum and to channel its results to the rapidly evolving audience for cultural studies.

New World Studies

Vera M. Kutzinski
Sugar's Secrets: Race and the Erotics of Cuban Nationalism

Richard D. E. Burton and Fred Reno, editors
French and West Indian: Martinique, Guadeloupe, and French Guiana Today

A. James Arnold, editor
Monsters, Tricksters, and Sacred Cows: Animal Tales and American Identities

J. Michael Dash
The Other America: Caribbean Literature in a New World Context

Isabel Alvarez Borland
Cuban-American Literature of Exile: From Person to Persona

Belinda J. Edmondson, editor
Caribbean Romances: The Politics of Regional Representation

Steven V. Hunsaker
Autobiography and National Identity in the Americas

Celia M. Britton
Edouard Glissant and Postcolonial Theory: Strategies of Language and Resistance

Mary Peabody Mann
Juanita: A Romance of Real Life in Cuba Fifty Years Ago
Edited and with an introduction by Patricia M. Ard

George B. Handley
Postslavery Literatures in the Americas: Family Portraits in Black and White

Faith Smith
Creole Recitations: John Jacob Thomas and Colonial Formation in the Late Nineteenth-Century Caribbean

Ian Gregory Strachan
Paradise and Plantation: Tourism and Culture in the Anglophone Caribbean

Nick Nesbitt
Voicing Memory: History and Subjectivity in French Caribbean Literature

Charles W. Pollard
New World Modernisms: T. S. Eliot, Derek Walcott, and Kamau Brathwaite